The Little Trials of Childhood
and Children's Strategies for Dealing
with Them

The Little Trials of Childhood
and Children's Strategies for Dealing with Them

Frances Chaput Waksler

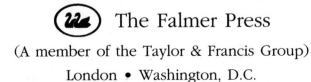 The Falmer Press

(A member of the Taylor & Francis Group)

London • Washington, D.C.

UK   The Falmer Press, 1 Gunpowder Square, London, EC4A 3DE
USA   The Falmer Press, Taylor & Francis Inc., 1900 Frost Road, Suite 101, Bristol, PA 19007

First published in 1996

A catalogue record for this book is available from the British Library

Library of Congress Cataloging-in-Publication Data are available on request

ISBN 0 7507 0453 5 cased
ISBN 0 7507 0454 3 paper

Jacket design by Caroline Archer

Typeset in 10/12 pt Garamond by
Graphicraft Typesetters Ltd., Hong Kong.

Printed in Great Britain by Biddles Ltd., Guildford and King's Lynn on paper which has a specified pH value on final paper manufacture of not less than 7.5 and is therefore 'acid free'.

Contents

Preface

Images of childhood dance in my head. Every memory is cherished. Such warmth, patience and love are truly gifts from God. However, focusing on the difficulties of my childhood is an entirely different experience for me. For some reason the frustrating times, the moments filled with stinging tears are easily forgotten but never erased. I believe that my bruises and cuts have left small scars. (Iris)

I do not remember very far back into my childhood for some reason but the things I do remember really stick out as being painful — not physically painful but things that hurt inside — and of course no one else knew except me how much they hurt. (Karen)

What is hard about simply *being* a child? My specific concern in this book is with certain ordinary childhood experiences that I call 'the little trials of childhood.' When I began exploring this topic, I must admit I had no clear expectations of what I would find, only a diffuse feeling that there ought to be something there. However, simply by asking adult informants what was 'hard' about being a child, I evoked a host of stories, including as well myriad strategies that children might use to exert some degree of control over those trials. A wide variety of trials emerge from my data: others' control over children's bodies, activities, and presentations of self; others ignoring, minimizing, distorting, and denying children's emotions; and restrictions on children's access to knowledge. In each chapter I present abundant, rich, and eloquent examples of the many kinds of trials that children may experience as well as strategies they may employ to minimize or avoid those trials. Readers may find these stories, as I have, surprising and yet familiar.

Adults in everyday life might view many of the trials described herein as trivial for children (not, necessarily, trivial for adults were similar experiences to happen to them). As I began to go through my data, I myself expected that I might be able to common-sensically categorize recounted experiences as either trivial or serious but, as I made every effort to suspend my adult perspective and take a sociological one, I found that the more I contemplated these stories, the less able I was to categorize any as trivial. Those that from an adult perspective initially appear cute, funny, or in some other way of little consequence seem to lose that quality when the recounted feelings of the teller are taken seriously. However adults might evaluate such experiences, from the perspectives of children they appear to be 'trials.' In the data I present, the 'littleness' of those trials emerges as a judgment *by adults,* one called into question as a formulation of childhood experiences *as they are lived.*

I make no quantitative claims about the applicability of my findings to all children. I am not concerned with frequency but have simply gathered stories to illustrate that, unsuspected by adults, children may be capable of a wide range of thoughts, plans, tastes, moral views, and emotions, as well as of actions directed to furthering their own goals, within which framework they encounter trials. The data I present is qualitative and, as Ambert states, 'Qualitative data may carry unexpected results; thus one of the major advantages of qualitative research is that it may open new vistas or enlarge existing ones' (1994, p. 7). It is just such vistas that I explore. 'We are trying,' writes Sacks, 'not to arrange things conveniently but to find out how they are arranged' (1975, p. 66).

The stories included in this book may appear to have been selected with a bias towards those that provide an especially negative view of childhood but, quite to the contrary, they are representative of all the stories I have collected. I have made minor editorial changes, mostly to correct grammar, give anonymity,[1] and provide clarification, and have omitted some repetitious or non-relevant details. I have also retained some colloquialisms and certain grammatical infelicities to preserve the spirit and voices of the stories. Otherwise the data I present is in the words of the respondents. This data displays children as far more than mere objects in the social worlds of adults for they emerge as full-fledged social actors in their own right, possessed of a range of pleasures and pains, knowledge, and methods for achieving their goals.

Acknowledgments

Portions of this book appeared in 'The hard times of childhood and children's strategies for dealing with them' (Waksler, 1991a). Drafts of some chapters were presented at meetings of the Eastern Sociological Society (1990, 1993, 1994, and 1995); of the Society for Phenomenology and the Human Sciences (1993); and at a workshop on Methodological Issues of Fieldwork with Children organized by Julie Gricar Beshers (1994). I have benefited from colleagues' responses, suggestions, and enthusiasm.

A number of people contributed in a variety of ways to this book: Malcolm Clarkson of Falmer Press, whose knowledge, support, and humor enhanced the pleasure of preparing the manuscript; Norman Waksler, who encouraged me throughout the project and provided invaluable advice; George Psathas, whose support I have always been able to count on; Erica Cavin, whose

---

[1] I have given pseudonyms to all informants and retain the same name for multiple quotations from the same informant. Pseudonyms reflect gender but not ethnicity.

extensive knowledge of the sociology of childhood I have drawn upon; those who read and provided commentary on draft chapters: Jeff Coulter, Gary Alan Fine, Christina Papidimitriou, Elaine Porter, and Greg Smith; Donna King, who provided me with wonderful data from her students; Emma Louise Provost Forrest and Zoë Young Kantor, who willingly gave descriptions of their on-going childhood experiences; Christine Cleary, who gave me a 'parent's reading' of chapters; Joan Duffy, who gave me a 'teacher's reading'; Brian Belson and Suzanne Zaroogian, who helped my computer realize its potential; Wheelock College Research and Development Committee, that provided me with time and funds; the many scholars upon whose work I have drawn; and, of course, my many informants, who gave thoughtful descriptions of their childhood experiences.

Frances Chaput Waksler
September, 1995

1 What Are the Little Trials of Childhood and Children's Strategies for Dealing with Them?

I remember wanting long hair and pierced ears. I wanted to buy my lunch instead of brown bagging it every day. I got lost in department stores, got caught telling little white lies, and got caught in places that were considered off limits by my parents. I was teased and teased others. I fell down in the hallway on the way to lunch. I threw up on Sammy Glasik's lunch-box standing in bus line. Kids dumped my books. I forgot my sneakers on gym days. I left my mittens on the bus. I left my homework on the kitchen table. I left my books at school. (Betty)

As a small child, I knew how to get adults to 'approve' of me. It was quite simple — be cute, do what you're told, and don't question authority. My third grade teacher was a firm believer in my theory — and she loved me! If that old woman only knew how I felt about her, it would break her mean heart. (Eleanor)

My goal in this book is to document that children, even very young children, may experience, in the ordinary course of their childhood, what they view as hardships. I want to make clear at the outset that when I use the phrase 'the little trials of childhood' I do not refer to experiences such as poverty, malnutrition, starvation, serious illness, neglect, and violence. In no way do I mean to minimize the severe physical and emotional hardships encountered by some children but simply assert that my concerns here are different. My project is to identify and examine some of the ordinary, everyday difficulties of simply *being* a child in relation to adults, other children, and the broader social world and some of the strategies that children may use to deal with those difficulties. I seek to learn about the lived experiences of young children, the richness and complexity of their lives, and the many spheres of their competence. My intent is not to reduce the importance of severe hardships nor to elevate little trials to an inappropriately lofty position but to grant to the latter a position commensurate with their importance to those who endure them. What then might children define as the little trials of childhood, the difficulties, struggles, and

1

problems? And what methods might children develop to offset, forestall, and endure those trials?

'Ordinary' hardships may indeed coexist with more severe ones. The following story, typifying what I mean by 'the little trials of childhood,' was offered by an informant whose childhood was characterized by severe physical and emotional abuse.

> My father would take my seven siblings and me for ice cream. When we got to the ice cream stand, my father would say, 'What kind of ice cream do you want?' We would give our choices: 'Chocolate.' 'Pistachio.' 'Peppermint Stick.' By the time my father got to the fifth or sixth request, he would simply say to the clerk, 'Kiddie vanilla cones for everybody.' The tease was part of the hard thing, as well as the frustration. A reward was turned into a punishment. We knew this would happen — it had happened before — but we still saw the slightest glimmer of hope, which was then nipped in the bud. And we were a party to it by having hope. It was hard that we participated in it, telling him what kind of ice cream we wanted. In this way it was like when he would say, 'Come over here so I can hit you.' We would participate in our own abuse, felt responsible for it, and were mad at ourselves. (Corrine, personal communication)

Corrine herself distinguishes between 'ordinary' and more serious hard times and, as well, describes continuities between them.

Analysis of the little trials of childhood and children's strategies for dealing with them brings forward knowledge obscured when sociologists (and other adults) fail to suspend their adult assumptions about children and fail to take children's experiences seriously. 'When one tries to observe what occurs between kids and adults in some relatively nonjudgmental way, being nonpragmatic, nonparental, and not institutionally motivated, the dominance of adult-authored versions of kids becomes immediately obvious. . .' (Goode, 1994, p. 170). My approach is avowedly partisan in that I seek *children's versions* (Cuff, 1994) of their experiences. Clearly, *adults' versions* may be dramatically different. My goal is neither to support nor to fault any version but to document versions that children might possess. This book is not about 'bad' adults and 'good' children; it is about experiences that children may have that they define as trials.

What Are the Little Trials of Childhood?

What kinds of experiences are described as difficulties, struggles, troubles, and problems of childhood? Holly, for example, speaks of 'all the numerous times adults made my decisions for me,' and Sally writes,

When I look back at my childhood, I can easily think of many experiences that I consider especially difficult. As I made a list of all the specific experiences that came to mind, I noticed they seemed to fall into three main categories. One category includes those experiences where I became fearful of a situation. The second category includes experiences where I felt a need to be accepted by my peers but was unable to because of parental control. Finally, the third category includes situations where an adult would not believe me although I was telling the truth.

Adults' claims that such experiences are trivial, even when adults are reflecting on their very own childhood, can obscure the experiences *as they were lived*. Pam writes of herself and her informants,

> The kinds of experiences I have identified are not ones that adults would necessarily characterize as hard for children. As one of my respondents noted, 'The experiences that I have told all seem so trivial now, like it was ridiculous to even have worried about them. But at the time they were so real, so important to me.'

As a way of demonstrating the non-trivial nature of these experiences, I offer a pair of stories. The first is what I see as a particularly clear example of an experience that might be viewed as fundamentally serious and non-trivial in adults' terms as well as in the terms of the teller.

> Something that really hurt when I was a child was when my grandfather was sick in the hospital. My father said I could go visit my grandfather. I got all ready to go and then my mother called and said I could not visit him. She said I was too young and could not handle it. But she did not understand how much I really wanted to see him, no matter what he looked like. I wanted to tell him I loved him and how much he meant to me. To this day it still hurts because I really wanted to let him know how I felt. (Inez)

Adults might readily term this story a description of a childhood trial. The story is not, however, in its manifest aspect, typical of the data I collected. I sought, and indeed found, far more manifestly ordinary data, but analysis had lead me to question this 'ordinary' aspect. Consider the following, *apparently* trivial, tale.

> In my second year of preschool I had a few problems. I remember drawing a picture of my family. When it came time to draw my father I couldn't remember if a mustache was over or under the nose. I was too embarrassed to ask anyone, so I think I put it over his nose. In the same year I had a 'homework assignment' where I had to color in

some people. I asked my mom what color do I color in the people's faces? She said, 'Red,' so I did. The next day I was laughed at by my teacher and my classmates because faces are not red, they should be orange. (Carol)

I myself smiled when I first read this story but the more I reread it in the course of examining my data, the more I empathized with Carol's feeling of incompetence, her sense of 'no way out,' the embarrassment of one in this predicament. In all the stories I gathered there is an element of seriousness for the participants that remains even in the face of others' amusement, trivialization, or denial.

The little trials of childhood may have many sources. Some of the stories I present describe roles played by siblings and other children[1] while other stories cite social structural sources, e.g., poverty in general, lack of money, and lack of opportunities. The prominence in what follows of *adults* as sources of childhood trials is not intended to minimize the importance of other sources but simply reflects my particular interest in adult–child interactions.

What Are the Strategies for Dealing with the Little Trials of Childhood?

Embarking on this study I never considered the possibility that children could develop a wide range of strategies to cope with what they perceive as trials. My informants, however, provide abundant examples of methods for exerting some degree of control over their circumstances. Some techniques entail extensive planning, work, or verbal skills, testifying to the competence of children, as in the following.

I can't forget the time when I was 4 and I finger-painted the bathroom and stained the walls. My mom came in and was totally shocked. She was so angry. I put on this innocent face and got teary-eyed, then made up my lie: I told her that I was outside playing and came inside to wash my hands. When I turned on the light I got dirt on the wall and decided to cover it with paint. Our walls were half wallpaper and the top was beige paint. I explained that the reason for using all of the colors was to try to match the color of the walls with the paint. When that didn't work I decided to do the whole thing — counter tops, shower, and all to match everything. My parents were upset, but not as upset as if they knew that I did it because I was mad at them for not letting me have my friend Joanie over. I schemed the whole thing

---

[1] Ambert's work on peer abuse (1994, 1995), for example, provides extensive documentation of hardships that can emerge in child–child interactions.

and got off scot-free while my parents had to re-do the entire bath-room. (Holly)

In order to exert control in spheres where that control is denied them, children may use a variety of resources, including their own bodies (as in faking ill-ness), their emotions (as in having temper tantrums), and their knowledge (lying). They may also draw on their knowledge of adults in general or of particular adults. Even very young children, for example, may recognize that adults can be manipulated; in the words of an anonymous 3-year-old spoken to a day-care worker, 'You can't be mad at me. I'm too cute.'[2]

Theoretical Background

The data and analysis provided herein emerge from a sociological perspec-tive, more specifically from the theoretical frameworks of phenomenology (Husserl, 1962), symbolic interactionism (Mead,[3] 1964; Goffman, 1959, 1963a, 1963b, 1967), and ethnomethodology (Garfinkel, 1967). *Phenomenology* di-rects attention to what Husserl describes as 'the originary right of all data,' the right of data to be apprehended as it appears. In studying children's experi-ences, a phenomenological approach involves suspending adults' perspectives and seeking children's perspectives. *Symbolic interactionism*, as the term implies, directs attention to the symbolic aspect of interaction, the meaning of interaction to participants. That meaning may well be different for children and for adults. *Ethnomethodology* focuses on members' practices. Concern here is with the details of children's practices in the world of everyday life. Of particular relevance is work in these three theoretical areas directed specifi-cally to the study of children as full-fledged social beings.[4]

The sociological study of children has traditionally adopted, implicitly when not explicitly, an *adult* perspective. Socialization, the predominant con-cept used by sociologists in analyzing childhood, has generally been pre-sented as an adult-directed process: adults socialize children. The assumption

---

[2] Erica Cavin provided me with this example.

[3] Although my perspective has been strongly influenced by the work of George Herbert Mead, my data suggests the need for some modification of Mead's ideas about the limited competence of *young* children. My data can be read as suggesting that children, even the very young, have at least a version of a self, that they too are capable of the spontaneous, creative action of the 'I,' from which in part they construct a 'me.' Al-though Mead saw the self as an achievement not attainable by very young children, indications of the 'I' and the 'me' are evident in the stories I gathered. Such evidence may reflect adults' additions to their stories of childhood; here I simply suggest that they may reflect children's experiences as children experience them.

[4] There is a growing literature on the sociology of childhood, to which I am indebted. Many important works are cited in the Bibliography and a more extensive list of sources is available in Waksler, 1991b.

that children are 'empty buckets' to be filled through the process of socialization — an assumption criticized by Wrong (1961) and empirically challenged by more recent findings, including my own — remains evident in the work of many sociologists. Sociologists' reliance on psychological theories about children further tends to reinforce an adult perspective on children.[5] The absence of children from sociological analysis except as objects of socialization conceals both children's lived experiences and the many similarities in the experiences of adults and children.[6] Attention to children's experiences brings to light social processes that are obscured when adults' taken-for-granted assumptions are adopted rather than suspended.

I have been particularly influenced by the critique of socialization offered by Mackay, who claims that socialization is not a scientific formulation but, rather, a 'gloss' and 'an expression of the sociologists' common-sense position in the world, i.e., as adults' (1973, p. 27). My work has also been influenced by Wattam, who, in her examination of adults' and children's versions of relevance, complains that 'On the whole, adult versions take precedence, and children's versions only achieve authority if they can be displayed as valid in an adult framework' (1989, p. 43). Mandell's study of negotiation of meaning in child–child interactions (1984) provides useful points of comparison and contrast with my own concern with children's negotiation of meaning in adult–child interactions, where power differentials are of particular significance. The works of Alice Miller (1981, 1990, 1991) have served as a useful framework for wondering about the 'littleness' of the 'little trials of childhood.'

Throughout this book I speak of 'adults' rather than 'parents' because my concern is with adults in general, not parents in particular. It is the 'adultness' in adult–child interactions to which I want to call attention and thus, for my purposes here, I take parents to be simply one kind of adult. In the words of one of my informants,

> Perhaps the most frustrating and unfair part of my childhood for me
> was dealing with all adults, not just my parents. The adults directly
> related to me (i.e., parents, older sisters, teachers, baby-sitters) were
> for the most part very authoritarian and bossy. They always thought
> they were right, I was wrong. The best example I can think of for this
> is the way adults spoke to me. For instance, if I was not allowed
> to do something and asked for the reason, frequent answers were

---

[5] Coser, Nock, Steffan and Spain, 1991, p. 123, to cite but one of many possible examples, in a chapter on socialization in an introductory sociology textbook, discuss the theories not only of Cooley and Mead but of Freud, Piaget, Kohlberg, and Erik Erikson.

[6] For a brief but especially lucid discussion of the distortions introduced by an adult perspective towards children, see Bluebond-Langer, 1978, pp. 3–14. Also useful in this regard are Atkinson, 1980; Bentz, 1989, esp. pp. 9–18; Goode, 1994; and Stainton-Rogers, R. and W., 1992.

'Because I am your mother' or worse, 'Because I said so.' Also frustrating was when I would try to defend myself when adults were angry with me. If I even opened my mouth, I would hear, 'Don't talk back to me!' Adults often also said such things as 'You're just a kid' or 'You don't know how lucky you are to be a kid and have no real problems.' They just assumed I was too young to understand anything and too young to have any real worries. (Gini)

In his analysis of the family, Schneider states that it is 'fundamental to distinguish between the father as a father and as a man, the mother as a mother and as a woman, etc.' (1968, p. 44). He claims that many characteristics attributed to spouses can be explained by gender roles. I want to make a related claim, that much of parental behavior is adult behavior. In choosing to focus on the broader category of adults I follow Mackay, who states, 'Writing about the process of socialization. . .has become for me an occasion for exploring the interaction between adults and children' (1973, in Waksler, 1991b, p. 27). I too explore relations between adults and children.

What is the theoretical significance of establishing the existence of the little trials of childhood? To determine that from their perspective children do indeed endure trials expands our knowledge of the social world, but this finding has further significance. First, it serves to document adults' limited knowledge about children. This limited knowledge may not be accidental for to some extent it is politically useful, enabling adults to act as they routinely do towards children. Second, the discovery of the little trials of childhood brings to light the social contexts in which these trials come about. Children's difficulties emerge in interaction, where children are misunderstood, both intentionally and unintentionally, and where they lack power in relation to others, especially adults. They may be expected to follow rules that they are not taught (see Mackay, 1973; and Waksler, 1987) and have limited resources for changing or bending rules. Third, if we think of adults as teaching children how to become adults, and if we recognize that children learn from what they observe as well as what they are told, then what do children learn from the kinds of experiences described herein? In a story about fear written by Rose, she describes her mother's statement, 'Don't worry. There is no such thing as a monster' not as a lesson that monsters don't exist; rather, in Rose's words,

I would wonder to myself about how she could be so stupid. I knew they were there and she didn't care. I cried myself to sleep for years. This was partly because I was so terrified and partly because Mommy didn't care.[7]

---

[7] The story from which this excerpt is taken appears in Chapter 5.

Unless Rose's mother was indeed trying to teach Rose that her mother didn't care, her teaching methods both failed to teach what she intended and taught what she did not intend.

And lastly, the discovery of the little trials of childhood displays the many similarities between children and adults, similarities that cannot be recognized when the sociological study of children is separated from the broader sociological enterprise. Children's trials and those of adults may not, after all, be so very different in their basic characteristics.

Methodology

The impetus for this book was a theoretical piece I wrote entitled 'Studying children: Phenomenological insights,' wherein I stated in a footnote,

> I have elicited some very promising data by asking adults to recall their childhood experiences with adults. I have used such questions as: What kinds of things did adults do that bothered you? How did adults treat you? What did it feel like to be a child? I think the limits of such retrospective data may be counterbalanced by the fact that adults have the power to speak of that which as children it was politically wise for them to conceal. (1980, p. 69)

At the time I wrote this footnote, my expectation was that someone else would take up this project but as I continued to address the topic in my classes, I was increasingly intrigued by what was said and written. Following a variety of spirited discussions in college classrooms and a large number of excellent student papers, I found myself pursuing this research. I was further encouraged when my description of the project to friends and colleagues elicited even more stories of childhood trials.

The primary source of the data I gathered is student papers written in fulfillment of an assignment for a freshman college course entitled 'Studying the Social Worlds of Children.' Students' writing of this assignment followed class discussion of the topic. In initiating these discussions, I offered examples such as 'being kissed by adults when you didn't want to be' and then simply asked students to reflect upon hard times of their childhood. Classroom response has customarily been knowing smiles followed by a flood of anecdotes. Then I asked students to write:

> *Report No. 1: The Experience of Childhood.* This report should focus on memories of one's own childhood, with particular emphasis on the 'difficulties' of being a child. What was hard? Unfair? Unable to be done? Pay particular attention to the difficulties presented by adults. Provide stories from as young an age as possible. Conclude this report with some general statements about possible difficulties of childhood in general. Avoid moral judgments. (From course syllabus)

Initially students were asked to write a five-page first person account of their own childhood. Later, other students were asked to write papers based on interviews on hard times in general or on related topics such as embarrassment, Santa Claus, and the shortcomings of adults. Although my initial concern was simply with identifying the little trials of childhood, it soon became clear that also significant for informants were strategies to offset, forestall, and endure these hard times. Unsolicited student reports of such strategies were accompanied by a seeming certain pride expressed in describing the effective use of such strategies. I therefore expanded my investigations accordingly and directed my informants to do so.

The topic of childhood trials does not seem to have been one about which informants had already formulated ideas, except of the quite different kind that adults routinely have about childhood. Events from childhood invoked in everyday life by adults seem typically to be those that are memorably good or bad. When publicly presented as recollections, the good experiences tend to be very good; the bad, very bad. Initially my informants spoke in glowing terms of their childhood.

> When I think of childhood in general, I automatically think of freedom
> and being carefree. Happy memories come to mind. (Gini)

My method of data gathering has been to ask respondents to use different selection criteria. Ambert writes, 'in any study using recollections, it is unavoidable that selectivity, as well as reconstructions of the past, take place' (1994, p. 8). In an effort to move beyond conventional recollections, I urged students to employ *directed looking* at childhood experiences, bracketing their adult assessments of those experiences. Guided by Husserl's directive to respect 'the originary right of all data,' I sought, and urged students to seek, and then to suspend, adults' ideas about children, and adults' reformulations of childhood.[8] Students were asked to go beyond adult reconstructions and attempt to recall the experiences *as they were lived at the time.* Thus Gini, quoted above, continues,

> However, when I stop and really think deeply, some hardships are
> quite prominent in my memory of childhood. Some of these hardships
> include friendships, physical differences, the pain of 'no' when other
> mothers said 'yes,' and the control of adults.

That cultural criteria are not readily available to frame such stories is evidenced by a recurrent theme in data gathering — adults' claiming an inability to recall little trials of childhood, followed by their offering an abundance of just such stories. Thus Ralph writes,

---

[8] For examples of adult taken-for-granted assumptions about children, see Mackay, 1973; and Waksler, 1986.

> One person whom I interviewed was a middle-aged woman. She thought the whole interview project was goofy and it took her a long time to think of a hard time of childhood. But when she thought of one it seemed to trigger a number of unpleasant memories.

Ralph then tells a story of his informant's mother cutting off 'my long beautiful blonde hair that everybody always complimented me on.' Her 'forgotten' story concludes, 'I'll never forgive my mother for that' (Ralph's informant). Granting legitimacy to the little trials of childhood *as trials* appears to facilitate their articulation while cultural criteria appear to support their concealment.

The following methodological excerpts suggest the data-gathering techniques used by students.

> I obtained my data from five college students and personal reflections about my own childhood. I gathered my data by asking people if they would mind sharing stories or memories. . .Often, I obtained data from conversation and shared some of my personal memories. This allowed the conversation to continue, because when I shared one story they often shared two or three. I also told people that I needed the data for a sociology paper. I recorded my data and separated it into categories. (Dora)

> Actually, it happened like this. . .I called my boyfriend [age 17]. . .over the phone and hit him with the magic question. There were three other people in the room, all college students, who just happened to be listening to my conversation. With curiosity, they begged me to tell them what I was talking about. I told them, which triggered a two-hour conversation. The following is the result of our story-telling time that, I must admit, was very funny. (Sandra)

Many of the students who provided data were enrolled in a program designed for those planning a career working with young children and therefore their familiarity with, interest in, and knowledge of young children may be greater than that of college students in general. My data, however, does not indicate that my topic was one about which they had already formulated ideas, except, as noted above, the kinds of ideas that adults routinely have about childhood. Most of those who gathered data or wrote of their own experiences are female; some of their informants are male. Thus I have considerably more data from females but have not noticed significant gender differences, although the specific content of some trials may be related to gender. In this regard, Bentz's comment in her study of maturity seems apt.

> This study is about human beings. . .These human beings were women. Some aspects of what they experienced are shared be all of us, some by none of us, some perhaps, only by women. (1989, p. 23)

My data does not allow me to make gender distinctions nor does it indicate that they are necessarily relevant. The modest number of male respondents has not produced data that is different in any significant way and males who have read versions of this paper have offered not objections but rather examples of the same sort of trials of their own. Clearly gender, as well as ethnicity, race, social class, and a variety of other factors are relevant to the *kinds* of trials children endure but do not appear to be relevant to the fact *that* they endure them. Being a child may be more relevant than other factors to experiencing the little trials of childhood.

To my surprise — and that of my students — disclosure of their experiences of the little trials of childhood to adults deemed responsible for them sometimes proved distressing. Those who 'told' reported arguments, some rather bitter, leading me to a recognition of the risks of such 'telling.'

> As I started to think about my own childhood I actually had a hard time thinking about my hard times of my childhood. As soon as I started to figure out some memories, they seemed to come rolling back. That was helpful to me but my mother was not too pleased when I kept saying, 'Oh, yeah, remember this. . .and. . .oh, I was so mad about that. . .' My mother, I think, was getting a little upset when I kept remembering things that were hard times to me. (Annette)

> After I collected my data I told the adults who annoyed and embarrassed me exactly what they did to make me feel this way. They were shocked and embarrassed themselves. They said they never realized that their actions could be interpreted in a negative way. I found the adults were surprised that as a child I had the competence and knowledge to understand I didn't like what they did. They assumed that because I was a child and they were the adults that they knew what I liked or didn't like. When I told my mother all the things she did that bothered me or embarrassed me she said, 'I'm sorry. Now that you point some of the things out, I can understand why you felt the way you did.' When I asked the people I interviewed if they were going to share their feelings with the adults who contributed to their embarrassment and aggravation they said no. They said they all felt that it would hurt the adults' feelings. They thought it was enough for them to have shared their feelings with me. I found it interesting that none of us ever told an adult our feelings when we were a child. (Tanya)

Although Tanya describes her mother's understanding and apologizing, her informants describe reluctance to risk hurting adults' feelings; other informants told of adults' surprise, anger, disbelief, and denial and of sufficiently serious arguments to make me decide to present future assignments with a recommendation that care be used in making disclosures. It was particularly because of the potential troublesomeness, even danger, of such disclosures for young children that I chose not to study them directly. *And thus a caveat.* Those interested in exploring the ideas presented in this book, either formally or informally, are urged to do so with some caution. Even discussing quite 'little' trials can lead to disputes and hurt feelings.

The little trials of childhood cannot be readily apprehended through direct observation. Rather, they appear in *accounts* of experiences. The data I have collected can thus be most accurately, if somewhat infelicitously, described as *responses to requests for accounts of childhood experiences.* Some accounts were provided directly, in written form, by students who experienced them; other accounts were gathered by students and written up by them; yet other stories were told directly to me. Given the exigencies of student life, some stories could be invented. Against this background, what remains are accounts of children's trials.

For a variety of reasons I chose not to study children's accounts as a part of this project.[9] The weaknesses of interviews with children, especially young children, lie in the distortions introduced by the mere presence of adults (interviewers, parents, teachers) and, more significantly, the potential risks to children in telling, or even thinking about, complaints about which they may be powerless to do anything. Informed by ideas presented throughout this book, interviews with children might be conducted with less risk and greater knowledge of what kinds of data might be sought. Direct interviews of children would of course be closer in time to the experiences themselves but they too would rely on recollections and accounts.

The data I have gathered could be analyzed in a variety of ways. 'Data sets are representations, or signs, or indexes of some actual state of affairs with which they may or may not be (in some practical sense of the term) "congruent"' (Goode, 1994, p. 137). The 'actual state of affairs' with which I am concerned are children's lived experiences of trials. Quite valid reasons might be offered for why accounts by adults cannot be taken to be literal descriptions of these experiences. Nonetheless, I am claiming that much is to be learned by reading the accounts I have gathered as reflections of *possible* children's experiences and perspectives. Stories were gathered by directing informants' attention to the lived experiences of childhood and away from social constructions derived from cultural criteria for childhood stories. The stories differ dramatically from adults' everyday formulations of children's experiences — whether these formulations apply to adults' own childhood or to that of children with whom they as adults associate — and yet have a familiarity about them in relation to one's own childhood experiences. Any one account could be questioned but taken together they display a wide range of children's feelings and actions that are not regularly investigated, attended to, taken into account, recognized, or even suspected by many sociologists

---

[9] Although I discouraged students from interviewing children, a few spoke informally with children they knew well. Thus in what follows there are some stories from children. See Appendix for data informally gathered from a first-grade class.

and by adults in their everyday lives. In the words of Gary Alan Fine (personal communication), 'One has come to terms with whether these are actual events, children's perceptions of these events, adult perceptions of these events, or adult recall provided for a particular purpose in a particular context.' I have chosen to present my data as *possible* children's experiences of the little trials of childhood and provide abundant data that speaks for itself. The appropriateness of my formulation of the data is best assessed by the insights it provides and the theoretical and practical consequences to which it leads.

Practical Implications

Adults who associate with children, in whatever capacity, may well find themselves asking again and again as they read: Ought adults to do something about these little trials of childhood and, if so, what? I see this question, important as it is, as not a sociological but a moral one, subject to many different answers depending on one's goals and perspectives. As Heap writes,

> For any article or presentation there is the question of why speak, why communicate (and why listen and why read). This question becomes salient because of the more general question of how one should live. The question 'how should I live?' can arise only within a collection of normative orders, a culture, where 'how should one live?' is a prior question. How one should live, is how I should live. Scientific inquiry cannot decide this question, nor is there an answer in general to this kind of question. However, inquiry can deliver some of what we need to know in order to make reasoned judgments in particular situations about how to act to achieve some end. (1990, p. 39)

Although I too see it as outside the sphere of sociology to dictate morality or to make claims about what ought to be, I do see it as appropriate to offer some comments on the practical implications that are — and are not — suggested by my data.[10]

Certainly adults are implicated in many of the little trials of childhood. It does not, however, follow that adults *are* villains, despite children's sometimes seeing them as such. Adults themselves, no doubt, endure the little trials of adulthood, of which children may be one source. Nonetheless, given the power of adults over children, the decision to do something — or not do something — about the little trials of childhood seems to lie primarily with adults. It is of course possible for adults to do nothing about these trials, to see them as inevitable features of childhood, perhaps as the necessary building blocks of

---

[10] In Chapter 10 I address in greater detail the topic of practical implications. Some may want to read Chapter 10 before proceeding to the rest of the book.

'character.' Adults may deny children's experiences, arguing that children's trials are 'not really trials' and that children ought not to so define them. Alternatively, it is possible for adults to strive to eliminate all childhood trials, although such a goal seems unlikely of achievement — just as it is unlikely that trials can be altogether eliminated from the lives of adults. I want to emphasize that I am arguing neither that children's trials should be ignored nor that adults should always defer to children, granting their every wish. I am claiming that children's trials exist and are worthy of consideration.

I am certainly not recommending that children be given everything they want. I am suggesting that what children want, what adults think children want, what adults want children to want, what adults want, etc., are very different from one another. These distinctions become readily blurred when all adults' behavior towards children is defined as 'for children's own good.' One way to read the stories that follow is to look for instances where it appears to be 'for adults' own good' to *not* notice that children are perceiving their experiences as trials and where adult decisions seem to be motivated at least in part by their own welfare, even when they claim otherwise.

Against the background of the data presented throughout this book, adults might choose to reconsider their own behavior. More specifically, they might ask *in any given situation* how children are characterizing their experiences. By setting aside taken-for-granted assumptions and ideological claims about children, adults can consider the grounds both of children's behavior and of their own. Knowing that children endure what they view as trials offers insight into the ways of both children and adults and their interactions together. Adults who do not understand how children are defining their experiences are limited in the help that they can provide.

When, for example, adults claim that they know what is best for children, they not only deny that adults themselves disagree about what is best but also deny children their perspectives as well as the alternatives that may be routinely granted to adults in the face of disagreement. By denying the little trials of childhood, adults deny to children the strategies for dealing with them that are known to adults. To tell a child that a medical procedure will not hurt when one knows it will is not only to lie and to deny a child's experience; it also prevents adults from assisting children in developing strategies for dealing with pain. Instead of denying future pain, adults might say to children, 'When I have to go through this procedure, this is what I do.'

Applying to adult–child interactions the moral framework applied to adult–adult interactions may lead to some modifications in the former. When adults ask something of a child, a recognition that the child finds the request a difficulty or problem may influence either what adults ask or how they ask it. (As an adult I may make a sacrifice for another but I may expect the other to recognize that a sacrifice is involved.) Adults may deem some children's trials avoidable, others necessary, but may find it appropriate to recognize and acknowledge the latter as trials. Adults may choose to change some of their behavior in relation to children; to retain other behavior but present it differently;

to understand more fully what they are asking of children; and to accord children more sympathy for their trials and more respect for the many and innovative ways they have developed on their own to come to terms with those trials. Accepting children as fellow actors in the social world also provides an alternative to the view that socialization — adults teaching children — is the only possible mode of adult–child interaction. Children thus become not 'other' but 'us.'

Earlier in this chapter I referred to a story by Rose in which she describes her mother's statement, 'Don't worry. There is no such thing as a monster,' not as a lesson that monsters don't exist but as an instance of her mother's not caring. My data, however, calls into question not only her mother's approach but also the alternative of adults' *pretending* belief in monsters. Just such pretense is recommended in the following advice to parents offered by Turecki.

> Because young children are much more suggestible than adults, they often respond well to *positive magical thinking*. Monsters may disappear with applications of 'monster spray'. . . (1994, p. 232, emphasis in original)[11]

Alternatives to denial or pretense could be crafted by considering how adults manage interactions with other adults when they disagree on what they take to be real (what Pollner, 1975, refers to as 'reality disjunctures').

The many insights provided in the data I gathered have changed my own interactions with children in ways that may appear minor but that attempt to employ a view of children as beings in their own right. I offer a few examples. Now, whenever possible, I ask young children if they want to be picked up — and find that they respond with either 'yes' or 'no,' and not necessarily the answer I would have predicted. The phrase 'whenever possible,' however, suggests that as an adult I may violate this practice if I deem it necessary to do so — but perhaps I offer an apology. When bringing food to a children's party, I bring 'good' food, i.e., adult food, and find that children happily select gourmet cakes and cookies. I, as one who regularly drinks soft drinks, bring them to the homes of friends who forbid such drinks for their children 'except when there is company'; I even plan that there will be some to be left behind. I try to include children in conversations that also include adults — although other adults often impede such attempts, answering for children, telling me what they mean, urging them to answer, and otherwise substituting themselves for the child. Sometimes, as is likely to be apparent, I offend adults while I please children; I am sure in the past I offended children as I sought to please adults. Now I am aware of having a choice. Rejecting the fiction that adults and children view the world in the same way, that the adults' way is

---

[11] Many books of advice to parents are readily available. A systematic analysis of such books against the background of the data I present holds promise for future research. I cite just a few works in this genre for illustrative purposes.

best, that the same thing can please both, I am attentive to different definitions of situations and am able to move among them.

As the data throughout this book indicates, children may well observe their world closely and fashion a variety of ways to function in that world according to their own standards. This data can serve to increase adults' respect for children's competence and children's ways of being in the world. It can also increase adults' awareness that children understand, make use of, and judge adults' words and actions. In the words of one informant,

> [Writing the assigned paper] made an impact on me because I will think more before I act when I am around children, because I know they are watching. (Kara)

Adults' recognition — rather than denial — of the little trials of childhood can influence their interactions with children in a variety of ways, many yet to be determined. Applying an understanding of the little trials of childhood to everyday interactions between adults and children is an exceedingly complex matter, best achieved *in situ* rather than by fiat.

* * *

Those who have endured severe childhood hardships might be tempted to see the little trials of childhood as no more than the petty complaints of the privileged. For one who goes hungry, being forced to eat one's peas hardly seems a trial. The data to follow, however, suggests both the seriousness of the apparently petty for those who experience them and certain surprising continuities with severe hardships.

There is some tendency among adults to balk at taking children seriously.[12] I mean to claim that the little trials of childhood are serious matters for those who endure them. I urge readers to consider what follows in relation to their own childhood experiences — not from an adult perspective but with faithfulness to the ways they are described as having been experienced. 'Allow the possibility of the facts,' writes Horace Walpole, 'and all the actors comport themselves as persons would in their situation.' Might childhood indeed be as it appears in what follows?

---

[12] Gottlieb (1994), for example, after a glowing review of Matthews' *The Philosophy of Childhood*, writes, 'Sometimes Mr. Matthews goes a bit far' and then rejects his central claims that children can be viewed as philosophers and artists.

2   Whose Body is It?

One difficulty is when you have a runny nose and it really hurts and someone always wipes it. You can squirm and wiggle but they will still wipe your nose. (Theresa)

When I was younger, I had this problem with biting my fingernails and cracking my knuckles. I did this whenever my hands were free. My mother used to tell me not to bite my nails because they did not taste good. To me, they tasted fine. My grandmother would tell me not to crack my knuckles because they would end up looking like hers. She has skinny fingers with big, fat knuckles. After about the third time she told me this, I finally stopped. The thought of having hands like that was pretty scary. I only found out recently that her hands are like that because of arthritis. (Veronica)

Adults make decisions about what foods children like and dislike and about whether children are hungry or full, sleepy or awake, dirty or clean. They control access to bathroom facilities and the activities conducted therein. They impede children's use of their own bodies (as in the case of fingernails and knuckles above). *Against children's wishes*, they pick them up bodily, move them from place to place, kiss them and require them to kiss others, pinch, tickle, and otherwise make physical contact with them. Children may view such 'liberties' as little trials of childhood and work to develop strategies for gaining some control over their own bodies.

Food

Abundant stories describing food eloquently testify to children's limited control over their own bodies — namely, what goes into their bodies. Coercive strategies that adults may employ, and the counter-strategies children may adopt, are exemplified in the following story.

For as long as I can remember I have hated food. I was always forced to eat everything on my plate, down to the last drop. When I could not eat any more, one of two things would happen. My mother would either suggest spoon-feeding me, saying, 'This spoonful is for Mommy,'

'This spoonful is for Daddy,' and so on and I would open my mouth wide to let her know that I liked eating for them. Sometimes we would go so far as to eat for all my relatives that are alive and most of the relatives that are deceased. The last spoonful was always for strength.

The other alternative was me refusing to play this childish silly game with her and not opening up my mouth. At that point I was ordered to sit in the kitchen with my food until I was done eating. Sometimes I would spend an entire day in the kitchen, poking at my food with the fork and watching it get cold as I was getting more and more disgusted with it.

Sometimes I would hold my nose with my fingers, put all the food in my mouth, tell my mother that I was done eating, and run to the bathroom to spit it all out. That would usually be followed by vomiting. I did not like to do that very much but, on the days that I had definite plans to meet with my friends in the backyard and play, that would be my only alternative. (Denise)

The distress attendant upon children's eating disliked food may go unrecognized by adults — but not by children.

I don't think I will ever be able to forget the feeling of those unchewed lima beans rolling down my throat. Even washing them down with milk didn't help. Every time I had to do it nausea set in and I always wanted to excuse myself from the table. Neither my mother nor my father would let me leave because they knew that if I did I would spit them into the toilet and flush them. I don't understand why everything had to be finished, in fact I feel it was wrong because to this day I refuse to eat lima beans. (Agatha)

What adults perceive as reasonable strategies for accomplishing the goal of feeding children may be viewed quite differently by the children involved. Denise (above) speaks of her mother's 'childish silly game.' Children may see in adults' practices injustice (adults serving foods that adults like without taking children's tastes into account) and adults' exemption from rules to which children are held (the 'clean plate' rule).

We always came together for dinner when I was young. I happened to dislike beets, cooked carrots, and roast beef. Of course, one of these almost always appeared on my plate. . .I tried to explain to my parents that I didn't like these foods. My frustration would turn to tears, stubbornness, and resentment. Why did I have to sit there and finish everything when my parents didn't always eat everything put in front of them? They also chose what they ate while I just got what they gave me. I still don't like those things and do my best to avoid them.

My parents said I had to eat them because they were good for me and I shouldn't waste food with all the starving people in the world. I'm healthy, so far, without them, and I'd gladly give my beets, cooked carrots, or roast beef to a starving person. (Holly)

Children may not only reject adult claims that certain foods taste good or are 'good for you' but view those claims — and thus adults — as presumptuous, their claims of superior knowledge dubious.

I remember at times I would rather starve to death than eat pea soup, cabbage and beans, broccoli, cauliflower, carrots or fish. Even the smell would gross me out. Getting it into my mouth was one thing, and then trying to swallow it was even worse. I use to feel myself gagging trying to get it down my throat. In fact I think I would be happier at times if I got sick so I would not have to eat that gross food. How could parents make you eat something so disgusting? It did not even look or smell good, let alone taste good. How could they possibly use the excuse that 'it is good for you'? I remember I used to think that my parents liked every kind of food. But I guess it was because they only made what they liked. How many adults eat food they do not like just because it's good for them? (Cindy)

When children's tastes *are* taken into account, children may see such consideration as luck rather than as something to which they are entitled.

I found it very troublesome to have adults tell me what food was good and what food was bad. Each person has their own taste buds so no one can decide for anyone else what is good or bad food. I was a fussy eater and would not eat many of the meals that my mother prepared for me. *I was lucky in the sense that my mom would make me something else if I did not like what she had made.* She always wanted me to try new stuff though. She would say it is good. Everyone used to tell me to eat my Brussels sprouts, for someone came up with the idea that they are good for you. I hate Brussels sprouts, they make me feel like I want to vomit, how can I be told they are good and believe it? Another food that I was told is not good is vanilla ice cream. Everyone says it is too plain and boring. I happen to love vanilla ice cream. How come people always tell me to get something more exciting and good? To me there is nothing better. I will always choose vanilla over all other flavors. I hated being told about foods that taste good, bad, or are or aren't good for you. It all depends on whose opinion you are going by. (Ruth emphasis added)

Although one might be tempted to see claims of nausea and vomiting as exaggerated, personal recollections may modify such criticism. (I certainly remember gagging on unhomogenized milk that had lumps of cream in it and bananas still make me gag.) The options that children see as open to them may be limited — eating, followed by nausea and vomiting, or not eating and going hungry, perhaps followed by being sent to bed or some other form of punishment. Children may, nonetheless, make choices from among their limited options.

Dessert's contingency on finishing the main meal is a way of using one food as a reward for eating other foods and using deprivation of a particular food as punishment.

> I could never figure out the meaning of 'no dessert until your plate is clean.' Why did my plate have to be clean before I ate more? I used to think up all kinds of schemes just so I could get dessert. One of my favorite ideas was while my mother wasn't looking I would shove everything I didn't like into my napkin. Then when the meal was over I would excuse myself in a very lady-like fashion. That way no one would suspect anything. I would then walk to the bathroom and either flush the whole thing down the toilet or throw it in the trash can. Even though this worked for a few meals, my parents soon caught on and refused to let me be excused. I also went a few meals without dessert even thought my plate was clean and so was my napkin. (Agatha)

Agatha's strategy for getting dessert, although of short-lived efficacy, displays her grasp of the importance of appearance in successful deception (her 'lady-like fashion' of excusing herself from the table) and the importance of dessert to her. Dessert deprivation as punishment (or, euphemistically, 'limit setting') may be urged by authorities offering advice to parents. Greenspan, in *Playground Politics: Understanding the Emotional Life of Your School-Age Child*, writes,

> Some parents are uncomfortable with the use of food, such as withholding desserts, as a punishment, fearing that it could lead to eating disorders. Actually, as long as your family's attitude about food, hunger, and other bodily functions is flexible and not rigid, it's perfectly fine to make dessert a special treat that can be withheld as part of limit setting. (1993, pp. 296–7)

That Greenspan treats dessert deprivation as 'perfectly fine' suggests unawareness of the seriousness with which children may view it. What adults take to be a minor deprivation children may view as major. Why is dessert a contingent food? As a child I imagined myself having two stomachs, a main meal one and a dessert one; the former could be full while the latter was empty. As an adult I still find such a distinction supportable. One of my informants adopted this formulation with her 8-year-old daughter and reported that both found it quite satisfactory.

An often obscured experience or one that is significantly reformulated by adults is children's experiences when they discover the sources of food. This knowledge may be concealed from children or children's scruples may be overridden.

> The first difficult incident of my childhood that stands out in my mind has to do with the fact that I grew up on a farm. When I was about 4 or 5 years old you could not convince me that I was at all a lucky child. At this time in my childhood, I happened to be a fussy eater. I refused to eat beef because I knew it used to be 'Betsy,' who was once my favorite calf. Also, I hated the vegetables that came from the garden because I had seen the potato beetles and other dreaded insects buzzing over the entire garden and munching on the plants. My problem was that I basically knew where everything that was on our dinner table came from. Unfortunately, my parents did not understand this and I was forced each and every night to clear my plate before I could leave the table. Oh, how I dreaded for the time to come when my mother would call me for dinner. I would wait anxiously until the last minute and would slowly saunter into the kitchen under the watchful eyes of my parents and the keen, intimidating glare of my older brother. Each night, after grace was said, my ultimate torture began. (Regina)

In addition to the hardship of offering prayerful thanks for food for which one is not thankful, this story describes childhood concerns with cleanliness and with morality. Indeed children may be *taught*, contrary to their own inclinations, that it is morally acceptable to eat meat (or, when possible, the source of meat may be concealed from them). When older and able to choose for themselves, they may return to their childhood predilections, gardening with greater care and avoiding meat.

As I read stories of mealtimes and the distress informants recounted, I became intrigued at the pervasiveness of the rules for cleaning one's plate and eating any food offered. It seems to me that at least some adults who enforce these rules are likely to have suffered under those very rules themselves and that my informants themselves may well enforce such rules for children in their care. Adults may offer nutritional reasons for their practices but children who develop successful strategies for avoiding eating may not be noticed by adults as lacking nourishment. Forcing children to eat, either in general or certain foods in particular, may not be necessary for the children involved, despite adult claims to the contrary. Indeed such coercion may serve to support adults' values (not wasting food), adults' presentations of self (as good parents), or adults' projects (facilitating clean-up procedures, streamlining food preparation). In the absence of coercion, do children starve or become malnourished? Perhaps taken-for-granted adult assumptions about feeding children could benefit from re-examination in the light of empirical evidence.

Sleep

Many and varied stories describe trials related to bedtime as well as strategies for dealing with them. One such trial is being required to sleep when one does not want to.

> When I was younger and up until about eighth grade, my two sisters and I all had certain times to go to bed on school nights. They were all about an hour apart. First my younger sister would go and that did not really bother me because then I would go into my older sister's room and sit and talk to her. But then the hour was up and it was my turn to go to bed. As quiet as I was my parents never seemed to forget to come and tell me it was bedtime. If I asked why I had to go to bed they said, 'When you get older you can stay up later, but for now it is bedtime.' I used to hate going into my bedroom (which my younger sister and I shared), having to be quiet. I never wanted to go to sleep. I always wanted to wake her up and have her talk with me. But somehow I knew that would cause trouble, so I never did. (Cindy)

Adults clearly do not have the power to *make* children sleep — and to that extent children have control over their bodies — but adults are certainly in the position to *encourage* children to choose to sleep.

> My mother always had us in bed by 7:00 every night until we were about 10 years old. This seemed so cruel because all my friends stayed up so much later and got to watch the 'good' shows on television while I was sleeping. We also had to take naps until we were old enough to go to school. I would beg and plead to stay up but Mom would always say, 'I know you are tired. Just lie down and shut your eyes.' Much to my dismay I would always fall asleep no matter how hard I tried to stay awake just to prove her wrong. (Theresa)

Sleeping when one is not tired, when one simply does not want to, or when one has more pressing matters to which to attend can be a problem for adults as well as children. Adults, however, may openly choose not to sleep; children may find themselves urged to subterfuge. Cindy's being quiet so as not to be noticed proved unsuccessful and Theresa's body betrayed her in her efforts to stay awake; others report more effective strategies.

> Bedtime was the worst time of the day. I never wanted to go to bed. I always wished I was the 'oldest' so that I could stay up with the 'old people.' Whenever there was a good television show on it seemed like that was my bedtime. I never got to watch the good shows like my older brother did. Whenever my parents made me go to bed I would make them leave the door open half way. They thought it was

because I needed a night light but actually it was so I could watch the television that was situated perfectly so I could watch it from my bedroom. (Marian)

Adults may quite reasonably maintain that children need their sleep, and indeed they may. If, however, children's strategies for avoiding sleep continue over time, any effects of less sleep, if indeed there are any, may be sufficiently insignificant to go unnoticed by adults.

Children may perceive naps and bedtimes as adults' inaccurate formulations of children's inner states and as occasions for adults to consign children's bodies to bed. When one's experiences are redefined by others, especially when those others have the power to enforce their definitions, frustration is a not surprising consequence.

I'd love to meet the person that decided children need a nap in the afternoon so I could punch that person in the nose. I hated naps! My naps were always an hour after lunch. Whenever I took one I woke up feeling awful — so tired and dazed. It took such a long time and so much effort to get rid of that feeling. The one thing that upset me the most was when my parents would blame my grouchy moods on not taking a nap or not getting enough sleep. That explanation would get me even more angry because then I'd end up in bed early again. They never thought that I just might have had a bad day, which was frequently the case. They still tell me today that I'm grouchy because I'm overtired. (Holly)

Nap time was an adult-imposed rule that I found especially hard to do. When I was 3 I was forced to take a nap during the day. Being a very active child, I could never sleep at nap time. It was so hard to lie still on my mat when I had so much energy inside me. The toys around me always seemed to be calling my name to come over and play, and consequently I had the reputation of being a hard-to-control napper. My mother even used to make me take naps on Christmas day after dinner but before we opened our presents from Grandma and Grandpa. I remember thinking, 'How do they expect me to sleep with all of these unopened presents?' (Irene)

When adults tell children that they (the children) are sleepy, children may be faced with trying to define what they are feeling as 'sleepy,' despite their evidence to the contrary, or trying in some other way to come to terms with a discrepancy between what they are told they are experiencing and what they take to be true of their experience.

Adults may, in their presentations to children, confound children's need for sleep and adults' need for children to be asleep.

> Bedtime for me was when my parents were tired and didn't feel like dealing with me anymore. I usually stayed awake in bed playing imagination games until I was tired. (Holly)

Perhaps the one who needs to sleep is the one who actually falls asleep.

> I had to take a nap until I was 5 years old. My mom took the nap with me. We would watch soap operas and fall asleep to them. My mom would, anyway. When my mom fell asleep I can remember moving off the bed a tiny bit every few minutes and then crawling on the floor and out of her room. (Brenda)

That children can, through a variety of strategies, not get the amount of sleep they are said to need and still function suggests that their 'need' for specific amounts of sleep may be more an adults' than a biological need. That adults fail to observe children's strategies for avoiding sleep — strategies that nonetheless keep children as quiet as if they were asleep — suggests either that adults are not particularly attentive or that it is in their interest to have children act as if they were asleep rather than necessarily being asleep. Clearly adults have needs but those needs are denied and children's experiences distorted when the sole reason for sending children to bed is said to be 'for children's own good.'

Unwanted Physical Contact[1]

Adults may take with children's bodies what would be called 'liberties' were they taken with adults' bodies. Unwanted kisses and hugs, being tickled, and being pulled, dragged, or picked up are some such 'liberties' described by informants. The following story describes another.

> One of my mother's friends always used to come straight at me and pinch my cheeks. I hated it. I wasn't allowed to say anything to her because it was not proper and it would be considered disrespectful. I saw it as a humiliating act that I was forced to endure because Mommy said so. (Irene)

Adults may use children's bodies to display affection or as a source of adult pleasure[2] — and children certainly may enjoy such contact. I am emphasizing

---

[1] Although physical punishment can be viewed as unwanted physical contact, my concern here is with actions that adults might *not* view as hardships for children.

[2] When adults treat children's bodies in *sexual* ways, their actions are subject to severe criticism. My data indicates that children themselves may also object to non-sexual uses of their bodies.

here, however, that *they may not.* Adults may enjoy kissing or other physical contact with children, unaware that children may view such practices as trials. Children may be encouraged to kiss others — adults or children — to the distress of one or both participants.

> Ever since I can remember, my family has been trying to put me and my cousin Nathan together. My family would take pictures of us holding hands or him kissing me on the cheek. Every time this occurred I felt like I was going to be sick. I could not stand Nathan and always refused to go and visit him.
> There was one particular incident, when I was about 6 or 7 years old. Grandma and Grandpa were taking me to visit the cousins, including Nathan. I begged and pleaded if I could stay home but they would not listen to me. I even told them that I hated Nathan and that he was always trying to touch and kiss me. They just laughed and said, 'Isn't that cute.' I felt frustrated because nobody would pay attention to my feelings.
> When we arrived at my cousins, I sat very close to Grandma. I was hoping I could not be bothered. But, sure enough, Nathan came over to me and I was forced to play with him. I was so angry and upset at this point that I threw a temper tantrum and we left.
> I am usually a very quiet, well-behaved child so for me to resort to a temper tantrum must have been the ultimate. But it worked. I have not seen my cousin Nathan since this incident. (Ellie)

When children's perspectives are denied by adults — Ellie herself does not describe her experiences with Nathan as 'cute' — their distress may be exacerbated.
'Washing with spit' appears as a not uncommon liberty taken with children's bodies.

> Every morning when I woke up and was getting ready to leave for school, my grandmother would come over to me, lick her hand, and wipe it on my face, like she was trying to get out a spot. I hated that so much but, because I was a lot younger than her, there was really nothing that I could do about it. (Richard, Naomi's informant)

> Bob told me how his mother is always licking her finger and washing his face with it. Daniel also told me the same story. I instantly remembered how my grandmother would do that to me. I always hated it. It seems so nasty. If anyone did that to me as an adult I would back away yet as a child I would always get in trouble for not listening to my grandmother. (Estelle)

Adults may, unthinkingly and with the best of motives, act in ways that children find both troublesome and unavoidable.

As an adult I may see as trivial what I call 'unwanted physical contact' — at least when it happens to children. When, however, I take seriously the childhood experiences described by my informants, it is clear that such contact, when unwanted, demonstrates children's lack of control over their own bodies and can be experienced as a little trial of childhood.

Bathroom Access

Adults routinely have access to bathroom facilities and, when such facilities are unavailable, know the ensuing problems, about which they may complain with varying degrees of vigor. Children cannot routinely take for granted such ready access. The following story shows the difficulties attendant on lack of knowledge of where facilities are, the embarrassing consequences, and the lack of resources for concealing those consequences.

> My first grade class was in art class and we had it upstairs where all the older kids had their classes. I think it was for the third to fifth graders. I can remember having to go to the bathroom very badly but I didn't know where the bathrooms were on the second floor. I asked the teacher if I could bring someone with me who knew where to go but she told me to just get directions and go alone or I couldn't go at all. I asked someone for directions but I still wasn't sure if I could get there and I was really nervous about all the big kids in the hallway so I begged the teacher to let someone come but she still refused. By this point I had to go so badly that I just left and prayed that I would find the bathroom. I ran as fast as I could down the hall with all the big kids, thinking that they were all staring at me and knew that I needed the bathroom fast. I couldn't find the upstairs bathroom because I was so panicked so I ran downstairs to our bathroom, but just as I reached the bathroom it was too late. I was so embarrassed and I had to call a friend's mother to bring me clothes. Needless to say my friend was smaller than I was so I had to wear highwaters[3] and naturally thought everyone knew what happened. If only my teacher had realized how important it was that someone come with me because I was so nervous about going alone. I think I will always think twice before I say no to someone when they have to go to the bathroom. (Karen)

Children may experience many situations where they are required to ask for permission to go to the bathroom and where that permission can be and is denied.

---

[3] Highwaters are trousers that are considered too short, ending above the ankle. They look as if they have been pulled up at the waist to keep the cuffs from dragging in water.

> In first grade, Debbie had to go to the bathroom and the teacher wouldn't let her go because it was the end of the day and the teacher wanted to go home. The teacher told her to wait until she got home. She had an accident on the way home and when she got home her mom was mad at her and Debbie said the teacher told her to wait and her mom said the teacher would let you go. Her mom believed the teacher, not her daughter. (Anonymous notes from class discussion)

Contradictory responses from adults, both of whom wielded the power to enforce their definitions of the situation, left this child with a problem without apparent resolution. The child was faulted both for wanting to go to the bathroom and for not going.

Adults may, for a variety of reasons, deny children permission to use bathroom facilities. Nonetheless, from the child's point of view, such denial can create a no-win situation, as in the previous and following stories.

> I can remember the time when my mother took me shopping with her. I was about 4 or 5 years old. I had gone to the bathroom before I left home but when I got to the store, I had to go again. (I was afraid of my mother then.) I wanted to ask her if she could take me to the bathroom but I was so afraid. So finally I asked her if I could go to the bathroom, and *she told me that I didn't have to go to the bathroom*. I told her if I didn't go to the bathroom that I would pee all over myself. She told me that if I peed all over myself that she was going to whip my behind, because I know I don't have to go to the bathroom. I peed on myself and she did whip me.
>
> Parents and adults have the tendency of telling children when they are sleepy, hungry, and when they have to go to the bathroom. Not too many adults know what they want to do and they don't have control over everything they do. Just because I went to the bathroom before I left home doesn't lead to the conclusion that I wouldn't have to go again before I got home. (Polly, emphasis added)

Adults' power to define children's physical states and act on those definitions can present problems for children whose experiences do not accord with adult definitions. How indeed do adults know when children have to go to the bathroom and when they do not? How does one in the position to grant permission decide when requests are warranted?

Children themselves may recognize that a need to use bathroom facilities is but one reason for requesting them.

> This experience happened in the second grade. I hated my teacher, and my teacher hated me, so it was a mutual feeling. Well, I was sitting in class one day and we were doing math. I hated math and my teacher knew it. I raised my hand to ask if I could go to the bathroom

and my teacher just ignored me. *Now I have to admit I had pulled this stunt before just to get out of class, but this time I really had to go to the bathroom.* I continued to raise my hand, and my teacher continued to ignore me. Finally, after about ten minutes of this, I blurted out, 'Excuse me Mrs. Shaw, but I reeeeally have to go to the bathroom!' She said, 'No you don't. You can wait until math is over.' I could not believe she was going to make me wait a whole half hour before I could go. I could not wait that long. All of a sudden I could not hold it any longer and I said, 'If you don't let me go, I'm going to go right here in class.' She said, 'Go right ahead,' and I knew she didn't think I would. You've got to know I was a very stubborn kid, and I never thought of the consequences. Well, I proceeded to pee right there in my chair. Then I saw the look on my teacher's face and let me tell you it was not a pleasant one. She sent me to the principal's office to call my parents to get some clean pants. While I was waiting it dawned on me that my parents were going to be mad and I started to cry. By the time my father got to school with a clean pair of pants, I was in hysterics. I proceeded to tell him how sorry I was, etc., and I was getting ready for him to yell at me. You know what? He didn't even get the slightest bit mad, he just sort of chuckled and said, 'See you at 3:00.' I couldn't believe it. I walked back into class and the whole class started laughing at me. I was so embarrassed, and all I could think of was that my dad had laughed at me too. (Tilly emphasis added)

That children can request to go to the bathroom for 'illegitimate' purposes indicates that children can use resources available to them to fulfill their own purposes. The cost of illegitimate use, however, may be the denial of legitimate use. For Tilly, a further cost was being embarrassed and laughed at. It is also noteworthy that Tilly seems to leave her father no 'acceptable' option for responding, for both anger and amusement are faulted.

The requirement that one get permission in order to use bathroom facilities can lead to recognition of adults' failings as well as to embarrassment.

I was in first grade. I was attending the public school in my neighborhood. I remember each morning I would walk to school with my friends in my neighborhood. Well, one day in particular I will always remember. I was sitting quietly in my seat listening to my teacher explain the lesson. I suddenly had to go to the bathroom in the worst way. The bathroom was right next to my classroom but I couldn't just get up and go because I would get in trouble. We were taught to raise our hand if we wanted something. So I raised my hand and waited for my teacher to call on me but she never did. I then began to wave my hand a little, but she still didn't call on me. By now I just couldn't hold it anymore. Well, that finally got her attention. She sent me to the bathroom, but what good would that do? I was done. She told me to wait there until my mom came with a change of clothes. When my mom came I began to cry because I was so upset that my teacher didn't call on me. I wanted to go home but my mom said no. I walked back into my classroom where I saw the janitor mopping the floor around where I sat. *The look he gave me made me want to cry again but I kept saying to myself, 'It wasn't my fault. It was the teacher's because she wouldn't call on me and let me go to the bathroom.'* (Judy, emphasis added)

Teachers may deny such permission for a variety of reasons that, in the context of school and the classroom, make good sense, for children may use permission for 'illegitimate' reasons such as getting out of class; teachers are responsible for knowing children's whereabouts and limiting their out-of-class time; children leaving class may constitute a disruption; and teachers may want to bring their workday to a close. Nonetheless, denial of permission may have serious consequences for those to whom it is denied.

In order to obtain their own goals, children may make use of the requirement for permission to use bathroom facilities. In the following example, Holly interprets permission as an absolute requirement, even though she knows it is not intended to be so taken. (Her failure does not compromise the innovative character of her strategy.)

I used to have to stay in my room on Sunday mornings until 8:30. That was a long time for me, considering I would wake up around 6:30. I would go crazy waiting to be allowed to go out and do something. Nothing in my room satisfied me. I had to get out. I would try to get my parents back for doing this to me. One time I had to go to the bathroom so I went in my wastepaper basket. My parents were so angry, but I explained to them that I wasn't allowed out of my room till 8:30 and I had to go (even though I knew I was allowed to use the bathroom anytime). This tactic didn't work but I eventually got my parents to realize that I could get up and do things semi-quietly. I would insist on getting cereal myself. They would leave a bowl down on the counter for me with a spoon. I would then turn on the TV until they got up. There would be, of course, a mess, but it was better than the little war going on previously. (Holly)

One consequence of children's manipulation of their 'needs' to suit their own goals may be that children encourage adults to not believe them or to see them as childish. In some circumstances, the goal may be viewed as worth these or other negative consequences.

Adults' control of children's use of bathroom facilities highlights adults' routine assumption that they know better than children what children's inner states are. Adults' assumptions about how much control children have over their bodily functions may be at odds with children's experiences. When adults' 'knowledge' contradicts children's experiences, children may find themselves in awkward situations, unable to act as they see fit. They may also discover that adults' 'knowledge' is limited or flawed.

Being Bathed

That adults bathe children does not initially appear to be an assault on children's bodies but, as a number of stories suggest, it can be so viewed by children. That a child may simply not want to bathe, and see no need to do so, is described in the following story.

> Another experience that I had a few times was when I was 6 years old until I was 10 years old and I didn't want to take a bath. I remember it was a daily fight. After 5:00 in the afternoon it was time for the daily bath. This was the time to run, to hide, and to scream. As soon as my favorite cartoon (*Tom and Jerry*) had finished my mom would come to get me with her sweet voice: 'Edna, it's time to take a bath.' As soon as I heard the first two words: 'it's time' I started complaining, and running and I remember it was a war. I bounced off the walls, I wanted to take my dog to the shower with me, I wanted to bath all my dolls, and I had a severe fever in five minutes. I remember telling my mom how bad I felt with the fever I had. As always my mom gave me two baby aspirins and put me in the tub with my dolls. The difficult thing about the 'shower battles' for me was the fact of taking a shower every day. It was so terrible for me to hear the word shower. I remember I asked my mom why I had to take a shower if I had taken one the day before. Why did my parents force me to take a shower? I was clean. This is a question that I asked myself through my childhood years. (Edna)

That standards of cleanliness may differ from adult to adult is exemplified by Edna's *daily* bath and, for Dawn in the following story, a *weekly* bath.

> One specific rule that I had to follow as a child wasn't really a rule, it was more like something that my sister and I had to do without asking any questions. Every Sunday we had to take a bath and wash our hair. I used to hate doing this because when I got out of the tub my mother used to rub my head with the towel so hard that it would hurt. Then when she would try to comb my hair there would be so many knots that it would take hours. I couldn't complain because if I did my mother would just tell me that 'I had to be clean' or 'It's for your own good' or even better, 'No teacher likes a dirty child in class on Monday morning.' That used to make my skin crawl. I hated going to school, especially on Mondays. (Dawn)

Children may object not only to bathing itself but, as Dawn notes, to the particular physical discomforts associated with it, or, as in the following story, to the negative consequences for one's body image.

> Another time regretted by me as well as by my brothers and sisters was bath time. Bath time was set for a specific time each night and each of my brothers and sisters had a certain night assigned to bathe my brother and me. No one liked this, especially my older sister. She always got shampoo in my eyes, I swear on purpose, and she made me dry myself. She refused to touch me. It made me feel like there was something wrong with me. I felt like a burden on the family, which I probably was. (Jane)

In the process of bathing, children's moral sensibilities may be offended.

> An incident that really bothered me was when I was around 10 years old. I use to go to the baby-sitter's every day after school when my mother was at work. One day I was supposed to sleep over because my mother had a date. My baby-sitter had two sons. One was a lot older and one was a year younger than me. That evening I was forced to take a bath with her younger son. I was very embarrassed as I stepped into the tub. The bath was humiliating enough but I had to wear her son's underwear and pajamas because I did not have a change of clothing. This was a very embarrassing situation for me and I was forced to do it. I will never forget the feeling I had as I stepped into that tub. (Ellie)

One of my own memories supports this experience.

> When I was about 5 we had a lodger who occasionally baby-sat for me. One night when my mother was out she gave me a bath. When I stood up in the tub to be dried, before putting the towel around me she said, 'Shame on you. Cover yourself up.' I remember thinking at the time that what she said was stupid. Of course I was naked. I was taking a bath. Nonetheless, I felt bad.

Even when children view adults as wrong they may take adults' claims to heart.

Although it is hardly unreasonable for adults to want children to be 'clean,' the relativity of cleanliness is obscured when adults use their power to establish as absolute the standards to which children are held (and with which children may disagree). How cleanliness is produced, at what cost to physical comfort and modesty, may be viewed by children as having negative aspects and as being beyond their control.

Medical Procedures

Medical procedures can provide a locus for adults' control of children's bodies as well as a locus for children's exercise of control over their own bodies and over adults. Although one might not want to argue that children ought to be able to refuse medical treatment, it may be useful to recognize that nonetheless children are subject to what adults deem proper medical care (and those adults might disagree with one another on what is proper). Publicity given to the children of Christian Scientists who view prayer as the medical procedure of choice, and of Jehovah's Witnesses who reject blood transfusions, focus on children's lack of choice. Coercion of children to accept Western medical techniques is equally a lack of choice.

Not only are children subject to the medical procedures accepted by the adults who care for them but they may have legal access to those procedures only with the consent of those adults. Furthermore, children may be required to adopt adults' methods for following medical procedures in situations where adults have some choice. Is it better to take off Band-Aids quickly or slowly? What is the best way to take pills? Adults may choose their preferred method; children may be coerced to adopt adults' preferred methods.

> I must have been around 4 or 5 years old at the time. I had just come back from the doctor, who had given me penicillin to take. My mother gave me the pill and a glass of orange juice. I was standing by the kitchen door with my coat still on. I am not sure why but I must have been ready to leave at any moment. I just looked at both the objects in my hands and thought of how much I hated taking pills. My brother, who had been taking penicillin for a couple of years, came into the kitchen and began explaining how to swallow the pill. So I put it in my mouth and drank some juice but the pill would not go down my throat. This went on for some time and I even spit the juice and pill out once. I ended up crying, my father was yelling at me, and my brother kept saying, 'Just swallow it. It's easy.' I kept thinking 'Why does he say it is easy? It will not go down.' My father finally left all upset, my brother got frustrated and left, and my mother crushed up another pill and put it in some more juice and forced me to drink the entire thing. This episode would happen every time I had to take pills until my mother realized that it would save a lot of time and aggravation if she just crushed up the pills in the first place. She was never happy about doing this and always asked me why I just did not swallow it like everyone else did. When I tried to explain that they would not go down, she would start getting mad and leave the room. Finally I realized that it was better if I just told them that I took the medicine and let my body take care of the illness instead of having to go through all that hassle every time. (Debby)

One reason for adults' refusal to crush pills might be that they view it as simply the 'wrong' way to take them; another reason, the quite understandable desire of adults to avoid such an 'unnecessary' task. One problem that arises for children is that although they have preferences, they may require adults' assistance to carry them out, assistance that adults may define as 'work.' What I find particularly intriguing about the foregoing tale is the strategy devised of simply not taking the medicine. Presumably this child would remain ill but just as presumably she did not remain sufficiently ill for her subterfuge to be noticed.

Adults may, wisely or unwisely, conceal their injuries, avoiding medical care and rejecting treatment. Such options are less available to children.

> Even when I hurt myself I tried not to attract attention to myself. I would hide and cover my cut or bruise with my hand. I wouldn't even look at it. I would crouch down behind furniture, lock myself in the bathroom, or hide wherever I could. My brothers would usually tell my parents where I was hiding. After they found me they would have to pry my hand from my wound. I can remember how they would try to con me into letting my hand loose. They would tell me that whoever was in the house — relatives, grandparents, neighbors, even they themselves — was a doctor or nurse. They would go into elaborate stories about which hospital they worked at, which war they had fought in, and always how many lives that they had saved. They would try to make me feel guilty or embarrassed by saying 'You don't want to offend x, do you? He/she only wants to help you.' This usually worked. I hated to feel embarrassment so I would let go. *It worked until I realized that they were lying.* When their stories started to change every time, I realized what they were doing. After that, whenever they told the story it would make things worse. I would cry louder and squeeze tighter. . .It is funny because I now find myself telling my 8-year-old sister or any child the same stories. (Nan, emphasis added)

Against the background of Nan's description of her distress at adults' actions and at discovering that adults had lied, it seems puzzling that as an adult she reproduces their behavior.[4]

Children's medical treatment, however necessary adults may judge it to be, can be characterized as *uninformed non-consent*.[5] Whether or not informed consent is possible or desirable, it indeed is absent. Its absence may be recognized by children, with important consequences for their control of their own bodies as well as for their views of adults.

---

[4] I address this issue in some detail in Chapter 10.
[5] How children inform themselves of medical matters despite adults' attempted concealment is eloquently described by Bluebond-Langer in *The Private Worlds of Dying Children* (1978).

Physical Comfort and Discomfort

I have collected just a few stories of children's comfort but they too show how children may be dependent on adults' definitions of children's experiences — definitions that may be at odds with children's own. Adults' views of warmth and cold, for example, do not necessarily reflect children's physical experiences but rather reflect either adults' experiences or adults' views of children's 'needs.'

> My mother seemed to be perpetually cold, even if it was April and seventy-five degrees outside. Because of this, she always made me bundle up to the extent where I felt like such an oddball because everyone else got to wear their spring jackets. This whole issue made me so mad not only because it seemed as if I had no say over what I could and couldn't wear but also because it seemed that my mother did not respect my ability to make a rational decision. (Pam)

> A child has no control over the clothes he must wear. During the wintertime I would have to get all bundled up in three layers of clothes before I could go out. Then Mom puts on one coat and goes outside. This makes no sense. Parents think kids need to be in several layers of clothes in order to be warm. I always wanted to take something off but I never could because I might 'catch a chill.' (Theresa)

Physical comfort emerges as an issue in a story of seating arrangements in a car. In this incident it is clear that the very disposition of one's own body in space can lie beyond one's control.

> At the end of the night we would pile back into the family car and drive home. I would always have to sit in the middle of my two brothers because I was the smallest. My brothers would always fall asleep, leaning on me and taking up all the space, so there was no possible way for me to get some sleep. I would argue with my parents, saying it was not fair for me to always be in the middle. I felt really upset that because I was smaller than my brothers I had to be inconvenienced every time. My parents never understood. (Ellie)

Children's arguments about seating arrangements in cars may be perceived by adults as trivial, mere sibling squabbling, a source of *adults'* trials, but, for the children involved, the consequences of where one sits may be viewed as significant for one's comfort. To base seating decisions on size means that young children are foreordained to get less desirable seating arrangements than adults or older children (an experience with which small adults may also be familiar).

The following story shows the kind of physical discomfort that children may endure under the direction of adults.

In and out my face goes to the water, my arms are curved just a little, my hands cupped, and my legs are doing the flutter kick. I'm so tired I want to stop. I do and the lifeguard yells to keep going. I have been swimming for hours, my sides hurt, my eyes sting from the chlorine. I stop only to be yelled at again. I can't do it any longer. I go under and drink about three gallons of water. I come up gagging and the lesson's over. (Mary)

Children may experience discomfort in a variety of ways. Adults may deny not only resources or alternatives for minimizing or eliminating the discomfort but also deny the very experience of discomfort itself.

*   *   *

Why do adults feed children according to adults' standards for children, put children to bed, subject them to unwanted physical contact, control their access to bathroom facilities, bathe them, subject them to unwanted medical procedures, and ignore their physical discomfort? If the obvious answer, 'for the good of the children,' is suspended, if these questions are taken *not* to be rhetorical, it becomes possible to address them as genuine questions, their answers to be sought within what ethnomethodologists call 'the locally produced activities' of which they are a part. When adults' assumptions about children are suspended, empirical study can begin.

In stories of adults' control of children's bodies, children emerge as a source, as indeed they are, of adults' 'work' — to be fed, bathed, medicated, their bathroom needs attended to, their sleep provided for. As adults carry out their work, however, children find themselves acted upon in ways that deny them control over their own bodies. Running through the stories I have collected, often as submerged streams, are adults' values, standards, tastes, and convenience. Adults differ from one another in the standards they set for themselves; children, on the other hand, seem to be held to whatever standards are set by those who care for them. Adults emerge as presumptuous, claiming to know better than children what children are experiencing. Adults are also displayed as flawed, presenting themselves as knowledgeable when they are not and able to be duped in a variety of ways.

Children's ultimate lack of control over their own bodies is brought to their attention when they pray,

Now I lay me down to sleep
I pray the Lord my soul to keep.
If I should die before I wake
I pray the Lord my soul to take.

In discussions, informants expressed their childhood dismay when they said this prayer. Would they die before they woke? Children may take the disappearance of their bodies, soul and all, to be a real possibility. In the absence of knowledge that everyone dies, children may wonder why they have been singled out for supernatural control over their bodies.

3   Presenting One's Self

Some of the clothing my mother bought me I could not stand the look of. I remember having this red coat with flowers on it and white fur around the hat. I hated it. She always made me wear it. I used to be so embarrassed to be seen in it. When I was in third grade, Levi's were the cool thing to wear and my mother bought me Toughskins jeans. I cried. (Inez)

Harriet was my best friend from first grade through sixth grade. Since we spent all of our time together, our mothers gradually became best friends also. At first we thought it was heaven. We got to spend much more time together and the four of us would do things on the weekends. This heaven, however, slowly became hell. By the third grade, Harriet and I had the same clothes, same teacher, played the same sports, and were in Girl Scouts together. To say the least, I was quite sick of Harriet for I was having a lot of trouble establishing my own identity. (Gini)

How do children establish their identities, both in their own eyes and in the eyes of others? A significant element in establishing and sustaining a sense of self, for both children and adults, is how one imagines that one appears to others, a process Cooley (1962) refers to as the 'looking glass self.' By controlling one's appearance one can affect others' perceptions. Limited resources or the absence of permission to control appearance can seriously affect the ways one is perceived by others and thus one's sense of self.

In *Presentation of Self in Everyday Life* Goffman describes the significance of appearance for how one is viewed: 'When an individual enters the presence of others, they commonly seek to acquire information about him or to bring into play information about him already possessed. . .[O]bservers can glean clues from his conduct[1] and appearance. . .' (1959, p. 1) and 'When an individual appears before others, he knowingly and unwittingly projects a definition of the situation, of which a conception of himself is an important part' (1959, p. 242). A fundamental aspect of this projection is what one looks like. With limited control over appearance, children may find themselves compelled to give what they see as false, even negative, impressions of themselves.

---

[1] The importance of conduct (activities) is discussed in Chapter 4 of this volume.

Adults routinely recognize the importance *to themselves* of how they appear to themselves and to others. Physical appearance, including clothing, hair style, and physical characteristics; being similar to and different from others; and the company one keeps are important aspects of presentation of self, over which adults may maintain considerable control. Children may share this sense of the importance of how they present themselves without so routinely being able to exert significant control over how they do so. Nonetheless, how children view themselves and how they think others view them are consequential for them. Empirical evidence documents that children's concerns may be warranted. Ambert, in her study of peer abuse, states,

> [C]hildren can be victimized for very trivial and random reasons that have absolutely nothing to do with their own personalities (but may occasionally have something to do with their physical appearance or clothing, for instance). (1994, p. 10)

> *[C]hildren can be rejected [by peers] through no fault of their own* but, for instance, simply because they do not belong to the proper race, religion, social class, or, even, do not wear 'appropriate' clothing, do not belong to the 'in' groups, and do not share in the values or pastimes of their peers. (1995, p. 186, emphasis in original)

The consequences for children of adults' decisions are illustrated in the following story:

> When I was in the fourth grade, about 10 years old, my parents insisted I wear these bright pink pants. At first, I did not mind this very much — until I was publicly humiliated. Every time we had recess on the playground a bunch of girls would gather to laugh at and tease me. How humiliating! I could not help it that I wore pink pants. My parents liked them and I could not hurt their feelings. The girls continued to call me a sissy and weird. I felt very alienated. I just had to wear them. It just so happened that it was the time of year that we all put our clothes that did not fit us into a garbage bag for Goodwill (an organization that collects clothes for needy people). I managed to slip those pink pants in there by telling my mom that they did not fit anymore. (Yvonne)

Yvonne's story describes important features of trials related to children's presentations of self: ridicule and humiliation by others; protection of adults ('I could not hurt their feelings'); and a strategy for resolving the problem (lying). Faulting children for succumbing to 'peer pressure' denies them the advantages of 'blending in' that adults regularly realize and employ. Not 'blending in' may have significant, even dire, consequences for children.

In discussing the self, Cooley (1962) emphasizes the importance of what one *imagines* are the views of others towards one — not what others' views necessarily *are*. In the following story the explanation offered may not be empirically supportable; nonetheless, Emily attributes her lack of friends to her clothing, *it may be so*, and, whether or not it is so, her attribution influences her behavior and sense of self.

> When I was young I didn't like the fact that some of my friends always had beautiful new clothes and I didn't. It was hard because a lot of the children would want to be friends with the ones who had all of the nice clothes and always look nice. I wasn't one of the ones who had nice clothes; therefore, I didn't really have many friends. (Emily)[2]

Stone, in 'Appearance and the self,' testifies to the significance of appearance for children, asserting that it 'is of major importance at every stage of the early development of the self' (1962, p. 88) and that 'Challenges and validations of the self. . .may be regarded as aroused by personal appearance' (1962, p. 92). That children recognize the importance of appearance is illustrated in the following story.

> I remember those endless days of worrisome fear about what my schoolmates would think of me, whether it would be the clothes I would be wearing each day, what reading group I would be in, or if the teacher would ever pick me to be first in line. The list can go on forever. But, there was one thing that, as an elementary school student, was more important than anything else in the world. It was something that every end of August your mother and you went to stores to find the perfect one — yes, it was the infamous lunch-box.
>
> I loved to pick my new lunch-boxes out. We would go to many different stores before I would actually make my final decision. I wanted so badly to have the prettiest lunch-box or at least one that my brother and his friends would think was cool. I didn't want one that the mean boys would make fun of or the snobby girls would look down on. I longed each year for the perfect lunch-box, one that I would be proud of, one that everyone would like. My decision sometimes took days and an awful lot of patience from my mother. After a while of me being picky though she would give me a final ultimatum, 'Find a lunch-box or you are brown-bagging it this year!' I would soon find a lunch-box that would meet all my requirements. I don't know why I made such a big thing about getting a lunch-box but I always did. I don't even remember if anyone ever made comments about my lunch-boxes. All I can remember is that incredible fear shopping for one. (Felicia)

---

[2] Experiences like Emily's might be marshaled in support of requiring school uniforms.

Adults who view children as indecisive shoppers may not realize the great importance of the choices being made.

The foregoing stories and those to follow document the importance that children attribute to their appearance and the restrictions within which they must act as they seek to present themselves as they see themselves and as they want to be seen. Adults' control of children's appearance may be viewed by children as compromising children's identity and acceptance by others.

Clothing

Who decides what children wear, whose standards apply, and with what consequences for children?

> I had some great little clothes in my time. I would wake up bright and early and dress myself in whatever clothes appealed to me at the time. I had no concept of matching or clashing. I just knew that was the shirt I wanted to wear and those were the pants for that day. Then I would leave my room, wake up my parents, and go to the family room to watch television. Then my mom would wake up and walk into the family room and take one look at my beautiful outfit and say, 'Celeste, let's find a new shirt or some new pants.' What she really meant was 'You picked out ugly clothes and I'm going to fix them.' I would always put up a fuss about changing my clothes because I could never see what was wrong with them. To me my clothes looked wonderful. I guess it's true when they say that beauty is in the eye of the beholder. I feel that children should be able to dress themselves. Who cares if a child doesn't match once in a while? At least this way the child would get some feeling of accomplishment and satisfaction. (Celeste)

Celeste seems to have seen her mother's strategy ('Let's find a new shirt or some new pants'), perhaps designed to save Celeste's feelings, as just that — a strategy — and thus Celeste saw herself as both deceived, albeit unsuccessfully, and insulted.

Clothing can have important negative consequences for a child's journeys into the world — discomfort, embarrassment, the inability to be distinguishable from others, and being taken to be what one is not (e.g., a boy when one is a girl, younger than one is). Nonetheless, children's decisions about what to wear can as a matter of course be denied and overridden by adults. Children's concern may be solely with appearance and adults' with *both* appearance and the work involved to create that appearance — although children too may weigh the attendant bother. Fundamental, however, is children's experiences of not looking the way they want to and being troubled by it, both for reasons of aesthetics and for the implications in presenting one's self to others.

If, as Stone writes, 'One's clothes impart value to the wearer, both in the wearer's own eyes and in the eyes of others' (1962, p. 92), that value may be negative as well as positive.

> My informant told me that her mother always made her wear these brown shoes that her mother said were really good for her feet. She said she did not need to wear them for any certain reason except that her mother made her. She remembers having her first grade picture taken and she was sitting in the first row with a pink dress on and the awful brown shoes. (Annette)

> One of the most hated things of my childhood was the green flowered bonnet. From the time I was 1 year old to when I was 3 years old, my mother made me wear a big ugly green flowered bonnet in the summer every time that I went to the beach. I HATED IT! I loved to go to the beach and look for starfish and play in the water but I was never allowed to do this unless I had on the bonnet. . .My mother claimed that she did it so my face wouldn't get sunburned. I could understand that but always wondered why my brother didn't have to wear one. Didn't she worry about his face getting sunburned? I can remember many instances when my mom would have to chase me all over the beach because I tried so hard to get away from her and that ugly bonnet. I was always embarrassed to wear it because I thought it was the ugliest thing I'd ever seen. I was also always jealous of my cousin because we were the same age and she never had to wear a bonnet. (Naomi)

Naomi questions not only the requirement that she wear something she hates but the explanation offered. Her story, as she tells it, does not provide a fully satisfactory explanation for her mother's commitment to her bonnet-wearing.

Annette and Naomi complain about wearing what they did not like. In the following story Pauline complains of not being able to wear what she did like.

> I recall difficult experiences shopping with my mother as a child and my frustrating limitations concerning my inability to 'present myself.' I remember that I had a strong preference and liking for gaudy clothes, which my mother called 'Spanish-looking clothes.' The outfits were full and flashy with sparkles and other adornments and were brightly colored. She never bought these clothes for me because her taste in clothes was in complete opposition to mine. I can still remember the incredible frustration I would experience shopping with her. (Pauline)

Pauline describes her sense of how she wanted to present herself. She also raises the issue of the importance to one's sense of self of making one's own decisions, as does Greg.

> I can remember distinctly loathing my mother picking out my clothes for me and trying to dress me as a young child. I remember wanting to pick out my own clothes, ones that I like, very badly. (Greg)

Practical considerations may compromise one's appearance.

> One thing I hated all through grade school was wearing boots to school, especially if it were only because of the rain and not snow. I hated my boots. I thought they were so ugly and I never wanted to wear them. At least my mom would let me bring my shoes in a bag to school. As soon as I got into the school building I would run into the bathroom and change from my boots to my shoes. I always wished there were some way I could change them at the bus stop but there was no way I could without getting my feet wet so I had to wait until I got to school. Actually I remember doing it a few times right on the bus. My sister and I would both sit there taking off our boots and putting our shoes on before we even got to school. (Cindy)

Adults who have dressed impractically in rain or snow for reasons of appearance can sympathize with Cindy. Adults, however, may have more freedom to make their own *unwise* choices.

'Seldom, upon encountering another, do we inquire concerning the other's gender,' writes Stone, perhaps more accurately of adults than of children. He continues, 'Indeed to do so would be to impugn the very gender that must be established. The knowing of the other's gender is known silently, established by appearances' (1962, p. 90). In the following story (and in others in this and the following section about hair style), just such impugning is described.

> In addition to my boyish haircut, most of my wardrobe was made up of hand-me-downs from my two older brothers. When all my friends were wearing flowers and ruffles, I was wearing Toughskins and T-shirts. This didn't help when I was already being mistaken for a boy. I can remember bringing a pair of high-heeled shoes that a friend of mine had given me to school and changing into them when I got to school. (Sally)

Alternatively, a girl's dressing like a girl may be viewed as both negative and unnecessary for accurate gender display.

> School as a young child was never one of my most favorite places, probably because my mother made me wear a skirt every day. Why she did this to me I will never understand. I always thought my mom dressed me like that because she wanted everyone to know I was a girl. Obviously everyone knew I was a girl because my name was Daisy. (Daisy)

Children's appearance may lead to their being taken for the gender they are or are not and in either case children may or may not mind. I was told by a long-haired boy of 12 who was regularly mistaken for a girl, 'I don't care. I know what I am.' Problems seem to arise when adults' concerns, or lack thereof, are directed towards children whose concerns differ.

Not being like others can be viewed as a problem; being like others can also possess the properties of a trial. As Gini described in the epigraph to this chapter, matching clothing may be viewed as strongly objectionable. For Cindy in the following story, matching clothing seems merely tiresome.

> In nursery school and as I got a little older, I remember my sister and I always had matching dresses. Whether my parents bought them, or other relatives, everyone seemed to think it was so cute to dress us like twins. Well, this did not seem to bother me but as we got older and outgrew these outfits, I did not get rid of mine. Instead, my outfit went to my younger sister and my older sister's outfit went to me. (We are all two years apart.) So, once again I was in the same outfit, only this time my 'twin' was my younger sister. (Cindy)

The following story describes matching clothing as an adult convenience.

> My mother and I differed many times in our taste in clothes. She used to always dress me and my sister, who is two years older than I, in matching dresses. My sister and I both didn't care for this but my mom found shopping for us quite convenient. (Eunice)

Adult–child disagreements over clothing may reflect different versions of that child held by each.

> I can recall a time when I was having school pictures taken and my mother had picked out the outfit I was to wear. It was something that I was strongly opposed to wearing but the more I argued against wearing it, the more my mother argued for it. I tried telling her it was ugly, made me look like a boy, and was way too tight. My mother insisted that I wear it because the pictures were for her. After the pictures, I was outside at recess and the seat of my pants split open. I was so embarrassed but I was more angry at my mother than I was embarrassed. She had to make me do something I didn't want to and I ended up being embarrassed in front of my friends because of it. It appears to me that she was trying to dress me in a way that reflects her as a good mother but her actions ended up hurting me. (Gladys)

Different versions of children may reflect different concerns. Gladys emphasizes avoiding such negative outcomes as looking ugly, looking like a boy, and embarrassment; she attributes to her mother a desire to appear to be a good mother. Adults' attention to children's clothing certainly may reflect concern with children's well-being but, as the above stories indicate, adults may also use children as an element in their own adult presentation of self. When adults control children's appearance, for whatever reasons of their own, children may be faced with two rather undesirable alternatives, namely, to present themselves as if their appearance were their choice (and thus as stylistically incompetent) or as if it were not (and, thus, as lacking power and control and as weak).

Hair Style and Length

Like clothing, hair style may have important implications for children's presentation of self. Stories indicate that those with short hair wanted long; with long hair, short; those with curly hair wanted straight, etc.

> A time when I remember being very mad and thought that it was very hard was when it was time to get a haircut. I wanted hair and my father insisted that I get my head shaven. I cried the whole time we were at the barber's and the whole way home. Every year until I was 12 I had to get a butch cut. It really made me mad. (Jack, Dottie's informant)

> When I was about 7 years old, my mother wanted to cut my hair short. I didn't want it cut because I liked it long. My mom said that she wanted it short because whenever she tried to brush my long hair, I would scream and cry. The truth is I didn't want her to brush my hair because she always pulled too hard and wasn't gentle and it hurt. I didn't think that it was fair that I had to have short hair just because she didn't want to deal with it. . .I remember visiting my great grandmother every few months in Connecticut. She was in her eighties and was going senile. When we would visit, she would always look at me and say to my mom, 'What a cute little boy you have. He's so handsome.' Because my mother had chopped off all my hair, I looked somewhat like a boy. I would get so upset when my grandmother said this, I would go into the back bedroom and cry and be so mad at my mom for cutting my hair. This upset me because I knew that I could do nothing about it. I couldn't get my long hair back and I couldn't yell at my grandmother because I'd get in trouble. I still, to this day, hold a grudge against my mother for the 'hell' that I went through with my short hair. (Naomi)

Like Sally in the foregoing section who was *dressed* like a boy, Naomi (as well as Gini and Sally, cited below) describe their hair styles as limiting their presentation of self *as a girl*. Naomi also describes adult obliviousness (to why she screamed and cried, or even that she did so) and her own impotence not only to do anything but to say anything.

Those who complained of having short hair cited 'everyone else' who has long hair but given the number of complaints I received, I wonder who was privileged enough to have long hair. Theresa was one of the 'fortunate' ones, though she paid a price for her good fortune.

> When I was young I always wanted to grow my hair long but my grandmother always liked it short. Well, guess what length my hair was? You're right, my hair was kept short thanks to my grandmother's power. Then when my mother finally let it grow long she would braid it almost every day. This really hurt because she pulled it so tight that I thought it would just come out of my head. It was definitely worth it though and, unfortunately for my grandmother, I liked my hair much better long. (Theresa)

One of Whoopie Goldberg's comedic sketches describes a Black child wanting long blond hair ('Whoopie Goldberg in Concert'). White informants speak of using the same strategy Whoopie did — putting something (a shirt, a blanket) on one's head as a facsimile of long hair.

> I always wanted to have long, straight hair like most of my friends did. However, my mother insisted on keeping my hair short because, she said, it would be too much trouble to take care of. I also wanted to have my hair straightened but my mother laughed every time I mentioned this suggestion. At the time I was very frustrated by the situation. Not only did I want to be like my friends but several times people who didn't know me referred to me as a boy. When I was at home, I would take a pink blanket that I used for my dolls and tie it around my head so I could pretend I had long hair. I also used to take my mother's old wigs that were stored in the attic and wear them when I was in the house. (Sally)

The facsimile strategy, however, is of somewhat limited use, for the most part restricted to solitary occasions and private settings. Its efficacy in the presence of others depends on their willingness to see 'a child with long hair' and not 'a child with a blanket on her head.'

In the following story, hair length is not the only object of distress; a 'bad' haircut compounds the problem.

> My mother loved cutting my hair. I always had the shortest hair while most of my friends had long braids. I hated having short hair but what I hated more was crooked bangs. My bangs always looked like an algebraic slope. On one side my bangs ended where my forehead began, on the other side they were regular length. Whenever my short

bang side got to be as long as my long side originally was, my mother would get the marvelous idea of cutting my hair again. I had no say in the length of my hair. (Ruth)

Not only length but also style may be viewed as a problem.

I hated how my mom would always put my hair in pigtails. She tied pink ribbons around the pigtails and I would always try to take them out when my mom wasn't looking. I would often hide them, in drawers or under my bed, but my mom would find them and yell at me for hiding them. She knew that I hated them but she made me wear them anyway. (Arlene, age 10, Naomi's informant)

Children's styles popular with adults — e.g., the 'Dorothy Hamill haircut'[3] — may be imposed on unwilling children. What adults view as suitable or 'cute' may not accord with children's views. Indeed children may not see 'cute' as the effect *they* want to achieve.

Our mothers took us [my friend and me] to get our haircuts together. The hairdressers were given instructions by our mothers to give us a 'Dorothy Hamill' haircut. The end result was Harriet and me crying for days, for we looked like a bowl was put around our hair and then trimmed around it. Not only did I look like a boy, but here was my best friend with the same ugly haircut. The fact that I was not embarrassed alone did not comfort me. Instead, it made me feel sick, for I couldn't even get my own, individual haircut — never mind the fact that it was a horrible haircut. (Gini)

Fitting in with one's peers is not offered as comfort by Gini; rather she describes looking like Harriet as an assault on her individual identity.

Children's resources for remedying perceived problems of appearance differ from those available to adults. Thus children might remedy short or curly or the wrong color hair by wearing shirts on their heads; adults might simply let their hair grow, straighten it, or dye it. Limited resources and the need for permission constrain children's choices and may leave them open to looking silly by adults' standards and by those of other children.

Pierced Ears

I have gathered (and heard in everyday life) a number of stories of children being told that they had to wait until a certain age — in the following story,

---

[3] Dorothy Hamill won a gold medal in figure-skating in the 1976 Olympics. She became a celebrity in the US. Her hair style can be described as a 'bowl cut'.

13; in other instances, 16, and in yet others, a range of ages — before they could have their ears pierced. And yet babies have their ears pierced without having so chosen. Whose choice is it and on what grounds is it made? What specific objections do adults have to such a choice being made by a child? How is the 'right' age determined? Ultimately the answers seem to lie in the vicissitudes of adults' preferences. The following story describes a child's seeing herself as being undesirably different from others, knowing that this difference can be easily remedied, but lacking the power to make the desired change. She selects from her limited resources a 'second-rate' remedy, and that it is second-rate is demonstrated in the outcome of the story.

> One problem I encountered was trying to convince my mother to let me get my ears pierced. In second grade, almost all the girls in my class had their ears pierced. My mother, however, felt I was too young to have mine pierced. She told me that when I turned 13, I could have them done. But I had already told my friends that I was going to have them pierced and every day they would ask when they were going to be done. One day when they asked, I told them I was having them done that night. I had decided that I would take two of the little silver sprinkles that my mother kept in the kitchen cupboard and I would glue them on my ears. The next morning before school I glued the sprinkles on my ears and ran out the door before my mother could notice. When I got to school, I proudly showed off my new 'earrings' to all my friends. All went well until Claudia Franklin insisted that she see the backings to the earrings. When Claudia knew that my 'earrings' were not real, the whole class knew. The entire class, including the teacher, seemed to find the situation hysterical. I, on the other hand, came home from school in tears. (Sally)

Unable to get her ears pierced and thus be like 'everyone else,' Sally lost face in trying to save face. The simple solution, but one unavailable to her, was to have her ears pierced.

Medical Matters

Medical considerations may lead to appearances that are viewed negatively by both the possessor and others.

> One of the earliest experiences I viewed as hard was being forced by my parents and the doctor to get glasses in the third grade because of my substandard eyesight. I remember the loss of control I felt when I entered the optometrist's office with my mom and sister to pick out my brand new glasses that I so desperately loathed. I begged and pleaded with my mother not to get them but she insisted it was for my

own good and that 'I was just too young to really understand the reason why I had to get them.' When the optometrist came up to me and asked me to pick out what color I wanted for my glasses, I told him I didn't want any at all and refused to pick out any color of glasses at all. Seeing this, my mother got upset and decided to resolve the situation by having my bigger sister pick out the color of glasses she thought I would like. I cried and whimpered as the doctor fit the bug-like yellow glasses to my face. I hated the color, I hated the glasses, and most of all I hated my mother and my sister because I knew all the kids at school would make fun of me. The next day when I went to school my friends nicknamed me 'Bug Eyes' and to say the least I got even more upset over the whole entire incident. (Jill, Greg's informant)

Taking children's experiences seriously does not necessitate acceding to their wishes, e.g., supporting their desire to not wear glasses, but does suggest the appropriateness of acknowledging children's distress and the ridicule that they may quite accurately anticipate. To dismiss children's objections as simply 'childish' and 'something they will get over' impedes any assistance that adults' might provide in searching for a solution that respects both medical and personal considerations. It also impedes the offering of solace.[4]

When children themselves are able to bring about desired changes, their views of themselves may change dramatically.

I felt I was not accepted as a child. I had braces, glasses, and very short hair. I was very uncomfortable with myself. When I was little I was judged by the way I looked and everyone made fun of me. I can remember my peers making fun of me on the bus. They would say that I was blind because my glasses were so thick. I never wanted to go to school because of it. I never talked on the phone and I never had friends until later in my adolescence. Finally I lost the braces, got contacts, and grew my hair the way I wanted it, long. Nobody picked on me anymore. I was comfortable with myself for the first time in my life. (Margot, Lydia's informant)

Age

The age that one is, that one appears to be, and that one is presented as being influences children's sense of and presentation of self. Age is a dimension of knowledge about one's self over which children may want, but do not have,

---

[4] In recent years some children have implemented their own solutions, offering solace and camouflage to classmates who have lost their hair through chemotherapy by shaving their own heads.

control. Adults may lie about their own age or about the age of children but children are somewhat limited by enforceable restrictions on lying and by frequenting settings where their age is already known to others.

Being presented as younger than one is may compromise one's presentation of self.

> Every time we went on a vacation, my dad would pass me off for a younger age to get the cheaper rates. I remember his saying 'Two adults, one junior, and one child.' My brother at the time was 12 and I was 9. 'Child,' however, was anybody under 8. I always wanted to yell out my real age because I wanted to be myself, not a 'little kid.' (Fern)

It may be difficult to present oneself as older when one is publicly treated as younger.

> Growing up the youngest of five children was not easy. . .I always felt like I was being 'babied.' It embarrassed me to have to walk home from school with my sister. It made me mad to have my brothers stick up for me with the neighborhood kids. I wanted to scream and yell and let the whole world know I could handle myself even though I was only 6. I thought I was a very mature 6-year-old. I hated having my sisters pamper me all the time. I used to wish I had a little brother to boss around so I invented one. (Lisa)

Like wearing a shirt on one's head, inventing a little brother is a resourceful, if interactionally limited, solution to a problem. Pretense is most effectively practiced in the absence of those who deny the pretense.

In the following story Judy is publicly presented as younger than she is, observable by all present as younger than she can be documented to be and than she perceives herself as being.

> My earliest memory of myself is when I was 5 and my brother was 3. My mother was into a 'diet mode,' a mode that made her want to lose weight and exercise, so she enrolled herself in the Gloria Stevens' program. This program would allow her to work out with a class and an instructor. The place was fully equipped with rowing machines, exercise bikes, exercise mats, and weights. That was only part of the reason she enrolled. The other part was that she could bring us and put us in a playroom. This is where I had a problem. I dreaded the day each week when my mom would put us in the car and we would head to Gloria Stevens. The playroom was about the size of a bathroom. The doorway was blocked with one of those gates that are used to prevent a baby from crawling down stairs. I was furious to be confined to such an area where most of the kids were younger than

I was and the toys were geared to toddlers. There I was, confined to a room where I was unable to get out because the gate was too high for me to get my leg over. I never threw a temper tantrum because I knew that would aggravate my mom so I would just stand by the gate waiting for the hour to go by. I would be in a bad mood the whole time I was there. It was no fun for me. I was too old to be in that small room with toddlers! All I wanted was to be on the other side of the gate but because I was a 'child' I was confined. I saw that I was different from the toddlers and could distinguish between the labels. I saw that I was not a toddler because I wasn't in diapers and I didn't talk in broken sentences. I also knew that 5-year-olds don't throw temper tantrums to get something or at least it didn't work in my house with my parents. (Judy)

Too old for the setting in which she is placed but also too old to use the only resource she sees as available, a temper tantrum, Judy 'just stands by the gate.'

The age one appears to be — and about which children, though not adults, may have little control — can be interactionally problematic.

Physical differences were a big part of the pain childhood at times gave me. I was always very tiny and small. I was several inches shorter than my peers and it made me feel very self-conscious. This was especially true in my pre-school and elementary years. I remember everyone saying I was so 'cute.' That wasn't the bad part, however. What hurt the most was when people would think I was younger than I actually was because of my short height...Even when I was 6 and 7 years old, adults would crouch down to my level and treat me as if I were years younger...Relatives that I had not seen in years would pinch my cheeks and say 'Look at Yooooou! Aren't yooooou a cuteeeeee! (Gini)

The thing that bothered me the most about when I was younger was my relatives coming to visit. All of my aunts and my grandmothers would always treat me like a baby. They would come to my house and pinch my cheeks and say, 'Oh my gosh, you are growing so fast! Last time I saw you, you were this small!' The whole time that they were visiting, they would say these things over and over again. (Arlene, age 10, Naomi's informant)

The resolution of the problems described by Gini and Arlene seems to lie with adults and is dependent upon their formulation of their behavior as a source of problems for children. Children have few options, for speaking out seems likely to result in being labeled 'fresh.'

The stories in this section describe the relativity of age; one is 'young' or 'old' in relation to others.[5] For adults, all children are young; for children, young children are those younger than they. Given the link between age and rights, it is not surprising that children may object to being labeled and treated as younger than they see themselves as being.

The Company One Keeps

In an examination of children's relationships with other children — siblings, friends, relatives, enemies — adults' standards and adults' concerns for their own well-being emerge clearly. Children's concerns about relationships can routinely be superseded by adults' concerns with those relationships or with other issues. Siblings and friends can be separated 'for their own good' (as defined by adults) and children can be forced into associating with undesired others for adults' 'own good.' Children's complaints about adults' choreography of children's relationships are described as having been routinely treated by adults as illegitimate. For children themselves, however, relations with other children have important implications for self-image and presentation of self to others.

Being forced to associate with younger siblings can compromise one's view of oneself as 'older.'

> For a good part of my early life, I was an only child. At the age of 5, all that changed. It was at this time that my mom and dad (by a process I couldn't explain) presented me with a little brother. His birth, however, was not the difficulty. Sure, he hogged the attention and kept me up with his crying, but that didn't bother me too much. Two years later, my difficulty in this area came to pass. Very often I would have a friend of mine over to play. When I was an only child, me and my friend were a happy twosome. With my 2-year-old brother around, Mom made it a point to make us a trio! Almost every time I'd have a friend over, my mom would let my little brother play with us. Just when we started to have fun, that 2-year-old terror came to play. I hardly ever protested this issue because Mom made it seem like I was doing her a gigantic favor. She would get sweet and sappy on me and I hated to burst her bubble. Deep down, however, I felt she was unfair and was trying to make my life unpleasant. I remember thinking that if she were in my place, she wouldn't want a little baby playing with her either. I thought of myself as a big guy at the time and felt that this situation was ruining my image. Regardless of my feelings, life went on. There are times, however, when I wish I had gotten a dog instead of a little brother. (Ned)

---

[5] Stories of being 'too young' to engage in certain activities are presented in Chapter 4.

Adults' common-sense knowledge might suggest that a child would view the
birth of a sibling as a trial and playing with a younger child as manageable if
not pleasant. Ned's assessment suggests just the opposite.

Children may complain not only of being with but also of being apart
from siblings.

> When my sister Pat and I were younger we did everything together
> from sharing a crib, clothes, and toys to making diagrams on the walls
> with toothpaste, cakes on the floor of the kitchen, and writing with
> markers on our parents' bedspread. We were like twins. We were
> only a year and three days apart and we were inseparable. But when
> it was time for nursery school, we were not allowed to go together.
> My mom wanted me to experience school alone and be recognized as
> an individual being. She wanted me to have friends and not have to
> be home all day with just Pat and her. I thought she was so unfair to
> send me to school without Pat. How could she think I would be able
> to survive without her? I didn't want to go to school. I was scared of
> being alone and having no friends. I cried all the way to school every
> day for two weeks but once I got there I was fine. Pat, on the other
> hand, resented the fact that I was leaving her to go to school and have
> fun. It was very hard on me because I wanted her to be there too and
> she was, the next year. We spent a year of nursery school together
> because I was too young to go into kindergarten so for a year we got
> our own way and spent every day together in school and made our
> parents' lives a living hell with our schemes. (Diane)

Unlike Gini (in the epigraph to this chapter), who complained of not being
able to establish a separate identity, Diane describes a separate identity as
insignificant when compared to her desire to be with her sister. Adults' efforts
directed towards a child's establishing a separate identity, however well meaning, may be viewed negatively by the child involved and may be undermined.

Not only may children be forced to associate with those, e.g., siblings,
whom they would rather avoid but they may also be denied access to their
friends, temporarily or permanently, for a variety of adults' reasons.

> I was in the third grade and I had a best friend named Jill. We did
> everything together. We would play together at recess and after school
> at her house or mine. One day in gym class we were practicing hitting
> a tennis ball against the wall with a tennis racquet. Well, Jill and I
> would go to the same wall and hit the ball and when the wall became
> too crowded we would move. The gym teacher came up to me and
> told me to stay away from Jill. She said I kept following her around.
> So she sent me to a different wall, where Jill wasn't. I was so mad. I
> didn't understand what I had done wrong. She didn't explain. I went
> to the wall where she had told me to go. I was there for a while until

it got crowded so I moved. The wall I moved to was where Jill was but I moved there because there was more space. Just as I got there the teacher came over and yelled at me and told me to go back to where I was. I tried to explain but she wouldn't listen. To this day I still don't like her and each time I see her I recall the tennis lesson. (Judy)

There was a big shed behind my house. I was 6 and playing by myself. I started throwing rocks at the shed. The kid from next door went running in front of the shed just as I threw one and it hit him square in the head. He went running home crying. Later on his father came over and yelled at me. We weren't allowed to play together any more. (James, Elizabeth's informant)

In both of these stories, adults not only separate children from their friends but do so, apparently, on the basis of misunderstandings.

Changing schools — to improve the quality of education offered, for religious reasons, or because of a household move — can permanently separate children from friends. Adults may see compelling reasons for a change but may be unaware of the nature and extent of attendant hardships. Children's experiences may be more — or less distressing — than adults suspect. Some children may view such a change as devastating — either temporarily or for an extended length of time.

When I was in elementary school, in the third grade, I had many friends and lots of good teachers that I had to leave behind. My parents were making me leave public school and go to Catholic school. I had no choice but to go. My parents were being so unfair to make me go to Catholic school. I was the new kid on the block and no one liked me. Everyone had their own group of friends and wouldn't let me play with them. I ate lunch by myself and played out in the school yard alone. Once in a while someone would speak to me but only to say I was in the way or 'You're in our play area.' I went home every day for a week crying because no one would play with me. My mom gave me some encouraging words and told me to be extra friendly. Finally the girls at school let me be an end-roper. I got to hold the rope and swing it over and over again but still they would not let me play. For about three weeks this went on and finally someone stuck up for me and let me play. (Diane)

I had been going to the same school since kindergarten and I had a lot of friends there. In the third grade my parents bought a new house that was across town. This would mean that I would have to change schools. No matter how much I fought they wouldn't let me stay at my school. I finally ended up switching schools and it was like I was starting all over again. It was hard to do and I was very upset. (Carl, Elizabeth's informant)

Some children may perceive changing schools not as a trial at all but as a positive experience. The following story describes changing schools as a successful way to run away from a problem — persecution by peers.

Obstacles to Changing One's Presentation of Self
by Emily

When I was in elementary school, up until about fifth or sixth grade, I was heavy-set. The kids in school constantly made fun of me. They took my things and destroyed them. I had a little pig pencil sharpener and someone took it from me and later threw it away. This pencil sharpener was so special to me. I loved it with all of my heart. I was always called a cow, pig, and just about anything else you can think of that was degrading.

When I was in the sixth grade my doctor told me that I was overweight for my age and for my height. He told me that this was unhealthy and that I would have to go on a diet. I didn't want to though. I never thought that I would need to go on a diet at such a young age. I ended up losing about 25 pounds and I looked great. I got so many compliments from my family.

When I went back to school after the summer, the kids still called me a fat cow and a pig. They didn't care whether or not I had lost any weight, they just kept picking on me and calling me names. I would try to tell them, 'I lost about 25 pounds this summer.' They never listened. It didn't make any difference to them. They saw me as they used to see me, overweight. This treatment that I received hurt me so bad, to think that after I lost weight I may have some friends and they still treated me the same. This treatment occurred until the middle of my freshman year in high school. There were some days that were just so bad that I would come home crying and tell my mother that I never wanted to go back and that I wanted to move. The only reason it stopped was because my parents decided that we were going to move. They had found a house in another town that they could buy rather than renting a house in the town we had lived in. The town that we ended up moving to was a very nice town. I met so many nice people and made so many new friends. People liked me and they talked to me and, most of all, my school work improved so much. . .I believe that if I hadn't tried to start over at this new school and start believing in myself, I may have never been able to make new friends and improve my school work.

* * *

When people, adults or children, try to change or modify their identity, they are likely to find that former associates resist and even impede the process, treating them as if they were 'just the same.' Changes in identity are facilitated by changes in associates. Adults may change jobs, residence, even friends for just this reason. As a child, Emily's opportunity to successfully modify her identity appears a welcome but unintended outcome of adults' quite different projects.

When adults choose to change the school a child attends, they may do so for a variety of reasons — for the child, for themselves, for the household as a whole, and because they must. I am not arguing that adults ought not to change children's schools — or that they ought to — on the sole basis of a child's desires. If, however, children's experiences are taken seriously, the importance given to children's role in the decision may be increased (or decreased). Were her parents to have known the positive consequences of a move for Emily, it would not seem unwarranted to have attached great importance to her desires.

Since how others perceive one is consequential for one's sense of self, control over who those others are — the company one keeps — takes on great significance for children, as it does for adults. Relations with others can present particular difficulties for children since they may not have sufficient control over those relations to bring about what they see as desirable outcomes. Further complicating such relations are the limits to children's presentation of self evident in their lack of control over their appearance. Children are thus denied resources that adults come to count on in their own presentations of self.

Why Do Adults Care about Children's Appearance?

For a variety of adults' reasons children's resources for affecting their presentation of self may be limited. Why are adults so concerned with the appearance of children that they override children's desires? Why do adults deny children permission to wear clothes of a particular kind, adopt a desired hair style, or have their ears pierced? Part of the reason may be related to adults' own presentation of self. The appearance of a child may well have implications for how others view the adult with that child. Perhaps adults control the appearance of children because they do not want to be seen as the kind of adult who would 'allow' a child to look like 'that.' Note, however, that such concerns seem to be for the benefit of adults, not children. Another reason for adults' control of children's appearance may be that at least some of the 'work' involved in the child's appearance may devolve upon an adult. Thus issues of time, cost, etc., may affect adults' decisions. Throughout the data presented are many claims about adults' preferences, adults' taste, and adults' convenience — not negligible factors but less for the good of the child than for the good of the adult.

Adults' concerns about the appearance of children with whom they are associated are mirrored by children's concerns about adults' appearance. Less commonly recognized, but eloquently spoken of in stories of the little trials of childhood, are the implications for a child's self-image of the appearance of parents or other adults in whose company a child is seen. One informant spoke of throwing out what she described as her mother's 'awful' yellow shoes. Others spoke of sending parents back to change clothes before going out with them. Some spoke of objections based on taste and style, others on parents' looking 'too young' or 'too old.' One might expect such complaints to be more characteristic of older children — indeed Jacqueline, in the next story, describes her mid-teens — but subsequent comments by Janet (age 12) and Lorraine (describing grammar school) express similar concerns.

> [Grace's informant, Jacqueline, is describing a situation that occurred when she was between the ages of 16 and 18.] Jacqueline told me that her mother wears her make-up, borrows her clothes, and acts like she's 21 when she's 44. She said it really embarrassed her when she dresses like her. She told me that she would rather her mother wear ugly 'typical' clothes that other 44-year-old mothers wear. That made me laugh because my mother is one of those 'typical' mothers and I wish she would get some style or something. At times I try to get my mother to wear my clothes. Because her mother looks the way she does, Jacqueline does not go out in public with her mother and rarely allows friends to go over her house. (Grace)

> When Janet, my 12-year-old informant and I talked about embarrassing and bothersome things about adults, her eyes rolled when I mentioned appearance. She told me that her dad just got a new motorcycle so he's into leather jackets with zippers and other things. 'Isn't that the worst thing?' She also told me that she hates when her parents go out at night because her mother dresses like a biker too. I also had a similar experience with my parents' appearance when I was younger. When I was in grammar school the kids called me the 'little rich girl.' This was because of my parents' appearance. (Lorraine)

Jacqueline's strategies of not going out with her mother and not having friends to her house testify to the seriousness with which children may take adults' appearance. Like adults, children may view the appearance of those with whom they are associated as having negative implications for how they, the children, are viewed. And like adults, children may be quite willing to impose their desires on others. Unlike adults, however, children may have less power to influence adults so that their appearance will be a credit, or at least not an embarrassment, to them, the children.

* * *

The stories in this chapter suggest that even very young children may be concerned with presentation of self and what Goffman (1959) terms 'impression management.' The stories also suggest that adults' and children's views, desires, and projects may differ and indeed be incompatible. At times there may have to be a winner and a loser. Adults who support their own desires by defining them as 'for the good of the child' and rejecting those of children as 'childish' may give themselves an unfair advantage of becoming the winner. Adults who deny children's requests with 'I don't care what everybody else does. You're not "everybody"' may be creating greater problems for children than they, the adults, realize. If, however, children's concerns are taken seriously, the way is open to negotiation. Whose wants are greatest? Whose trials are greatest? Whose turn is it to prevail?

4   Activities

Being a child meant being told what to do, having all of my fun snatched away before my little hands were able to touch and grab on, and waiting for the day Mommy and Daddy would allow me to participate in a desired activity or maybe do it all by myself. Being a child also meant coping with two 'big people' who removed anything and everything that might perhaps prove to be interesting to my senses and entertaining to my probing little fingers, anything and everything that might perhaps taste good in my eager little mouth. Now, if you ask me, that was cruel. They put me on the floor to crawl around, explore and maybe have some fun, but they took away all the good stuff. So I sat there on the rug for a moment, smelling the pet smells that rose up from the carpet, and began to cry. (Gwen)

I am 8 years old and at camp, thousands and thousands of miles away from my nice warm bed at home in Delaware. I have been up for hours and I can't sleep. My sleeping bag smells like the attic, my nose is frozen, I hear noises outside, it's dark, someone is snoring, and I have to go to the bathroom and am scared to wake the counselor up. Don't Mom and Dad love me anymore? How could they do this to me? (Mary)

Adults may offer many and compelling reasons — moral, religious, educational, safety-related, practical, and personal — for controlling children's activities, even in the face of children's objections. Nonetheless, their control may, for children, serve as occasions for the little trials of childhood. Stories from my informants describe children's lack of control over many aspects of their activities: being prevented from taking part in desired ones, being interrupted, told *how* to undertake them, required to engage in unwanted ones, and finding desired activities contingent upon 'good' behavior. The following story eloquently illustrates the vicissitudes of adults' control.

When I was 12 years old, I wanted to sign up for cheer-leading but my parents said they did not have the extra money. They did have the money to sign my brother Tom up for football though. I wanted to take flute lessons. My mother said, 'What do you want to do that for?' Tom later took drum lessons and Phil now takes guitar and piano. My father did find the money to sign me up, without my consent, for basketball and soccer. Sports were important to him. I wasn't aggressive, hated competition. He would say 'If you'd only try harder. You have the potential.' I tried to tell him how much I hated sports, especially when I was the only girl on the team. He just didn't listen. (Linda)

For whose good are activities urged upon children?

The year I was 10 I might as well have had a job because I was always being driven to some other activity. Didn't my parents know kids just like to sit around and do nothing some of the time? On Mondays it was gymnastics lessons, on Tuesdays it was guitar lessons, Wednesdays were swim day, Thursdays were Girl Scouts, Fridays were art class, and Saturday mornings I played basketball. All I wanted to do was play the piano. I don't want to do all these things, I am not a superkid, I am just a kid who wants to play the piano. (Mary)

To claim that activities are urged upon children 'for their own good' is to obscure children's experiences as well as other possible answers, e.g., to meet community expectations, for parents to present themselves as good parents, or for children to meet parental standards, even those for which they may not be suited.

The extent of children's lack of control is demonstrated when their participation in desired activities is contingent on other behavior chosen by adults.

I remember numerous times that I was told I could go over my friend's house or stay up late if I was good. This threat was constantly held over my head. Any time I stepped out of line my parents would quickly remind me how they held the strings so I had best get my act together soon if I wanted these 'privileges'. (Holly)

Children's activities thus take on the character not of rights but of privileges.

Both adults and children may simply like to do some things and not like to do others, for the activities in which people engage can be valued in themselves. Activities, like appearance, are also important as indicators to oneself and others of the kind of person one is (and is not). As Schutz writes, 'In order to communicate with Others I have to perform overt acts in the outer world which are supposed to be interpreted by the Others as signs of what I mean to convey' (1967b, p. 218). Goffman similarly claims that 'when an individual appears in the presence of others, there will usually be some reason for him to mobilize his activity so that it will convey an impression to others which it is in his interests to convey' (1959, pp. 3–4). When adults control children's activities, children may be denied pleasurable or meaningful activities, urged to undesired ones, and also deprived of resources for their presentation of self.

Being Denied Participation in Desired Activities

For a variety of adults' reasons — to which children may or may not be privy — children may be denied participation in a multitude of activities that they see as pleasurable and as important to their presentation of self.

> I wouldn't call my parents strict, but they certainly were not lenient. This was especially true while I was 11 years old and ready for a social life. The big deal when you were 11 years old was to go to a local roller-skating rink. Not only could you stay out until 10:30 at night, but you also got to skate with boys during the slow songs! To me, this sounded like paradise. I say 'sounded like paradise' because at the age of 11 I never saw this paradise. Every Friday night, I'd ask the same question, 'Can I go to the roller-skating rink?' and every Friday night it was the same answer, 'NO!' This was especially painful for me because it seemed virtually everyone else could go. It was humiliating when they would ask why I wasn't there. My parents, but most especially my mother, had a hard time letting me experience, experiment, and grow up. . .My mother constantly worried and overreacted during my childhood. (Gini)

> My informant Bruce said he wanted to go on big trips to Disney world and he couldn't because his family didn't have enough money. He had to face all his friends at school after summer vacation asking where he went on vacation. He told me he felt ashamed to say that he went to work on his uncle's farm. He said he had a good time there but still had to clean the pool and work on the farm every day. He said he felt that wasn't an exciting or fun enough place to tell his friends where he had gone over vacation. (Lucy)

How does one explain to others that one cannot engage in certain activities? How does one avoid humiliation and shame before one's friends? Gini and Bruce describe the problem but not the resolution.

Restricted Access to Television

As discussed in Chapter 2, bedtime may be viewed not only as a hardship in itself but also as an intrusion into activities that are both intrinsically meaningful and consequential for one's relations with other children.

> Bedtime produced a few problems because it usually involved turning off the TV. Being in grade school meant knowing all about the good shows that came on between 8:00 and 10:00. I never got to watch these shows because my mother was (and still is) against prolonged

usage of the television. She wouldn't let me watch a lot of shows because they came on too late (anything after 9:30 was too late) or just because she said so. Frequently, I would be laughed at by my classmates because I hadn't seen 'The Dukes of Hazzard' or whatever late night movie came on. The worst part about the 9:30 deadline was that if the show started at 8:00 but went through 9:30 I couldn't watch it. I think the limited TV usage was my biggest handicap. It left me at a disadvantage with my classmates, who didn't have this problem . . .Even today, my mom gives me a hard time about certain shows and she won't allow cable or a VCR because 'we'll watch too much television.' She isn't swayed by the fact that no one really lives at home anymore. (Alan)

I was 7 years old and I can remember my friends all talking about some TV show that was on at 9:00 at night. Of course I wanted to watch it too so I went home that night and instead of going to bed at 9:00 like I was supposed to I begged to stay up for an extra half hour. My parents wouldn't let me and I threw a temper tantrum. Unfortunately this made matters worse and I had to go to bed at 8:00 for a week. (Carl, Elizabeth's informant)

Not seeing certain television shows can put children at a disadvantage in interactions with other children. Carl's use of begging and a temper tantrum, although unsuccessful — indeed counterproductive — nonetheless indicates the seriousness with which children may view their problem. Although adults may offer a variety of compelling reasons for restricting children's television watching, either in general or with respect to specific programs, children may experience such restrictions as a form of 'cultural deprivation,' for they may run the risk of disclosing themselves to other children as lacking the cultural knowledge that those others share.

Children may discover, and be distressed to discover, that standards change for their younger siblings.

Television shows, movies and going to bed later are many of the privileges my two sisters have had. Time after time I watched my parents give them permission to do something I was never allowed to do at their ages. When I was 11 years old, my favorite TV show was 'Three's Company.' My mother would not allow me to watch it because the show had too many double meanings about sex. There were many times when I would sneak around just to watch it. I got caught watching 'Three's Company' and was grounded from watching television for two days. I was also not allowed to see R-rated movies until I was seventeen. Many of the Eddie Murphy movies had come out when I was 12 and all my friends were seeing them. I couldn't because my parents felt there were too many swears, violence and sex scenes. Of course now my younger sister is permitted to watch anything she wants including soap operas. In fact she spends about 5 hours in front of the box. My sister, who's only 12, has seen many R-rated movies at the theater and on our VCR. My parents don't seem to monitor her TV and movie intake as much as they did when I was a kid. (Diane)

'Relative deprivation' refers to the experience of *deprivation in relation to what others have or do*. Children denied the opportunity to see television programs that other children are allowed to see may experience relative deprivation. Children may also experience, as Diane illustrates, what might be termed *retrospective relative deprivation* when they see younger siblings allowed what they were denied. The complexity of the problems that arise when one takes children's distress seriously is especially clear in this example of parental standards being changed for younger siblings. Eliminating the distress of older siblings would seem to require that parents *do not* change (even when they see it advisable to do so) and that younger siblings experience the same distress that older siblings did — a questionable policy. Any solution seems to require someone's distress.

Talking as a Restricted Activity

Both how one talks and that one talks can be sources of the little trials of childhood. Control of the volume of one's voice may be such a taken-for-granted feature of the adult world that it is difficult at first for adults to see that children may find it a hardship to control their voices.

I always used to talk a lot, talk fast, and talk loud. It was just something that I couldn't gauge very well. This did not happen at any particular age. It started from the moment that I learned how to talk — until now. I would be in a restaurant, at church, in school, or at home and someone would shout, 'Shh. Don't talk so loud.' I was so embarrassed that I wanted to crawl under a rock and disappear. (Irene)

Note that Irene describes the 'Shh' as *shouted*, suggesting that adults need not always follow the rule they espouse. The following story displays recognition of this non-reciprocity of standards, here applied to talk itself.

Another recollection I have of my childhood was not one incident but occurred many times. From as far back as I can remember I have loved to talk. Loving to talk got me in trouble quite a few times because I didn't know when to talk and when not to talk. I constantly interrupted people and when I interrupted someone I got scolded. I felt bad about interrupting people (and getting scolded) but I would get so excited that I couldn't contain myself. I felt that I had to talk right then or I would explode or even worse I might forget what I was going to say. Nonetheless I was scolded. I never thought that scolding me for talking would do any good and it didn't. I just grew very self-conscious of myself and went on guilt trips because I couldn't control my mouth. Deep down inside though I always wondered why if everyone expected me to hold my thought while they finished talking why couldn't they hold their thoughts while I talked instead? (Kate)

What begins as a trial may, however, be turned into a resource.

My parents had this thing about keeping me quiet whenever we went on trips. Everyone in the back seat had to have 'back seat voices.' They used to tell us that if we kept quiet we would get a quarter. I thought this was the greatest thing until I finally realized they were only giving me and my sister money to keep us quiet. After I realized this nothing could shut me up. The only way I would be quiet was if there were dollar bills involved or I could sit in the front seat. That was great because then I knew I had put my parents in their place. (Dawn)

Being Too Young

Being 'too young' may be offered to children as a self-evident and sufficient explanation for excluding them from activities.

One of my sisters was nine years older than I was, and my other sister was thirteen years older. The age difference was so great that I was always too young to do something or go somewhere. I can remember my sisters going out at the same time that I was supposed to go to bed. I always wanted to go with them to a basketball game or to a movie, and it was always past my bedtime, and I was too young. (Irene)

'Too young' may indeed be the reason that adults exclude children from activities but it may also be a euphemism for 'I don't want you to do that.' Children who attempt to determine the rules that govern 'being too young' may be undertaking a fruitless task.

I always hated it when my parents thought I was too young to do something or go somewhere. I will never forget the night my parents went to our school book fair and took my sister but left me at home with a baby-sitter. I couldn't understand how I was old enough to go to school but not old enough to attend my own book fair. It wasn't

even past my bedtime. I cried the whole time my baby-sitter was at
our house. No matter what he did to make me stop, I refused to do
it. I was so upset that my parents left me at home. I felt like I wasn't
important enough. When my parents returned home they had all kinds
of presents for me but I refused to take them. If they could be mean
enough to not take me then I could be mean enough to not take their
presents. (Dawn)

One outcome of the 'too young' restriction is that same-age friendships are
encouraged, different-age ones discouraged. In this way the system of age-
grading adopted in school is reinforced. Friendships with 'older' children are
risky for 'younger' children for there is always the danger that adults will deny
to the younger permission to engage in activities allowed to the older. The
acceptance younger children may have been granted — perhaps hard won
and important — may be endangered or destroyed.

One of the worst times I had as a child is when the older kids were
allowed to ride their bicycles on the road. I felt that I was old enough
to do this. I was probably between $6\frac{1}{2}$ and 7. The older kids were 10
and 11. My mother said that I could not ride my bicycle in the road
until I was 7 and I could not understand this because our road is not
busy at all. Back then, we were lucky if we saw five cars pass on our
road during the whole day. I think I could have accepted the fact that
my mother told me that I could not ride my bike on the road, but
when I told the other kids that my mother told me I could not, they
began to call me 'baby' and stuff like that. I was so upset with my
mother, because I thought she was the only person to blame, that I
snuck out of my driveway and went to find the other kids. My mother
was so angry when I came back because I had ridden my bike on the
road, but she was more mad that I took off without telling her. I was
grounded for a month. (Allison)

When adults deny children the opportunity to engage in certain activities, they
may also deny them the opportunity to face their fears.

There were many times that I was forbidden to do something because
I was 'too young.' I remember one instance when my family and my
best friend's family all went to Florida together. One day we were at
Busch Gardens and they had a roller coaster that made a loop so at
one point you were actually upside down. Ann, her brother, and her
sister were all going on and they asked me to go too. I asked my mom
and she said no. Her reason was the same old thing, that I was 'too
young.' In a way I was kind of relieved that my mom had said no
because I had never been on a roller coaster before and I was not
exactly the type of person to go on big, scary rides. I was also angry

with my mom because I was actually willing to try to go on this ride and to get rid of my fear but it seemed like she wasn't willing to let me try. It was another time when the only reason she gave was that I was 'too young.' (Cora)

Given the restrictions attendant on being 'too young,' children may come to attach great value to being 'older.' Adults may use this valued 'oldness' to their own advantage, urging children to engage in activities by claiming that they are appropriate to those who are older (but perhaps are simply desired by adults).

The one thing I hated to do was hang my towel up after I had used it. As much as my parents yelled and screamed, I wouldn't do it. Sometimes just to be obnoxious I would hang my towel in places where my parents wouldn't miss it — places like the kitchen table, the door of the refrigerator, the television set, and my parents' bathroom sink. Whenever they found it they would bring it to my room and put it on my bed with a note saying, 'Big girls hang up their towels. You must not be a big girl since I found this on the floor.' After receiving three of these notes I began to hang up my towel because the one thing I wanted to be was a big girl. (Brunella)

The disadvantages of being 'younger' are described by Stella, age 10. Asked, 'If you could change something about your age, what would you change?' she responds,

I want to be my brother's age [17]. He gets away with everything. If he gets yelled at, he leaves. He can do whatever he wants. He doesn't come in 'til late when I'm sleeping. (Stella, Roxanne's informant)

Restrictions Based on Gender

Like being 'too young,' simply *being* a girl or a boy may be offered by adults as a self-evident explanation for restricting children's activities. This explanation may not be self-evident to children.

I am an only girl with three brothers. I think my mother's favorite excuse to give me was 'No, you're a girl.' I could never understand; it was so frustrating. I always thought, 'Big deal. What is the difference if I am a girl or not?' My brothers were always allowed to do things before I could. (Inez)

Gender and age may be linked, what is acceptable (or unacceptable) for a young girl or boy viewed as otherwise for an older one.

When I was about 4 years old I wanted to be with my brothers every minute of the day. I would play cops and robbers, cowboys, trucks, you name it and I played it. My brothers had no qualms about this but the adults in my family did. They would say that I was a little girl and little girls should not be playing in the mud and getting dirt underneath their fingernails. I should be playing with dolls or playing house. I had fun with my brothers not because I liked getting dirty or being tied to a chair but because as the only girl I was lonely. Whereas my brothers always had each other to play with, I had no one (of the same sex that is). I remember that I would always beg my mother to let me sleep in my brothers' room so I would not have to be alone. Sometimes she would let me but as I got a little older she would not let me anymore. I did not understand why and all she would say was that I was a girl and they were boys. I would think to myself, 'Wasn't I a girl before?'

When I was 7 now I was older and had learned the difference between boys and girls. I now wanted to spend time with my girl-friends and not my brothers. I enjoyed make-up and dressing up and no more boys' games. I was beginning to think that my brothers were pests. In actuality I became very nasty toward them. The adults in my family did not like this either because I was not supposed to treat my brothers this way. They would tell me I was being selfish and self-centered. There came a point where my mother told my brothers not to talk to me anymore if I was going to be that way. That was fine with me because now I had them out of my hair.

But still the same I was confused once again. First they (being the adults) kept telling me to act like a lady, don't get dirty, and play with girls. Now because I wanted to do all of this I am mean or selfish. I just did not know what to do anymore. (Ann)

Children are routinely held to standards for gender behavior espoused by the adults in whose care they are. When children encounter differing gender standards, whether based on age (as with Ann, above), or place (home, school) or associates (friends, relatives), their own standards, inclinations, and opportunities may be challenged or they may experience confusion and frustration.

* * *

Quite obviously, adults may deem it necessary, important, or desirable to restrict children's activities. Adults' own concerns, however, may obscure some of the consequences of their restrictions both for themselves and for children. Children, for example, may come to see adults as unfair, employing double standards (for adults and children, older and younger siblings, boys and girls) or vacillating ones ('too young'). Children's selves and friendships may also be compromised. How do children explain, to themselves and to others, why they are denied participation in activities? Saying 'my mother won't let me' is of limited utility when one is trying to present oneself as an independent self. 'My parents can't afford it' presents one as 'poor.' Being advised 'not to care what others think' may not help if one agrees with those others. Children might benefit from adults' assistance in developing *interactionally useful* strategies to account for denied activities both to themselves and to others.

Activities Interrupted

Not only do informants report being denied participation in activities; they also describe engaging in desired activities only to have them interrupted. In the following story the actions of the adults might appear quite reasonable and those of the child 'childish,' but what also emerges is a difference in perspectives and preferences.

> My earliest memory is of my third birthday. I remember standing on the table dancing and feeling powerful and strong while my relatives were all gathered around the table, applauding me and humming a birthday song. As the dining room door opened, my mother entered the room with a cake in her hands. My uncle took me off the table so that my mother could place the cake there. I was quite unhappy with being taken off the table. I was not done dancing. Everybody started eating the cake while I sat there scheming how I might get myself back on that table. (Ruth)

'Everyone knows' that the highlight of a birthday party is the cake, but for Ruth the highlight appears to be her dancing on the table, a preference that appears to have gone unnoticed by adults. The following story also illustrates the substitution of adults' 'knowledge' for children's.

> The one thing that really stands out in my mind is when my mom used to call me at my friends' house and tell me to come home because I was 'wearing out my welcome'. . .When I was little and in the middle of playing a very important game my mom would call me and tell me that it was time for me to come home. This really bothered me because if my friends didn't want me there they would tell me to go home or tell me they had things to do. I never 'wore out my welcome.' Whenever I came home after my mom called me I would be so mad. I would tell her that she ruined my fun and I was never going to talk to her again. She would just tell me very calmly to find something to do in my own house or have my friends come play at our house. I would promise myself to never forgive her but I always

ended up talking to her until the next time I went to a friend's house. (Dawn)

Adults' may interrupt children's activities by offering unwanted instructions on *how* to engage in those activities. Adults, for example, may tell children how to play games even when children themselves seem quite satisfied with the rules they have formulated and are employing.

> Children can want to win and thus losing can be difficult for them. Arthur remembered one such incident in his childhood. One after-noon Arthur, Elvira, John, and I were playing 'Pay Day' [a board game]. He landed on the space requiring him to put fifty dollars in the pot. 'It was my last money, and I didn't think it was fair that I had to put it in,' he recalled. The rest of us children did not make an issue of his not putting money in the pot. However, his mother, who was 'stuck on the rules,' told him that if he didn't pay he couldn't play. At this point Russell sent the game board flying across the room with one sweeping motion of his arm. 'I was just so mad at the whole thing. It didn't seem very fair,' Russell said. (Amanda's informant)

Adults' commitment to written rules for games and activities (often described as the 'real rules') indicates a kind of inflexibility that children may reject, preferring instead to modify rules for the pleasure of participants. Adults' in-vocation of 'real rules' may destroy children's pleasure in the games they have developed *in situ*.[1]

Although adults may find their own activities more important than those of children, children may not share that assessment. Adults may have the power to interrupt children's activities but may not be aware that children can view adults' actions as intrusive, rude, presumptuous, and insulting.

Being Required to Engage in Unwanted Activities

Informants offer an array of tales concerning activities required of them and the consequent anger, embarrassment, discomfort, frustration, and boredom. Adults might readily associate some activities required of children — work, religious services, school, homework, etiquette, and lessons (music, dancing, etc.) — with virtue or privilege, self-evidently 'for the good of children' (and for the adults they are expected to become). In a long-range view they may indeed prove to be so but children, nonetheless, may view the experiences as trials. It would, of course, seem foolish, if not downright irresponsible, of adults to respond to children's concerns, 'Fine, you don't have to attend

---

[1] For further examples of *children's* ways of being with other children, see Mandell's careful observational studies of preschool children, e.g., Mandell, 1984.

religious services, do homework, etc.' To deny the difficult aspects of such experiences, however, is to deny children support for their difficulties, alternatives, and assistance in developing strategies for dealing with trials, both those of childhood and those to come in adulthood.

Housework

Housework is one activity described as a trial, a designation that adults may well share. Of particular concern to children may be that they are held to standards that they do not accept, standards set by others, namely, the adults who assign the work.

> Keeping my bedroom clean was a major problem in my life. During the week my room was the biggest mess. You could barely see the floor. When it got towards the end of the week and I wanted to go out on the weekend I wouldn't be able to unless my room was spotless. This was such a chore for me. The hardest thing for me to do was clean my room. (Brunella)

One strategy for dealing with this trial is to merely appear to meet others' standards, for Brunella continues,

> Sometimes I would just throw everything in the closet and close the door. My parents would never look in the closet. They would be so happy just to see the floor of my bedroom.

Some adults' standards may be based on cleanliness or health considerations but others appear more clearly a matter of personal preference, e.g., in the above story 'spotlessness' and, in the following, 'immaculateness.'

> At age 11 all the responsibilities of taking care of my sisters and house chores were laid on me. I had to do a good job because I was accountable for the well-being of my sisters. . .Every week my sisters Pat and Joan and I had to clean our rooms. Usually this was done on a Saturday. This consisted of vacuuming, dusting, and changing the sheets on the beds. Pat and I shared a room and my little sister Joan had her own room. When doing our room I had the duty to make sure our room was immaculate. I also had to help Joan because she was the baby of the family and didn't know how to do it on her own. Pat would never help Joan because they did not get along. My mother always knew I would help my little sister because we got along so well and I was also very protective of her. (Diane)

Adults may claim that they are teaching children 'good habits' but adults themselves differ over what constitutes such habits. Children, however, may be limited in their opportunities to differ from the adults with whom they live. Adults' concerns with their own preferences and with what visitors might think suggest that the standards to which they hold children may serve functions other than the instruction of the children involved. Furthermore, the requirement that children keep their 'own' rooms clean compromises the 'ownness' of their rooms.

The amount of work required of children may be viewed as a trial. In the following story, however, Joyce complains not about the work itself, extensive as it is, but of its consequences for an activity she wanted to engage in and for her relations with her friends.

My father injured his back at work, had surgery when I was 10, and could not work after the surgery. As a result, my mother had to work two jobs and I had to do all the housework, go to school, take care of my father, find time at home to do my homework and have a social life (which was really difficult when I had to be home every day to cook, clean, and take care of my father). One day during the six and a half years that I did all the housework and so on, my friends were going to see a movie after school and they wanted me to go with them. I had really wanted to do certain activities with them but always had to say no because I had to be home to make dinner or do the laundry or check on my father or any combination of these. This day I wanted to go see this movie more than anything in the world. I knew I couldn't go but I still went through every possible way I could go to this movie. I was more frustrated, upset, hurt, and angry about not being able to do this than I had been in my whole life (up until that time). I still said I couldn't go and they walked away with disappointed looks on their faces. The next day, one of them asked me if I didn't like hanging around the group after school. I told her that I would have loved to go to the movie the day before but I had to be home to do laundry and cook dinner. Then I explained to her my situation and she apologized for having thought I didn't like her or the group. (Joyce)

Joyce was denied an activity she judged very important and, as well, was led to an inaccurate presentation of herself as not liking those she considered friends. Joyce's distress might have been significantly eased not necessarily by a reduction in workload, for she does not complain of the work, but by an occasional day off to engage in desired activities with her friends.

Housework in itself may be viewed negatively; when it serves as punishment for children, it is likely to take on a negative (or even more negative) cast. Greenspan, a child psychiatrist, describes his clients' deliberations for which he offers approval:

Joey and his mother. . .discussed some automatic punishments that went right into effect when his teachers complained of fighting on the days when he was supposed to be trying to avoid trouble. For each report of a misdeed, he had to do a half-hour of household chores. (1993, p. 296)

Greenspan does not say whether his recommendation is gender-specific. If housework is used as a punishment for boys in particular, it may have interesting consequences for boys' views both of housework and of those who routinely do it.

What is to be done under the rubric of 'housework'? How much housework is too little or too much (for either adults or children)? Adults and children may both offer answers to these questions but adults have greater power to act in terms of their answers and to have children do so as well. Adults faced with housework may lower their standards (although they too are subject to community standards), modify or defer the work itself, and solicit help from others — and children, willing or unwilling, may be just such others. If children's and adults' experiences of doing housework are similar, the strategies that adults employ to deal with the unpleasant or difficult aspects or to make the work more pleasant or easier might be of benefit to children.

Religious Practices

Adults may value and possess religious freedom; children, however, are routinely limited to the religious beliefs and practices of those adults responsible for them. Adults may see themselves as introducing children to the values of religion, sharing with children their own important and valued truths, beliefs, and practices. Other adults, not religiously inclined, have been known to engage in religious practices solely for the good of children, to provide them with religious 'opportunities' — 'opportunities' that those same adults nonetheless reject for themselves. Children, however, may take a negative view of the religious beliefs and practices to which they are urged and may, when they become adults, make quite different choices from those made for them as children.

> One thing that I was forced to do because it was proper was going to church. I used to have to get all dressed up in an uncomfortable dress and tights that pinched. I would sit in the pew, bored, listening to my mother say, 'Shh. You have to be quiet during the sermon.' (Irene)

> When I was about 6 or 7 I had no say in going to church. I had to go. I remember feeling angry and resentful. I had a knot in my stomach that I named helplessness. (Tammy)

> I am sitting in the eighth row on the left side of the sanctuary, the same place we sit every Sunday. I am dressed in a Polly Flanders

dress, tights, and red buckle shoes. I sit and sit same as every Sunday only today seems infinitely longer. The same questions pop through my head: Why does Daddy have to be a minister? Why can't he be a school-bus driver like other dads? Why does Mom have to sing in the choir? Why does she make me sit with this old lady? Why do I have to get all dressed up? Why can't I stay home and watch cartoons? Why are these benches so hard? Why do I have to sit still? Why, Why, Why? (Mary)

Although the adults involved in the above stories might argue that attending religious services is beneficial for the children, their attendance seems also beneficial for adults' presentation of self. Adults' self-interest may not go unrecognized by children.

My mom always dressed us for church on Sundays. We always had to dress up. I would argue that God loves us for what we are, not what we wear. My mom would blurt out something about respect. I always knew it was just to show off in front of the parish. Almost everyone did the same thing. (Charity)

Homework

Not surprisingly, doing homework is described as a trial, at times greater than the trials attendant on not doing it.

I hated bringing homework home. I used to sit at the dinner table for hours listening to my parents try to convince me to do my work. As much as they told me I had to do it, I never did. I used to pretend I did it, but when conference time came around and my parents talked to my teacher and found out that I never did my assignments my parents would come home and be very disappointed, which made me feel very guilty. (Brunella)

Getting help with homework can also be fraught with difficulties. In the following story, a child is described as wanting help but finding herself required to participate in a far more time-consuming, and futile, activity:

As a child, I remember going to my father whenever I had a math problem that I could not figure out. He would be lying on the couch watching television or just about to fall asleep and I would go into the room and ask him if he would help me. He would sit up, turn off the television — so I would not watch it — look at the problem, and begin explaining how to go about solving it. But as he began to solve the problem, my father would take another example — something that pertained to real life but had absolutely nothing to do with the math I was supposed to be doing. My father would continue to solve this new problem and go on for about an hour. I remember watching the clock, thinking about all the other homework I had to do. When he finally got an answer to HIS problem he would go back and find the answer to the original problem. By this time, I would be completely lost but when my father would ask me if I knew how 'we' came up with the answer, I would say yes just so I would not be there for another hour. He would ask me again and tell me that I had to know how to get the answer in case I got called on the next day in class. I just reassured him that I knew and prayed to myself that I would not get called on. (Debby)

Adults may view homework as self-evidently important for children and see adults' help as altruistically offered and effective. From children's perspectives, the importance of homework may not be clear — indeed some homework assignments may be didactically questionable — and what adults offer as help may better meet adults' needs (e.g., to display *themselves* as knowledgeable) than children's needs.

Etiquette

Following rules of etiquette is a particularly interesting little trial of childhood, for in urging such rules upon children adults may disclose themselves as supporting practices that are sources of difficulties and for which they cannot provide specific justification.

Another thing I hated about dinner time was putting my napkin in my lap. I thought this was the dumbest thing. Why put your napkin in your lap if you just have to pick it up again to wipe your mouth? It always fell out of my lap anyway. The only reason why I kept it in my lap was because my father always told me that if I didn't I wouldn't grow up to be a lady. (Marian)

Etiquette practices may enable one to present oneself 'as a lady' or 'as a gentleman' but how is napkin placement related to *being* either? Etiquette rules seem to make sense only when viewed within the broader context of etiquette as a social resource for both children and adults, easing social relations and rendering them predictable. When unaware of this broader context, children may find any given rule simply silly.

Justification for etiquette rules governing the writing of thank-you notes may be clearer, especially when the explanation offered focuses not only on obligation but also on the pleasure it gives to those who receive them and the distress to those who do not. The conditions under which thank-you notes are or are not necessary, however, may be open to disagreement.

I loved getting Christmas presents but I hated writing thank-you notes. When I was about 7, my mother would always sit me down after Christmas and make me write thank-you notes. It angered me because I felt that I had more important things to do. I also couldn't understand why I had to write a letter when I had already thanked them in person. (Irene)

Irene's view is supported by etiquette authorities, one of whom writes, 'If a gift is given in person, the recipient makes his thanks then and there, though, of course if he wishes to write a note after the donor has left, it makes a nice, spontaneous gesture' (Vanderbilt, 1954, p. 412). Another concurs, 'Written thanks are not required for. . .presents delivered in person' (Martin, 1989, p. 520).

The advantage to children of writing thank-you notes — and thus its use to them as a strategy for obtaining gifts were they to know of it — is illustrated by the following exchange between an etiquette authority and one who sought her advice.

Dear Miss Manners:
Having followed instructions and taught a child to write thank-you notes, I call on Miss Manners for help in dealing with an unexpected side effect. My daughter, now 6, writes her own notes and expresses delight in most gifts, even new toothbrushes, so it is fun to give her presents. Her grandmother and godmother enjoy it so much, that they give her several gifts each month. Even if a child could keep her toys picked up, it is physically impossible to keep forty dolls in our two bedroom townhouse. They are occupying the dining room and scouting the living room. I have tried to remove the least favorite toys, but I feel heartless at best, and she now regularly checks all wastebaskets and bookshelf tops. It must be inappropriate to blame family and friends for a domestic problem, but what is the proper perspective?

Gentle Reader:
First, may Miss Manners borrow your child for a short while? She wants to trot her around the country, saying to all the other little children, 'You see what happens when you write thank-you letters? Do you begin to understand what an investment that is?' We won't tell them of the other result — your perfectly reasonable desire to end this flow of booty. Miss Manners thinks it admirable; she just doesn't want to sabotage the lesson on greed she is teaching the others.

Let us hope that it won't warp your daughter's attitude if you feel that you can pass on a tactful word to her admirers that token presents and attentions, such as letters, would actually mean more to her than adding to the doll overpopulation. Your daughter is ready for advanced etiquette. You have taught her the joy of receiving, and now you might try teaching her the joy of giving. It is cruel to confiscate toys she has already become attached to, but before a major influx of presents occurs you could suggest that she have the fun of choosing what she wants to keep and deciding what she can give to other children — say, through a hospital or other institution. (Martin, 1989, p. 518)

For adults, as well as for children, etiquette rules may involve hardships but they may also involve benefits. Children might be at a particular disadvantage in understanding the benefit of etiquette rules if they are expected to follow rules that adults do not follow in relation to them. It may be significantly easier, for example, to write a thank-you note when one has also been the recipient of one.

In informants' stories of etiquette, adult motives for requiring the described behavior may appear self-evident: children are being taught 'socially appropriate behavior.' The stories indicate, however, that children's perceptions of the hardships attendant on appropriate behavior may differ from those of adults — or may not, for some adults may share the perceptions described by children. Adults may also resent writing thank-you notes and indeed not write them. Adults, however, have control over the redefinition of 'socially appropriate behavior' and may even choose to behave 'inappropriately.' The children in the foregoing stories seemed to possess neither resource.

Lessons

Being required to participate in lessons, even those one initially wanted, can be a source of a variety of hardships. Lessons may present particular problems for children who have little talent for or interest in what is being taught. The boredom of 'practicing' lessons is especially difficult to endure if one is unaware that boredom is a not uncommon feature of practicing that practicing has long-term positive consequences, or if one does not see those consequences as positive. Characteristics of those who teach lessons may also be a source of trials.

One hardship of mine while growing up was piano lessons. At first, the idea of piano lessons was wonderful, then they became a nightmare. Practice, practice, practice was all I ever heard, from both my parents and my teacher. Not only was practicing horrible but seeing my teacher was a scary sight. My teacher was quite a large woman from Yugoslavia with a mustache as thick as my father's. Her house smelled like cats and her body odor was not the most pleasant thing in the world to inhale for forty-five minutes. The one thing that bothered me the most was when she stood over me and played over my shoulder with her armpits in my nose. I was forced to hold my breath while she was playing the piano in this position. Every day after my lesson I would complain, but it didn't make a difference. My parents would say, 'You're lucky to take piano lessons. I wish I could have been given the chance. If you quit you are going to regret it. Besides, you sound very good.' The lessons lasted two and one half years; until my teacher moved away. I'm sure if my teacher hadn't moved away I would still be taking lessons. (Celeste)

Celeste's difficulties might have been significantly alleviated by a change in piano teacher but that option was apparently not available to her. Mary might have benefited from a similar solution.

> If this lady hits me on the head with a tissue box one more time, I'm going to pick up that vase and hit her back. We begin 'The Waltzing Parakeet' again for the tenth time. Finally we get through it, my lesson's been over for twenty minutes, now will she let me go? No, we must practice it a few more times so that we have it perfect for the recital in a few weeks. Auuugh!
>
> In fifth grade, my parents finally agreed to allow me to take piano lessons. I was so excited, until I went to my first lessons. Entering her little brick house was like entering the dark ages. Her wallpaper was faded, her house smelled of mothballs and she had no heat on ever, only a small fire in the fireplace. Once the lesson began, I was seated at one of the two grand pianos or harpsichord in her small living room. The first few weeks we played simple scales and things were basically OK. Unfortunately as time went by I began to make more and more mistakes. My mistakes did not go unnoticed. If I dared play a wrong note she hit me over the head with a tissue box, if I looked at my hands she would cover them with a dirty dishcloth, and if I had bad hand position she would make me play with a paperweight on my hands.
>
> My parents, who never went to a lesson, loved Monique. I, who went to the lessons, hated her. Mom and Dad thought she was the nicest, sweetest lady. They also loved her because she only charged two dollars for a half an hour and kept you over an hour. I hated her and cried and screamed before every lesson. (Mary)

Adults, quite reasonably, may grant more importance to some factors (e.g., cost, convenience) than do children. Alternatively, children may have more knowledge of the situation itself than adults have — or want to have. To accept a child's complaints about a teacher presupposes adults' recognition that a teacher may act differently with adults and children or may have qualities that only emerge in close association. Adults might object to the very characteristics that Celeste and Mary fault in their piano teachers. Accepting a child's complaints, however, may involve adults in unwanted activities: finding another teacher, perhaps paying more, coordinating schedules and transportation. Adults who do not want to face such changes are served by their denial of children's experiences. Another consequence of this denial, at least for Celeste and Mary, is that their initial enthusiasm turned to distress. For Felicia, in the following story, even initial enthusiasm was lacking.

Dancing Lessons
by Felicia

A 'sour' event that still is alive on the lower side of my memories was my dancing lessons. I was one of those little girls for whom flying around in tutus never caught my eye. When I was about 4, I went to my first dancing lesson, the beginning of an unwilling and unwanted period of my life. I can remember my mother's exaggerated grin. . .as she held up a glowing green leotard and said, 'You're going to dancing lessons.' The grossest words I'd ever heard. Being a youngster subject to my parents' horrible will, I had no choice. Within an hour we were in a bright pink room with large mirrors and oodles of anxious girls in colorful outfits. My stomach rolled and pirouetted better than I ever did on that first day of my dancing career. I detested my mother on dancing days and I couldn't understand for the life of me why she would make me do something I hated so much. Why didn't she take the dancing lessons instead of me? She always got more excited than I ever did.

I would wake up on dancing days with a knot in my stomach and it would get tighter and larger as the day went on. I would be miserable all day long and petrified that one of my friends in school would find out that I took dancing lessons. During recess I wouldn't play because I was afraid that some-one would accidentally see what I was wearing underneath my school clothes — the infamous skintight leotard that shone a neon green through my slacks. Not only did the lessons cause anxiety and discomfort, but they nearly ruined my social life — no swing-sets and hopscotch for me — I stood quietly aside worrying about my after-school nightmare.

Not only did I not like the dance lessons, but I was a terrible dancer. It may not have been as bad if I could have at least done 'able pie' (a simple dance step) but my pie looked more like a waterlogged pizza! My instructor always yelled at me — 'No, No, No, not like that, dear — like this. Gee, you're a clutzy little girl, aren't you?' The whole experience was agony — from day one until I finally stopped four years later.

The most embarrassing single moment from dancing happened one day in school right before lunch. Before we went to lunch, we all had to take our brown bags and lunch-boxes from the shelf and file out to the lunch room. Not before, of course, the teacher checked the shelf for leftover lunches. Usually, it wasn't a problem — what hungry little kid would leave a peanut-butter and jelly sandwich and a Twinkie in the closet? But one day there was a brown bag. The teacher wouldn't let the class go because someone didn't have a lunch. We all had to go back to our seats and put our heads on our desks until the 'culprit' claimed his food. Finally, after ten minutes of quiet and wide-spread fear, the teacher threatened to open the brown bag and expose the perpetrator. Still nobody claimed the lunch. It was opened and out popped my pink ballet slippers. My face turned florescent red as the class erupted in a chorus of hoots and hollers, not a pretty sight for second grade.

Soon after, my mother finally realized what her little girl was going through. Her dreams of having a ballerina as a daughter were shattered — but after, she did have a much happier little girl.

* * *

Adults' choreography of children's activities — denying access to desired ones, requiring participation in undesired ones, interrupting, and providing inappropriate 'help' — may serve as a source of many little trials of childhood. It may also serve as an explanation for some instances of what adults term children's 'short attention span.' ' "Attention," ' writes Lane, 'seems only a label we use when a person responds to some things and not others: he is not "paying attention" if the cues influencing him at the moment do not interest us' (1976, p. 103). There may be many reasons for children's not paying attention; adults' practices in relation to children may go unrecognized as one such reason. Indeed the term itself may embody adults' biases, for adults may be more likely to identify a 'short attention span' when children are shirking adult-directed projects than to identify a 'long attention span' when children are playing video games, watching TV, or engaging in other activities they have chosen for themselves but of which adults are critical.

Children live in worlds peopled by others, adults and children, who may be perceived as having greater control over their own activities. Children who can engage in certain desired activities and do not have to engage in other undesired ones can make life unpleasant, even miserable, for children who face greater restrictions. By recognizing children's trials, adults gain greater understanding of and sympathy for the *fact* of children's distress, even when they dispute the *reasons* for it. Although children may develop their own strategies for dealing with the kinds of trials described in this chapter, adults who recognize the depth of children's difficulties may be able to provide them with other strategies, for adults too have experiences of being included in activities from which they would prefer exclusion and of being denied that which they want to do.

5 Emotions Ignored, Minimized, Distorted, and Denied

I had Brownie meetings once a week and I always loved going. We did all sorts of projects and of course we sold Girl Scout cookies. Well, it came to the time of year to go out and sell the cookies and I was all excited. I went around knocking on doors trying to sell them, but no one would buy them from me. They always either said, 'No, we're not interested' or 'No, we already bought some.' So by the end of the month we were supposed to sell them, I had only sold 10 boxes of cookies and 5 of them were to my parents. . .I went to the next meeting and handed in my small order, and I distinctly remember the scowl on my group leader's face. She said, 'This is all you sold?' I said yes and started to cry, and she said, 'Well, in order for you to "fly up" [graduate] to Girl Scouts you were supposed to sell at least 25 boxes of cookies. You will have to stay in Brownies next year.' Well, all of my other friends had sold the required amount of cookies and were going to 'fly up' so of course I was very upset. I went running out of the meeting and went home crying to my mother. She did not take it seriously at all. She started laughing and said it was no big deal, yet it was a big deal and I couldn't believe she was laughing at me. I was crushed. (Tilly)

Children may respond to objects and events with a strength, depth, and range of emotions of which adults are unaware or that they deem inappropriate. One might speak of adults possessing taken-for-granted 'rules' for children's emotions — rules that govern the emotions that children ought and ought not feel and the objects and events towards which they ought and ought not feel them. That children themselves may neither follow nor indeed accept the legitimacy of these taken-for-granted rules is demonstrated in the stories to follow. Adults' explicit claims about emotions may further obscure children's experiences and, moreover, lead children to see adults as odd, if not misguided.

I still can't understand why adults told me that my parents were showing their love for me when they spanked me. It always seemed like they were showing their anger. That's not my connotation of love. Nor do I understand why my parents would say it hurt them more than the spanking hurt me. I never believed that one. (Holly)

Frank writes, '*to be a child is to have one's states of being. . .defined in others'* (e.g., adults') *terms*, rather than from one's own perspective' (1981, p. 113, emphasis in original). When adults, implicitly or explicitly, define children's emotional states of being from their own (adults') perspective, they risk ignoring, minimizing, distorting, or denying children's emotions.

Many of the stories presented throughout this book include descriptions of children's emotions; in this chapter I focus on emotions to which informants direct specific attention: embarrassment, anger, and fear. Children may find already existing trials of childhood exacerbated and experience further trials as they attempt to deal with difficult emotions — and without being able to count on the kinds of help that adults accord one another.

Embarrassment

The stories in this section provide evidence that adults may see children as incapable of embarrassment, may fail to recognize the depth of their embarrassment, or may fail to see specific situations as ones that might engender embarrassment. Children's experiences of embarrassment, however, remain, as shown in the following story.

A Night of Humiliation
by Iris

Since the age of 7 my sister Madeline and I have sung in the church choir. Offering my gift of song to God was a truly beautiful experience. This glorious moment could only have improved if the choir director remembered my name. She was so concerned with Madeline and choosing Madeline's solo that my name was irrelevant. . .As a result of our close relationship, and much time spent together, Madeline and I developed the same interests and pursued the same talents. Trying to find just one thing I really enjoyed at which Madeline was not skilled became an important mission. I wanted to spread my wings, fly with freedom and love to a place where Madeline had never been. Being the oldest meant always being first. Madeline would always be older and knowledgeable of what I had yet to experience. It was a long time before I was recognized and my name was remembered. Looking in the mirror and seeing the words 'Madeline's sister' was far from an appropriate reflection of self. As the years went by, my appreciation and respect for Madeline grew. I began formulating my own dreams, experiences and pursuits of truth. My love and admiration for my sister drew sharp lines around my own personality.

The realization that I didn't have to be a duplicate of my sister began in the fourth grade at a Christmas concert. Suddenly I was standing alone waiting for the music to begin. My entire family sat in the front row, eyes so full of love and encouragement. This was my song, my chance. Tragically this was also

one of my most embarrassing moments. Mr. Pappas, our music director an-
nounces, ' "My Favorite Things" from *The Sound of Music* will be performed
by Iris Henderson.' My eyes scanned the crowd, completely surprised by their
enthusiastic applause. They knew I wasn't Madeline but continued to clap. My
light pink satin dress suddenly became very itchy. What has been described as
'butterflies in your stomach' felt more like elephants. All the parents stopped
bragging about their own children and focused on me. Struggling not to be
controlled by fear, I opened my mouth. I sang the first verse with happiness
in my heart. 'Raindrops on roses and whiskers on kittens. . .' Yes, these too
were some of my favorite things. Caught up in the magic of the song, smiling
at relatives, I listened closely to the musical interlude. . .what's the words to
the second verse? La La La La La La. . .I don't remember. The words to every
song I had ever sung in my entire life flashed through my head. 'Happy
Birthday to You.' No! Something about things. . .What kind of things anyway?
The pianist repeated the interlude, mouthing the words to me. I was horrified
at my mistake. I wanted people to remember my name. Oh yes, Iris Henderson,
the girl who couldn't remember the words and ran out of the auditorium
humiliated and disgusted.

My concerned parents found me crying hysterically in the hallway. 'That's
okay, honey, nobody noticed,' my dad explained. Nice try, Dad, but I stood
there thinking about the words to 'Happy Birthday.' My mother hugged me.
She was crying too. 'It's okay, Iris. Why don't you try to remember the words
now and give it another chance?' Didn't they realize there was nothing they
could do or say to save me? The sound of my sister's new high heels got
louder. Click click, clack — she wasn't used to walking in them yet. She
lovingly called my name, a name that I wanted to forget instead of the words.
'I'm proud of you' was all she said. She was just pitying me. Didn't she see
what happened? 'The first verse sounded beautiful and I know if you remembered the words, the second would have been even better.' Her smile was a
message of love and, yes, of approval.

I'll never forget that night of humiliation, mistakes, and most importantly
appreciation of self. Everyone makes mistakes that can't be denied. But not
everyone makes them in front of a hundred people and can still sing about
that today.

*   *   *

It is illuminating to view Iris' story in relation to social practices governing
adults' management of embarrassment. Goffman (1967) states that in everyday
social interactions adults (1) strive to conceal their own embarrassment; (2)
expect to receive assistance from others in that concealment; (3) expect to
receive from others who recognize the embarrassment assistance in repairing
the situation; and (4) may experience the dissolution of an encounter in the

face of unrepaired embarrassment. Iris was unable to conceal her embarrassment. She was also unable to make use of the assistance in concealment offered by others ('Nobody noticed,' 'it's okay,' 'I'm proud of you') because of its discrepancy with what she knew to be true. Despite the love, approval, and solicitude of others, without acknowledging her embarrassment they could provide her no assistance in repairing the situation. Thus the encounter was dissolved, for she 'ran out of the auditorium humiliated and disgusted.' Iris nonetheless may be seen as fortunate in being offered some, albeit unhelpful, assistance, for children may not be able to count on any assistance from adults in concealing or repairing embarrassment. To document this claim, I juxtapose Goffman's statements about adults' practices among themselves with stories of children's experiences.

(1) *Concealing one's embarrassment*

[T]o appear flustered, in our society at least, is considered evidence of weakness, inferiority, low status, moral guilt, defeat, and other unenviable attributes. . .[U]nderstandably the flustered individual will make some effort to conceal his state from the others present. (Goffman, 1967, p. 102)

In the story to follow, Irene's source of embarrassment — bed-wetting — might appear to be a reasonable one by adult standards. Adults with urinary lapses, however, might avail themselves of the many sanitary products on the market designed to conceal such failings. Without resources for concealment, Irene is left to give 'evidence of weakness, inferiority, low status, moral guilt, defeat, and other unenviable attributes.'

The most embarrassing childhood memory that I have was being a bed-wetter. Up until first grade, no matter what theory my mother tried, I still wet my bed. Every night my mother had to get up in the middle of the night and change my sheets. When I went to visit my friends overnight, I would wet the bed. It was extremely embarrassing. (Irene)

Children's attempts to conceal their embarrassment is undermined by adults who use embarrassment as a technique for 'curing' children's bed-wetting. Adults thus reveal the very thing that children are trying to conceal.

One time, I must've been around 3 years old, my mom was tired of my wetting my pants so she decided that she was going to stop it one way or another. My mom bought diapers, made me lie on the table, and put a diaper on me. She told my brother and sister to come in and watch her do this. I was crying the whole time. I was so embarrassed and angry at her for doing this to me. Then the next day Ann's mom was baby-sitting me and my mom gave her the box and told her that if I wet my pants to put a diaper on me. I was never so angry with her. Even now as I am writing this I can remember how angry I was. I was only 3 years old but even 3-year-olds know what anger and embarrassment are. (Cora)

Adults frustrated by children's bed-wetting may be unaware that children too find their failing a matter of concern and, as well, a source of embarrassment. Adults' methods for resolving the problem can simply add to that embarrassment.

(2) *Others' assistance with concealment*

Since the individual dislikes to feel or appear embarrassed, tactful persons will avoid placing him in this position. In addition, they will often pretend not to know that he has lost composure or has grounds for losing it. They may try to suppress signs of having recognized his state or hide them behind the same kind of covering gesture that he might employ. Thus they protect his face and his feelings and presumably make it easier for him to regain composure or at least hold on to what he still has. (Goffman, 1967, pp. 102–3)

When adults call public attention to that which embarrasses children, they deprive them of assistance with concealment, offering instead revelation and the very thing that children are trying to avoid — embarrassment.

A specific incident that I remember very well happened to me when I was 6 years old. My mother was an elementary teacher in the school that I went to. I would often forget my lunch money. One day when I asked if I could go to my mother's room, my teacher yelled at me for forgetting my lunch money. She made me eat a piece of cheese and drink a carton of milk that was free from the cafeteria. All the children laughed at me and I was very embarrassed. (Irene)

Calling a characteristic to public notice may be a particular source of distress to those who see that characteristic as true of themselves *and* as a failing.

A painful memory associated with my height happened in the third grade. My teacher was measuring students' height to make a 'Growing Tree' for the classroom bulletin board. This 'Growing Tree' chart ranged from 4 feet on up to 6 feet. No one was expected to be shorter or taller than those margins. As I stood underneath the 'Growing Tree,' my teacher laughed aloud and commented to the whole class that Gini was not yet four feet tall. Needless to say, I hid my head for days. (Gini)

Adults may fail to provide children with assistance in concealment, may reveal what children want to conceal, or may, as in the following story, be the very source of the embarrassment itself.

> When I was 8 I had a big birthday party. When I was opening my presents my mother told me to take whatever I got out of the box and show everyone what it was. I came to one box and when I opened it I was horrified to see 6 pairs of neatly wrapped underwear. I started to close the box but my mother insisted that I show everyone what I had gotten. I was so embarrassed! After I had finished opening all of my presents my mother apologized since she hadn't known what was in the box. I was still really embarrassed. (Elizabeth)

If adults do not recognize the potential sources of children's embarrassment (e.g., if they fail to recognize children's sense of modesty), they are hardly able to assist with concealment.

Although adults may deem it appropriate to pretend to not notice the embarrassment of other adults, in some adult–child interactions no pretense is involved. Rather than failing to hide their knowledge, adults may simply not know that children are embarrassed. With pretense, the pretender may be counted on for help; with lack of knowledge, such help is not possible. On other occasions any pretense is abandoned and children's embarrassment is openly noted. Adults who do notice children's embarrassment may dismiss its seriousness, finding it 'cute.' Since being embarrassed may itself be embarrassing, embarrassment can be readily compounded. Whether adults are unaware of children's embarrassment or actively contribute to it, children are left on their own to manage their emotions.

(3) *Receiving assistance in repairing a situation*

> [T]he individual whose self has been threatened (the individual for whom embarrassment is felt) and the individual who threatened him may both feel ashamed of what together they have brought about, sharing this sentiment just when they have reason to feel apart. And this joint responsibility is only right. By the standards of the wider society, perhaps only the discredited individual ought to feel ashamed; but, by the standards of the little social system maintained through the interaction, the discreditor is just as guilty as the person he discredits — sometimes more so, for, if he has been posing as a tactful man, in destroying another's image he destroys his own. (Goffman, 1967, p. 106)

Unlike Goffman's adults who assist one another in repairing a situation, the camp owner in the following story is described as placing the child in an embarrassing position, recognizing and indeed highlighting the child's loss of composure, and making it difficult if not impossible for the child to regain composure and repair the situation.

> When I was 4 years old, my mother sent me to day camp. I didn't want to go. I wanted to stay home with her like my younger sister did.

My mother told me that she thought the best place for me was camp. I disagreed. From the time the bus picked me up until the time I came home, I cried. I remember sitting on the steps of the baby pool and screaming for my mother. The counselors thought I was afraid of the water, but I already knew how to swim. After a few weeks of trying to get me to stop crying, the owner of the camp took me inside, held me up to a mirror, and asked me if I wanted people to see me like that. I was so embarrassed I cried even more. For the first time, in all that crying, I felt that I was ugly and no one would like me because I cried so much. All I wanted was to spend time with my mother and no one would listen to me. (Nora)

When embarrassment is used as a method for controlling or punishing children, those children can hardly look to those same adults for assistance in repairing the situation.

(4) *Experiencing the dissolution of an encounter in the face of unrepaired embarrassment*

[J]ust as the flustered individual may fail to conceal his embarrassment, those who perceive his discomfort may fail in their attempt to hide their knowledge, whereupon they all will realize that his embarrassment has been seen and that the seeing of it was something to conceal. When this point is reached, ordinary involvement in the interaction may meet a painful end. . . .(Goffman, 1967, p. 103)

Adults may find that dissolution of an encounter, while perhaps painful, does result in an end to that encounter and a departure from the scene. A particular problem described by my informants is to experience unrepaired embarrassment *and* to be required to remain in the encounter.

When I was in the first grade, my reading group was going to put on a Christmas play for the school and parents. There were try-outs and everything. I was really excited. I went to try-outs and read the part of Mrs Claus. I thought I did pretty well too. I had one problem though; out of my whole reading group I was the second to worst reader. My teacher of course held this against me, and when parts got handed out I was not given the part of Mrs Claus. I was given the part of one of Santa's helpers, and my name was Tweedle-DUMB. I was convinced that this was because I was so stupid when it came to my reading skills. I went home and told my parents the part I got and they were excited that I even got a speaking part. They did not understand how mortified I was that my name in the play was Tweedle-DUMB. All they cared about was that I got a speaking part.

When it came time to put on the play, I did not want to go on stage. All the kids had been laughing at me and I didn't want the audience to laugh at me too. My parents, however, made me go on stage and the audience did laugh at me. They laughed at me because I was supposed to be funny, but I did not understand that. After the play my parents told me how proud of me they were and took me out for ice cream. I could not understand though. How come my parents were rewarding me when all I had done was embarrassed myself? (Tilly)

The adult onlookers in the following story may not have recognized the child's embarrassment but by attending to him in his embarrassment they contributed to the 'painful end' predicted by Goffman, an end that itself required an adults' assistance.

We were all eating dinner in a restaurant when 3-year-old Pete fell off his chair. He began to cry. People stopped eating, gathered around, asked if he were hurt, and generally made a fuss. As he became the center of attention he hid his face against me. I knew he was not hurt but simply embarrassed and wanted the incident ignored and forgotten but I had great difficulty in moving people away. (Paraphrased from a story told me by Maxine)

Children's embarrassment may be tripartite: (1) the initial embarrassment; (2) the embarrassment of adults' attentions, even those apparently motivated by kindness, concern, or sympathy, that violate the rule calling for the pretense of not noticing; and (3) the continuing embarrassment occasioned by children's inability to escape the encounter by departing the scene.

When I was younger, my parents used to fight all the time. I hated it. I used to think I was the only one who was going through this. I remember devising plans in an effort to make them stop fighting. I used to get sick, because I figured they would have to worry more about me than themselves. I used to ask them, behind each other's back, if they really loved each other. Once, at an amusement park, my parents got into a huge fight. We were sitting in the parking lot of the park when they started to fight. My father didn't want to stay because he hates amusement parks. My mother said, 'Fine, let's go!' Then she asked how he could do that to us (take us to an amusement park and not let us go on the rides). My mother got out of the car, took my sister's hand and started walking into the park. My father was walking about a block behind and I was in between the two of them, crying hysterically. It was so embarrassing, because all of the people were watching me cry and telling each other to look at me and saying how sorry they felt for me. Some of the people even wanted to help me. I was so humiliated. I hated my mother for doing this to me. (Sara)

According to adults' conventions, if a social encounter is to be sustained, the parties will cooperate to overcome problems caused by embarrassment. When those problems are not overcome, adults may dissolve the encounter by departing the scene. In adult–child interactions, however, encounters can be sustained even in the face of children's unconcealed and unrepaired embarrassment. Unable to hide their embarrassment, denied assistance with concealment and repair, perhaps even having their embarrassment made public, and without power to dissolve encounters, children remain in them, left on their own to endure what they cannot escape.

Anger

Adults certainly accept the possibility that children can feel anger, but the thoroughgoing, enduring, and consequential aspects of anger described in the following story may come as a surprise.

> When I was in nursery school or kindergarten, I don't know which, I can remember one day in particular that is probably responsible for me hating school throughout my life. I had been playing with a group of children in the playhouse that was set up for us. It was like a giant doll house with a kitchen area and everything like that. There were a lot of children in the house on this particular day and everyone was being louder than usual. I can't remember if the teacher had come in before and given everyone a warning, but she came in at one point and started yelling for everyone to quiet down. Then she told me to leave and go sit at a table outside of the house. I was the only one she asked to leave and I wasn't even the loudest in there, if I was even making any noise at all. She made me go sit with a girl that I hated and help her with a puzzle. I was so mad at my teacher and I have hated her ever since and I can't even remember her name. I used to tell my mother these things but she would always say something like 'I'm sure the teacher had a good reason for what she did.' I don't think she ever knew how mad I was about that day. (Karen)

Adults may also fail to recognize that they can be the quite unintentional source of a child's anger.

> I remember when I was in kindergarten, towards the end of the year, we had to practice our bus route for the first grade because it was going to be different. Well, I was supposed to switch buses and I didn't, so the driver had to take me back to my house after everyone else. When I got home my family was all giggly, they thought it was such a cute thing to do. I was so angry. I wish they hadn't laughed. I didn't think it was funny. (Sybil, Pearl's informant)

Being laughed at emerges as significant in a number of stories, a source of anger as well as embarrassment. Like adults, children may find it distressing to be laughed at.

Adults' commitment to their own understanding of a situation when they are mistaken can be another source of children's anger. In the following story, that anger is increased by the adult's failure to recognize that the child is following the very rule established by the adult.

A Story of Anger
by Peg

One of my earliest childhood memories is when I was 3. My brother Ray and I were playing hide and seek in our apartment. We were running around the house and being very loud. My mother was in the kitchen and asked us to quiet down. We started to whisper and giggle and I remember it being quite fun. It was my turn to hide so I hid in the bathroom. My brother saw me and slammed the bathroom door, yelling 'I got you, I got you' over and over. What he didn't realize was that my right hand had been on the door frame. He had slammed the door on my hand.

I remember screaming and crying when the door closed on my hand. I heard my mom yell from the kitchen for us to quiet down. My brother giggled louder. My mom yelled that if we didn't stop she would spank both our bottoms. This made me angry. I was scared and hurt and I had not done anything wrong. My mother had told me never to call for help unless I really needed it because no one would believe me otherwise. I had always followed this rule and now, when I really needed help and was asking for it, she wasn't coming.

I heard her coming down the hall and yelling at my brother. I tried desperately to reach the doorknob but my arms were too short and it hurt too much. My mom picked up my brother and carried him to the bedroom. I was so frustrated and tried repeatedly to get out but I couldn't. I couldn't even scream anymore and simply cried. Finally, my mother opened the door and I distinctly remember the deep sense of gratification and self-justice I felt when I saw my mother's face. It changed quickly from angry to shocked concern as I held my bleeding and swollen hand to her. I was so happy to be heard and justified that I barely cried on the way to the hospital. That is what my mother says she remembers best, how brave I had been not to cry. She will never know that I was simply happy to see her so upset and apologetic after I had been feeling so very powerless and helpless. It's funny that I can remember these feelings so clearly but not the pain I felt. I guess the feelings were deeper.

I can still remember which finger was fractured, the pattern of the wallpaper in the bathroom, and the look on not only my mother's face but also on my father's several hours later. This memory is my first of a conflict with rules. I had followed my mother's rules about calling for help but she showed me that rules aren't always inviolable. I learned the hard way that I couldn't always depend on others.

One other important realization I've had was how adults decide how children feel. I can still hear my mom's praise of how brave I was, not crying or yelling the whole time we went to the hospital. I knew this was not an act of bravery but satisfaction at being proven right. Children remember many details adults don't give them credit for. My mother thought I would remember the pain and that's all. I remember the strong feelings that I probably didn't even know the names of then. I don't remember anyone apologizing (except my brother because my parents made him) for making me so angry and not believing me.

* * *

When adults recognize that they have been wrong in their definitions of situations, they do not necessarily offer apologies.

> I feel to me what was hard about being a child was most of the time I was seen, not heard. I remember one incident when my father accused my brother and me of scraping off paint from the cabinet door in the kitchen. We pleaded with him to listen to our story but he would not hear of it. He told us to go to his room and wait for him there. We knew what was going to happen next, his belt was going to come off and he was going to whip us. He was about to do so when my aunt came through the door and told him not to whip us because her daughter, who was 2 at the time, did the scraping. My brother and I were so happy that my aunt came through the door because she basically rescued us from getting a beating. Till this day, my father has not apologized and still does not admit that he was wrong for not believing in us. (Norma, Lillian's informant)

Adults may, however, coerce children into apologizing, even when children do not see an apology as warranted.

> I was in the sixth grade. I had just moved and had to start in a new school. A girl who lived up the street, Eva, had introduced herself to me when I moved in and had introduced me to the other kids in the neighborhood. She quickly became my new best friend. One morning, while waiting for the bus, Eva, the other kids at the bus stop, and I were having a snowball fight. Eva threw a snowball in my face, which got me slightly upset, so I kicked her in the shins. The bus came as Eva fell to the ground crying. She was such a pitiful sight that

I couldn't help but laugh. Eva made her way onto the bus and sat down. When we got to school, Eva wasn't speaking to me. I told my friends what had happened and most of them 'took my side.' Through-out the school day, my friends laughed at and called Eva every name in the book. I stayed out of it because I knew Eva would tell her parents, who in turn would tell mine. That afternoon, when we got off the bus, Eva ran home crying. That night, Eva's parents showed up at my house and told my parents that I had beaten Eva up and had been harassing her at school. I tried to tell Eva's parents what had really happened but they wouldn't listen. They told my parents that I should be grounded for 3 to 5 days. Thankfully, my parents believed that I didn't beat Eva up so I did not get grounded. However, my mother insisted that I call Eva and apologize for harassing her. I refused to apologize for something I had not done but my parents wouldn't believe me that I hadn't been harassing her. They made me call and apologize to Eva even though I hadn't done what I had been accused of. (Sally)

Wrong in their definitions of situations, amused by children's misfortunes, requiring children to offer unwarranted apologies and not offering children warranted ones, adults may seem to children worthy recipients of anger.

Fears

Adults may disagree, among themselves and with children, over whether any given object or situation warrants fear. Guided by their own assessments, adults may ignore children's fears or call them 'silly,' even though other adults may have just such fears.

On one beach. . .you could walk for miles and miles into the water and it would be up to your ankles. I found sand dollars, rare conch shells with animals in them, and many other beautiful shells that were the colors of the rainbow. When you were standing in the water, gazing at the breathtaking beauty of this beach, you had to watch out for the sand sharks. . .because this was their territory. My dad started going after these sharks to take pictures of them. I was screaming at him because I was afraid he would get bit. My dad ignored me and said that nothing would happen. But I was petrified because we were on this deserted beach and we were miles away from other people and I did not know what to do if my dad got bit. I was really upset because my father would not listen to me, so I ran to the car and pouted. My dad came after me and I did not talk to him for the rest of the day. (Ellie)

When I was in third grade my parents decided that we were going to visit our relatives in Hawaii. It was my first plane ride and I had to leave my friends. I was really scared of the plane and of what I would do while I was in Hawaii. . .While in Hawaii I can remember my uncle lived on the side of an active volcano. When we started walking toward the volcano we could see smoke rising from it and I was really scared. I told my mother that I didn't want to go up there and she and my father told me that I was being silly. Needless to say, they forced me to visit my uncle that day. (Joanna, Elizabeth's informant)

Adults who fear sand sharks, emergencies for which they are unprepared, volcanoes, or airplanes may have greater resources for avoiding these 'dangers' or for avoiding the designation 'silly.' When adults take their own fears as reasonable and children's as unreasonable, the grounds for children's fears are denied but their fears remain. 'Don't be afraid' is advice no more helpful for children than for adults, its offer suggesting that fear is a matter over which one has greater control than it may seem to those experiencing it.

Although adults may routinely acknowledge some children's fears, e.g., of the dark, they may nonetheless minimize or dismiss them, denying their basis in 'reality.' The following story documents the depth and significance that such fear can possess.

Monsters never existed during the day when anyone else could see them but every night when Mom tucked me in, shut the light off, and went downstairs I could feel the presence of the monsters. I could feel them, hear them, and sometimes even see them. What did Mom say when, after what seemed like hours went by, I finally started frantically screaming? She said, 'Rose, don't worry. There is no such thing as a monster.' I would wonder to myself about how she could be so stupid. I knew they were there and she didn't care. I cried myself to sleep for years. This was partly because I was so terrified and partly because Mommy didn't care. (Rose)

In establishing the truth or falsity of a claim, children, like adults, may seek out authorities. In the above story, the child's mother was sought out but rejected as an authority, apparently in the face of the child's strong evidence for the existence of monsters. What *was* Rose feeling, hearing, and seeing? Was it *nothing*? I am reminded of a statement in Kinney's *How to Raise a Dog in the City and the Suburbs*:

[If a puppy] thinks he hears a noise in the kitchen, for instance, take him out to the kitchen in your arms and show him there is nothing there. (If there is something there — a burglar or something — you are on your own as to how to explain your way out.) (Kinney, 1938, p. 70)

I do not plead for the reality of monsters but do assert that to take children's experiences to be *solely* imaginary and *totally* groundless is both to deny their experiences and to impede any quest for alternative explanations. For those who eschew supernatural explanations, natural ones can be sought. Learning that houses settle, and creak as they do so, may be one useful explanation for sounds that a child indeed does hear but attributes to monsters.

Children may maintain their versions of the truth even in the face of adults' versions (and in so doing may also find it necessary to construct explanations for adults' claims and actions — for Rose, above, that her mother didn't care). What evidence can children offer that monsters do or do not exist? In the stories read to them,[1] in the knowledge and experiences of their peers, and with what can be taken as adults' confirmation, evidence for the existence of monsters may seem quite compelling. It appears to have been so for the child in the following story, wherein belief in monsters seems to have been created by the adult — who apparently did not believe in monsters but made them up to further his own projects. Regardless of adults' expectations, such inventions may be received as fact by children.

> Behind our house was a tall fence and on the other side of the fence were railroad tracks...For as long as I can remember, my parents always told me, 'Stay away from the railroad tracks,' and so I had. I used to climb my jungle gym to try to see the trains passing but no matter how high I climbed I could never ever actually see the trains. I could hear them but I never saw one.
>
> One night, when my parents were going out, I had a baby-sitter named Jimmy. He was the last person that your mother called when she was searching for a baby-sitter and almost every child's unfavorite sitter. Jimmy came and my parents left, leaving plenty of instructions on the kitchen table. I played for a while, watched TV, did all the things kids do when their parents aren't at home. Eventually it was bedtime. I went upstairs without complaining. While brushing my teeth, I wondered if Jimmy would let me go outside and climb once again to the top of the jungle gym to look for trains. I ran downstairs and asked him but he told me not to be ridiculous. He said there were no trains outside my house and laughed and said, 'That's what your

---

[1] Children may take the stories read to them as sources of knowledge. Mackay, for example, discussing standardized tests, describes how the children he studied read test questions from within contexts that included the children's books to which they had access. When asked in a standardized test to select the picture to go with the sentence 'The bird built his own house,' some children selected the 'wrong' picture (of a birdhouse) rather than the 'right' one (a nest) based on knowledge they had gained from children's books. As their teacher states, 'well in fairy stories quite often a rabbit builds his own house...Monkeys do it we just read a story where monkeys didn't want to build their house' (Mackay, 1974, pp. 244–5). Children's stories replete with monsters may serve children as grounds for the facticity of monsters.

parents told you, isn't it?' He went on to tell me that behind the fence lived monsters, big ones and small ones, and the noises I heard all the time were really monsters. And they could run over the fence any time and steal me. And then he told me I'd better go to bed before he called them over. I ran upstairs and hid under the covers, terrified, until I fell asleep. It was at least a year before I told my parents what Jimmy told me and, each time I heard the distant sound of a train approaching, I ran into the house, so afraid that that was the time the monsters were going to get me. My dad finally put me on his shoulders and stood by the big fence until I could see a train go by. (Betty)

Fears judged imaginary by adults can be taken by children as having a quite legitimate basis in 'reality,' supported both by their experiences and by authorities. Betty suggests that children may be willing to entertain alternatives to monsters when they are provided with evidence that they find trustworthy.

Sources of Emotions

Adults' rules for children's emotions may govern not only the emotions children ought to feel but also the events and objects towards which they ought to feel them. If adults judge an object or event trivial, then they are likely to see a display of strong emotion by children as excessive. Conversely, if adults see an object or event as important, they are likely to attribute strong emotions to the children involved. Children's assessments of triviality or importance, and thus the emotions they experience, may violate adults' rules.

Adults may, for example, see divorce as unquestionably an important event for children, as indeed it may be. In the following story, however, a quite different assessment is offered, for divorce is described as not of great emotional importance — not, at least, until other adults make it so. (It is, of course, possible that Tammy is denying her feelings but it is also possible that she is not.) This story makes clear how great the discrepancy can be between the emotions of children and the emotions attributed to them.

The strongest memory I have is one involving my parents' divorce. When I was really young, I didn't pay much attention to the fact that I didn't have my father around. Nobody made a big deal about it. I wasn't sad, I didn't feel as though I was missing out, and I felt content. As I got older and started school, however, all that changed.

'All right, class, today we are going to make Father's Day cards,' my first grade teacher announced. I felt my stomach tighten and silently I raised my hand.

'Mrs Downs, I. . .I don't have a father who lives with me.'

'Oh! Oh, you poor child. Well, I guess you can just draw a picture then,' she told me. I nodded, but I was shaking inside. Was I different?

Did I fit in anymore? Why didn't the other kids just draw pictures? Why couldn't I have a father too? These were only a few of the feelings and questions I had.

'Tammy, I'm so, so sorry that your dad isn't living with you. That must be awfully hard for you to deal with.' After these words were spoken to me, I wanted to tell the adult that it was no big deal. It really didn't affect me. After hearing the two comments just mentioned, I began to think more about not how I really felt but rather how everyone else thought I should feel. I started missing a man I didn't even know, I started to cry about not having a dad, and I also developed feelings of jealousy. I hated hearing about what my friends did with their fathers because it made me feel empty and sad. (Tammy)

Thus may adults, through misunderstanding, not only fail to provide solace and support but make a manageable situation *more* difficult.

The importance of particular objects to children may be taken by adults to be out of proportion to their 'real value.' Adults' failure to appreciate children's value schemes can lead adults to minimize children's feelings, to view children as overly sensitive or emotional, or to respond in what children see as insufficiently serious ways to their problems, losses, and distress. The following story provides abundant detail about the strong emotions associated with what others might view as 'just a doll.'

The Doll
by Karen

I think one of the most traumatic things that ever happened to me when I was a child was when my oldest brother Donny punched the head off of my favorite doll. I must have been about 5 years old when it happened. I remember that my mother was at work so the older kids must have been baby-sitting me. I came downstairs and I had been playing house or something and I had my doll with me. I walked up to Donny and held out my 'baby' for him to admire and I think I said something like 'Kiss my baby.' Well, he wound up his arm as much as it would go and punched my baby as hard as he possibly could in the face! She has a cloth body and soft velvety skin and her head was hanging by a single thread. As I'm sure you can imagine, I screamed bloody murder and tried to beat him up myself but, needless to say, since he was much bigger than I was, the attempt was futile. I immediately ran hysterically to the phone and called my mother at work. My mother told me to put Donny on the phone and she told him that he had to sew the doll's head back on before she came home from work. This made my brother even more mad because he had to sew something and that was supposed to be a 'girl's' job.

To this day that doll's head is tightly sewn on and almost as good as new. However, the trauma never ends. Just last semester, while I was at school, my brother's dog (yes, the same brother) somehow got into my room and caused a little destruction. I went home that weekend to find my doll lying on the floor. I thought to myself, 'This is strange,' knowing there wasn't supposed to be anyone in my room. I went to pick her up off of the floor and noticed that one whole leg, the foot of the other leg, one whole arm and the hand of the other arm had all been chewed off. I immediately suspected Shag, my brother's dog, and I ran downstairs to show Donny what his dog had done. He laughed in my face and acted like it was no big deal. He probably went home that night and gave Shag a treat or something and told him what a good dog he was. By this time I was in tears because I was so angry and frustrated and I went in to show my mother what Shag had done. She was sincerely sorry for me but I could tell she thought I was overreacting. Well, I wasn't! I have had this doll since I was 4 years old and I had already planned to give it to my own daughter when I have one. But luckily my mother realized how upset I was and immediately offered to arrange for her to be fixed. We called a woman who has a small antique doll shop and who renovates broken dolls. She took one look at my doll and said she probably wasn't worth the money it would cost to fix her. Was not worth the money! I was furious at her and I still wish there was a place where I could get her fixed. I don't know if I could bring myself to give my own daughter a doll with only one leg and one arm. I suppose you would have to grow up with her in order to appreciate her now.

* * *

The strength of Karen's feelings for her doll is demonstrated by the endurance of her emotions (from age 5 to 17 and promising to continue) despite their trivialization by her brother, her mother, the doll shop owner, and, depending on one's anthropomorphic predilections, Shag.

Children who value an object — in the following story, a playhouse — may want others to value it as well and be distressed when they do not.

When I was 3 years old, my mother made me a playhouse under the stairs of the recreation room. When I woke up from my nap and I was led down to this area that was all mine, I felt so happy and responsible. I played down there the rest of the day, until my daddy came home. I was so excited to show my daddy this wonderful little place that I greeted him at the door with a big smile, and I said, 'Daddy, come see what Mommy made for me.' My daddy was not interested. He said he might look at it later. So, here I was left with a feeling of rejection and unimportance. All Daddy did was read the newspaper and watch television in his chair. Mommy finally saw how unhappy I was and had a talk with Daddy. Daddy did come down to see my

secret place but I knew he did not really care and that my place was
unimportant to him. (Ellie)

Ellie describes being unconvinced by her father's pretense; apparently she was
after a genuine response. Adults may certainly have sympathy for an exhausted
father but might also consider that his desire for relaxation is facilitated by his
minimizing the importance of his daughter's wishes.

Adults may not recognize the symbolic significance of objects to children.

One hard time I remember from my childhood is when my thoughts
and feelings weren't being recognized as valid. The clearest example
of this is the time that my first and only pet goldfish died the month
after we moved away from the neighborhood where my best friend
Joel lived. I remember feeling especially distraught. . .because it was
a gift from my best friend Joel before we moved away to our new
house. The goldfish to me was symbol of Joel and my relationship
together and the friendship we once shared as best friends and of my
hometown where I had spent the first years of my childhood. I remember feeling especially upset and distraught over having to move
away from Joel and my home because of my father's job. I remember
feeling especially vulnerable, helpless, out of control the day that we
moved away and the day that my goldfish died. The dead goldfish
served as reminder to me of my fading friendship with Joel, that was
no more. Looking back, I guess I wanted that goldfish to live on
forever just like our friendship but I realized the day that that goldfish
died that our friendship had died also.
    What I found truly hard about this experience is that my parents
took the goldfish's death very lightly, as if it did not matter. What I
couldn't make my parents understand was that that goldfish was much
more to me than just a 'goldfish.' It was part of me. What my parents
couldn't and wouldn't possibly ever understand was the day that
goldfish died, part of me died also. The day that I buried my goldfish
I wept for many things. I wept for me, for Joel, and the death of our
friendship. . .Looking back, that experience was one of the most trau-
matizing and hard episodes of my early childhood for me to deal with
because there was no effective method of coping that I could think of
at the time to employ. (Greg)

For Greg, the goldfish does not seem to have been of great importance for
itself, its value primarily symbolic. Other children may have stronger feelings
for their goldfish or for other pets and find themselves deprived of solace
when their pets die. Like children, adults differ in the strength of their feelings
for pets and their responses to their loss. Adults whose own feelings for pets
are minimal may minimize the grief experienced, whether by children or adults,
at the loss of a pet. For adults and children who deeply mourn the loss of a

pet, the sympathy they receive depends upon the seriousness with which others receive the news. Adults who feel deeply the loss of a pet may respond with a long grieving period, seek out similarly inclined adults for sympathy, or soon acquire another pet to comfort them. Fortunate the children who feel as do those upon whom they depend for solace and help.

*   *   *

Inaccurate assumptions about children's emotions coupled with power over children make it possible for adults to overlook children's emotions without so great a risk of destroying social encounters as is likely in adult–adult interactions. Unaware of the emotions that children are experiencing, adults may not only deny children assistance but make worse already difficult situations. Children's emotional responses to objects and events may be much more understandable to adults when they can see matters as do the children involved. In the absence of such knowledge, adults may judge children as responding inappropriately — a judgment that cannot but confound any efforts to assist, teach, or solace them. Adults who accept as legitimate the sources of children's emotions may find children acting much as adults would. If, for example, adults were to fail in the realm that Tilly did — the selling of Girl Scout cookies (described in the epigraph to this chapter) — they might indeed view the failure as trivial. Comparing adults' and children's experiences by taking into account their contexts, however, suggests that the emotional significance of a child's failure to sell Girl Scout cookies might be more accurately compared to an adult salesperson's failure to meet a sales quota and thus not 'fly up' in the company. Both differences and similarities between children and adults are obscured when adults ignore, minimize, distort, and deny children's emotions.

6   Knowledge

> My parents must have known that I loved to hear praise. They would
> get me to do things for them by making me think that I did them
> better than anyone else. So the dishes never sparkled, the coffee never
> tasted perfect, and the furniture never shone as bright unless I did it.
> This worked until I was about 12, then I realized that my parents were
> using me. (Nan)

This epigraph, brief and modest as it is, nonetheless illustrates knowledge[1] as
it changes over time. According to Nan, initially she knew that she did her
tasks to perfection, for her parents told her so. As she acquired new knowledge of her parents' motivation for praise, doubt was cast on her prior knowledge of her skill at household tasks. She also came to know things about her
parents — that they knew she loved to hear praise and that they were using
her.

   Concerns related to knowledge can emerge for children in a variety of
ways and through a variety of experiences. Informants describe in negative
terms the many ways whereby adults obscure children's knowledge: children
are lied to, told they are lying when they see themselves as offering the truth,
restricted in their access to information, and provided with discrepant information.[2] Such experiences are consequential for children's knowledge of the
world and themselves, as well as for their views of adults.

> I remember feeling angry that my parents would lie to me. I always
> thought of my parents as gods; they could do nothing bad or wrong.
> But when I discovered that they were lying to me it destroyed my
> perception of what they were. They would tell my brothers and me
> that it was wrong to lie and that we would be punished for lying. Yet
> they could lie to me. I couldn't understand how they could be so
> hypocritical. They had really disappointed me. (Nan)

---

[1] I adopt here the convention of Berger and Luckmann, who write, 'If we were going
to be meticulous in the ensuing argument, we would put quotation marks around
...[knowledge] every time we used...[it], but this would be stylistically awkward'
(1967, p. 2).
[2] I use the term 'discrepant information' to refer to contradictory ideas presented (generally with authority) by different adults or by the same adult at different times.

Children may find the achievement of knowledge a painful as well as obstacle-ridden undertaking.

In this chapter I consider children's knowledge within the framework of the sociology of knowledge as set forth by Berger and Luckmann in *The Social Construction of Reality*. I employ their claims about knowledge, including the following:

> It will be enough, for our purposes,. . .to define 'knowledge' as the certainty that phenomena are real and that they possess specific characteristics. (1967, p. 1)

> It is our contention. . .that the sociology of knowledge must concern itself with whatever passes for 'knowledge' in a society, regardless of the ultimate validity or invalidity (by whatever criteria) of such 'knowledge'. (1967, p. 3)

> Sociological interest in questions of 'reality' and 'knowledge' is. . .initially justified by the fact of their social relativity. (1967, p. 3)

To assess the validity of knowledge — whether children's or adults' — as one empirically investigates it is, in the words of Berger and Luckmann, 'somewhat like trying to push a bus in which one is riding' (1967, p. 13). Thus I speak of children's *knowledge*, whether or not it contradicts adults' knowledge. I suspend any claim that reality is a unitary phenomenon, knowable in absolute terms, and readily accessible (at least to adults). Just such a claim pervades advice offered to parents, teachers, and other adults. Greenspan, for example, writes,

> If all goes well, as they move into the grade-school years, children have already established not only a rich fantasy life, but also an ability to determine what's real and what's not real. (1993, p. 194)

Such a view, by rejecting the status of children's knowledge (e.g., what they *knew* prior to the grade-school years) *as knowledge*, impedes an appreciation and understanding of children's 'certainty that phenomena are real.' My concern is with what is known to children themselves, whatever that may be, free of adults' self-proclaimed 'superior' knowledge. What *do* children know, how is that knowledge achieved, and what roles do adults play in transmitting, concealing, and falsifying knowledge? How do children construct their knowledge, especially when it conflicts with the claims of adults or with 'reason' (i.e., 'reason' as defined by adults)? I explore these questions in this chapter and the next.

As children work to construct reality, to establish truth, and to define for themselves and for others the situations in which they find themselves, they draw on the resources they have available. Like the adults described by Sacks, children may, for example, 'monitor' what others say.

> One is responsible for knowing some things on one's own behalf, in contrast to the situation in which one is treated as likely to be repeating what another has [said]. . .The notion, then, of 'monitoring' attempts to come to terms with the difference between things that are heard as things you know on your own behalf and things that are heard as things you know by virtue of another's having told you. ('Everybody has to lie,' 1975, p. 72)

The knowledge at children's command is seriously compromised, their efforts at monitoring made both more necessary and more difficult, when what others tell them routinely includes lies and discrepancies or when others do not tell them at all. Knowledge so grounded may present problems for children as they seek to understand and act in the world. As well, however, children may come to discover the practices of lying, concealment, and deception and employ these practices themselves. They may lie to advance their own projects. They may conceal their knowledge from adults, as when they discover what adults have been lying about or hiding from them and, as in the following story, hide from adults that they (the children) have made such discoveries.

> I had lost my tooth during the day and I went to bed early so the tooth fairy could come and give me money. I laid in bed for a long time but I was too excited to get to sleep. After a while I could hear my parents getting ready for bed. My mom came into my room, slid her hand under my pillow, and took my tooth, replacing it with a dollar bill. After she had left I checked under the pillow and found the money. I was upset since I had found out that there was no such thing as the tooth fairy. The next morning I tried not to let on that I knew but I was still upset. (Carl, Elizabeth's informant)

In the data that follows, the pictures of children and of adults that appear may contrast sharply with adults' renditions of both children and adults themselves.

Being Lied To

One source of knowledge upon which children may depend is other people. When those others lie, children's knowledge is both limited and distorted. Bok, in her philosophical work entitled *Lying*, writes,

> Lies may. . .eliminate or obscure relevant *alternatives*. . .At times, lies foster the belief that there are more alternatives than is really the case; at other times, a lie may lead to the unnecessary loss of confidence in the best alternative. Similarly, the estimates of *costs and benefits* of any action can be endlessly varied through successful deception. (1989, p. 19, emphasis in original)

To the extent that knowledge gives power, to that extent do lies affect the distribution of power; they add to that of the liar, and diminish that of the deceived, altering his choices at different levels. (1989, p. 19)

When one learns, either at the time of the lie or later, that others lie, one does gain new knowledge (of others, namely, that they can lie) but also loses prior knowledge (what one took to be knowledge is now seen to have been a lie). Doubt may be cast on prior knowledge in general, for how many other times has one been lied to?

Adults may lie to children in order to achieve what they want for themselves or what they want for children. Some lies may obviously serve the liar, as Nan (in the epigraph to this chapter) and Lisa discovered.

> My older sister had me convinced that I could run up four flights of stairs better than anyone she knew. I never made the connection between my running up the stairs and her needing something on the fourth floor. I also firmly believed that I had to keep in practice or maybe one day she would find someone quicker than I to run up the stairs for her. Eventually I offered to run and get things for her so she wouldn't even need to ask. I'd say things like, 'Karen, you look uncomfortable. Do you need your pillow?' or 'Boy, Karen, you look cold. Do you want an extra sweater?' (Lisa)

Other lies may be justified by adults as 'for a child's own good.' Indeed they *may* be but they are not necessarily or exclusively so.

> When I was about 5 or 6 years old, I was a very picky eater. My parents had trouble getting me to eat dinner, so if I hadn't finished eating by the time they had cleaned up, they would set the timer on the oven for five minutes. They told me that if my plate wasn't clean within five minutes, the police would come and get me. Although my parents knew that I wasn't going to be taken away, I did not realize that it was only a threat and ate so fast that I often ended up with the hiccups. (Sally)

To fulfill the nutritionally questionable requirement of finishing one's meal (described in Chapter 2), Sally's parents impart what for Sally becomes knowledge — known to be false by those who gave it — that police arrest children and that they do so for the infraction of not finishing one's meal.

When children (and, equally so, adults) take a lie to be the truth, actions and feelings are guided by that knowledge, with consequences that may go unnoticed by the liar. (Note that in the following story the child also lies, apparently without detection.)

> One situation I think I will remember for the rest of my life occurred when I was about 7 years old. . .My mother and I were in the drug

store and I felt an unexplainable need to have a box of chalk. I asked my mother if she would buy me one, but she said no. I took her answer in stride, or so she thought, and went back to the school supply aisle. I looked around to make sure no one was watching and I slid a piece of chalk into my jacket pocket. Once my mother and I were safely out of the store and in the car, I pulled the piece of chalk out of my pocket and said, 'Look what I found in my pocket, Mom!' My mother told me she had just washed my jacket and that there wasn't a piece of chalk in the pocket. She also told me that I could be sent to jail for stealing, unless I took the piece of chalk back into the store, returned it, and apologized for taking it. I decided that this would be better than going to jail, so I went back into the store, planning on returning the piece of chalk. However, when I walked back into the store, I realized that no one in the store even had to know that I had taken the chalk. I decided to hide it inside the pages of a magazine. I picked out a magazine, opened it up, put the chalk inside the magazine, and put the magazine at the bottom of the pile. When I returned to the car, I told my mother that I had returned the chalk and had apologized for taking it. After that, the incident was never mentioned to me again. For months afterward however, I cringed every time I heard a siren, thinking 'they' were coming to get me. The following summer, my parents had some friends over. I had been sent to bed but was sitting at the top of the stairs listening to the conversation going on between the adults. I heard my mother telling some of her friends the whole chalk incident. I ran to my room crying, thinking that my life had been ruined because everyone knew I was a thief. (Sally)

Adults who threaten children with police or jail may not be aware that children take such threats as real. For a child to come to know that young children can be jailed for the theft of a piece of chalk or, if the stolen item is returned, still jailed for not apologizing — a process complete with rushing cruisers, sirens blaring — may prevent future thefts but also gives a child a view of the criminal justice system reminiscent of *Les Miserables*.

When a child wants something that an adult does not, adults may lie to conceal their own antipathy to the child's want. Children who want a pet and live with those who are not similarly inclined may find themselves lied to and deceived — and without a pet.

When I was 5, like many other kids I wanted a dog. My parents, however, were very much against this desire. I heard almost every reason in the free world why I couldn't have a dog. It seemed the more they rebutted my request, the stronger my desire became. I pleaded long and hard, but nothing worked. Finally, after two years of doglessness, my effort paid off. Mom and Dad surprised me with a little dog just near Christmas time. I called her Mandy and I loved her the second we met. We played together constantly. (I even let my brother play with her.) I was happy because I knew this was a sign of Mom and Dad's love. If this is getting too sentimental don't worry, the difficult part is close at hand. After a few short weeks, things took a turn for the worse. My parents informed me that Mandy missed her mother and her owners had to take her back. Shortly thereafter, Mandy was just a memory. I cried a great deal and seemed very sad, but inside I held very strong feelings of anger. I was mad at both Mandy's owners for taking her away and my parents for letting them do it. Even though my mom and dad said it was best for me, I felt I was hurt more having the dog taken away than the dog would have been staying. For a brief period, I even played with the notion that my parents didn't love me. They acted sympathetic but, as I saw it, they weren't even close to feeling the way I did. . .

While reminiscing with my mom about this situation, a new twist developed. My mother informed me that the reason the owners took Mandy back had nothing to do with her missing her mother. The real reason was in part that they didn't want to keep her. I for one was shocked, not so much that they fibbed but that I believed it for so many years. I guess these things are bound to happen when searching through old memories. (Ned)[3]

At the time of the event described, Ned came to some new, if questionable, knowledge: that puppies can miss their mothers so much that humans cannot overcome it and that a puppy's well-being necessarily outweighs a child's. He also came to question his parents' love. Much later he learned that he had been lied to — and seriously so, given his distress — and thus knew that his parents were capable of such consequential deception.

What Bok says of adults seems, on the basis of the stories presented in this chapter, to be equally applicable to children.

Those who learn that they have been lied to in an important matter . . .are resentful, disappointed, and suspicious. They feel wronged; they are wary of new overtures. And they look back on their past beliefs and actions in the new light of the discovered lies. They see that they were manipulated, that the deceit made them unable to make choices for themselves according to the most adequate information available, unable to act as they would have wanted to act had they known all along. (1989, p. 20)

---

[3] Ned's insights here illustrate the risks of exploring childhood experiences with the adults involved.

Lying to children can serve adults in a variety of ways: to bring about what adults see as 'good' for children, what they see as 'good' for themselves, and as a way to resolve conflicts between adults and children. It allows adults to achieve what they view as desirable by defining situations in such a way that children's agreement is achieved. In the process, however, children come to *know* what adults *know to be false*.

Being Taken to Lie

Like adults, children can experience frustration as well as distress when others reject the truth of their assertions and thus their knowledge. Adults may take some children's claims to be lies, others to be mistakes; from children's perspectives the distinction may be meaningless, for in either case they are taken to be offering, whether intentionally or unintentionally, falsehoods. When adults use their power to enforce and implement their own views of truth and when they take for granted that adults routinely and self-evidently 'know better,' children may be further frustrated and distressed.

A number of stories describe children not being believed when they say that they need to go to the bathroom and when they say that they are ill.[4] An interesting dilemma arises here, for a strategy that children (as well as adults) can use to avoid or escape unpleasant situations is to lie, claiming to be ill when they are not and to need to go to the bathroom when they do not. Thus with any such claim a certain ambiguity is possible. Just such ambiguity is illustrated by the following story. Mary may or may not be ill (she may, for example, be mistaking nervousness for illness) and she may or may not be lying (she may be faking illness to avoid school). Nonetheless, the truth of her claim that she is ill is simply rejected by both her mother and her brother and she is offered no alternative explanation for her pain.

> It's breakfast and I'm crying over my Corn Flakes because my stomach hurts so much. Kenny, my big brother in the third grade, hits me and tells me to shut up. I cry and cry and tell my mom I'm sure I'm going to be sick in school. Mom calmly tells me I won't. She is getting used to it after three straight weeks. Kenny, however, is getting a little tired of it. Mom collects our school bags and jackets and shoves us out the door. We walk, Ken ten steps ahead of me, trying to pretend he does not know this wailing 6-year-old behind him. We finally arrive at the bus stop and I stop crying but am still convinced my stomach is filled with three hundred butterflies. I finally arrive at school and as soon as

---

[4] Bathroom stories offered in Chapter 2 can also be read as instances of children's not being believed. Stories of children lying and being believed to be telling the truth are presented in Chapter 9.

reading, math, and the threat of having to stay in for recess are over, it goes away. (Mary)

Children may, however, have medically confirmed illnesses, know they are ill, and still not be believed.

> I was in second grade. . .I was in and out of hospitals throughout the school year. I was finally diagnosed as having three ulcers and a hiatal hernia. I would get sick often and my teacher knew that. One day I got sick while we had a substitute teacher. I asked her if I could go to the bathroom. She told me that I would have to wait until the entire class went all together. I tried to explain to her that I felt sick. She told me that the feeling would pass and that I should go back to my seat. I started to cry. The other children in my class tried to explain to her that I was really sick. By the time that she believed me it was too late. I vomited three times before getting to the trash can, once on her desk and twice on the floor. I can remember her sending me to the nurse after apologizing many times. The other children in the class were running around screaming. I was so embarrassed. I couldn't believe that she wouldn't let me go to the bathroom. . .My parents, the nurse, and my teacher told me that I should be aware that everyone doesn't know that I get sick a lot, that if I had persisted more and explained the problem better the incident may have not occurred. They made me feel like it was my fault. (Nan)

In the face of children's claims to illness, adults (even those with limited information) may designate themselves as those who 'really know' children's internal states and may reject children's own proclamations.

Children's claims can be denied in a variety of other settings.

> When I was in third or fourth grade, I had a red four-square ball that I had received for Christmas. This ball was my pride and joy. I had written my name on the ball in black marker in case I lost it. One day out at recess I did lose my ball. I was quite upset about it. A few weeks later I saw a girl in my class, Sara, with my ball. The black marker I had written my name with had faded quite a bit and was barely visible. Sara had written her name on the ball, also in black marker. I told my teacher that Sara had taken my ball. I tried to show her where my name had been, but she just said, 'Sally, this ball has Sara's name on it. I believe it is hers.' I did all I could to try to convince the teacher that the ball was mine, but she stayed convinced that the ball was Sara's. (Sally)

Sally presents clear evidence to support her knowledge that the ball was hers; her teacher, conversely, seems to have relied on more superficial evidence, perhaps accompanied by taken-for-granted assumptions about children in general (they lie) or about Sally (she lies) or Sara (she is neither thief nor liar). The assumption by adults that their own knowledge is superior to that of children also appears in the following story.

> My sister and I were in kindergarten. Every day we drove up a street with my mother to get home. The people who lived on the corner grew sunflowers. The sunflowers were huge. That year in kindergarten the teacher asked the class, 'What is bigger, a flower or a tree?' My sister and I said 'a flower' because the sunflowers that we saw every day were in fact bigger than the trees. The next day the teacher called my mother and told her that she thought we were weird because we thought that flowers were bigger than trees. My mother then explained the sunflower story to her. The teacher then took my answer and my sister's answer as correct. (Camille)

What Mackay says of those who construct standardized tests is applicable to Sally and Camille's teachers.

> The assumption of one correct answer is based on the. . .faith that. . .[the test constructor; here read 'teacher'] and the students share a common symbolic environment in which objects have only one meaning which is apparent to all. In this perspective meaning is given, not negotiated and built up over the course of interaction. (1974, p. 233)

In trying to assess the validity of children's claims, adults may routinely rely on their own taken-for-granted knowledge about children and children's competence — knowledge that may be false. In the following story, the adult's assumption seems to be that in a dispute between a younger and an older child, *the younger is to be believed* because young children do not lie.

> When I was 5 years old my sister and I were playing in the sandbox and my sister poured sand all over her head and told my grandmother that I did it and I got in trouble and I didn't do it and she did it again and each time I got in worse trouble. When I told my grandmother that I didn't do it, she said that my sister wouldn't pour sand on her own hair on purpose. I felt so powerless — I couldn't prove I was right. So I had to take the punishment and my sister kept on playing in the sand and laughed at me because I couldn't play. (Anonymous notes from class discussion)

An opposite taken-for-granted assumption that adults may employ is that in a dispute between a younger and an older child, *the older is to be believed*, as in the following.

I was with my cousins playing and we decided to go to the playground to play volleyball. We were playing and having fun but suddenly my cousin started to fight with her sister and I was in between them trying to separate them. As soon as my aunt saw us she came rapidly to separate us. Yes, us, because she thought I was fighting too. When the fight was finished, my aunt spanked me and then she asked my older cousins who started the fight. She spanked me because she saw me holding my cousin's arm and thought I was fighting with them. This time I was really surprised because I didn't expect her to spank me. It wasn't my fault, but because my cousins were older, my aunt did not listen to a child: me. (Claire)

In both of these stories, the child possesses greater knowledge of the situation than does the adult but has less power to establish it as knowledge.

Another taken-for-granted assumption adults may employ is that in a dispute between a younger and an older child, *the older is to blame.*

I can remember up until like eighth grade whenever I got into a fight with my younger sister I always got blamed. She could start the fight and hit me first, but as soon as I hit her all she had to do was cry and call my parents to tell on me and my parents would stick up for her. I would always be the one sent to my room. I always hated that. I thought it was so unfair. Just because she was the youngest they thought I was to blame. Every time she would start a fight I would try to hold out because I knew I would be the one to get the blame but as soon as she would hit me I would have to hit her back. (Cindy)

Adults' rules for believing children and for assigning blame suggest that knowledge gives way to other considerations, namely, *social rules for determining knowledge.* Such rules include believing the older child (who is more 'mature'), believing the younger child ('children don't lie'), and believing adults more than children. Use of any of these rules may not advance knowledge — indeed may impede it — but can provide adults with guidelines for action in resolving problems to *adults'* satisfaction.

When an adult and a child offer different versions of knowledge, whose version is accepted? In the following stories, adults accept the claims of other adults, even though, as presented, their claims appear to be less compelling than the child's.

When I was younger, I was very sick. At first, no one knew what was wrong with me. After a series of tests, the doctor found out I was allergic to sugar. He told me not to eat anything with sugar over the third ingredient. When I was at school, I was on my word to watch what I ate. After about a year, I went back to the doctor. He first told me I was too thin (I had lost over 30 pounds). He told me if I lost any more weight he would put me in the anorexia ward. I wasn't scared at all, I was angry with him because it was all his fault I had lost so much weight. I gave up sugar like he told me to. I was mad at him for trying to blame me for the condition I was in. I told him I had not had any sugar, except twice, once for my birthday and once by accident. My mother said, in front of the doctor, that she didn't believe me. I was mortified. I couldn't believe that she thought I had been lying for a whole year. Never again did I feel she trusted me. As for the doctor, I never wanted to go back and see him. I thought he was an idiot and I refused to go back and see him. He gave me nightmares. (Sara)

When I was 7 years old and. . .a Girl Scout, one day I went to the pharmacy with my mom wearing my Girl Scout uniform, and I was playing with a little box of these skinny stars that teachers used to put on my exams. The owner of the pharmacy saw me playing with the box and suddenly he started to yell at me. . .He told me in bad manners not to steal any of the stars inside the box. At that moment I hardly spoke; I was only playing with the box and to hear the man yelling at me was a shock. I think my mom heard the man yelling at me and she rapidly came to see what had happened to me. The man didn't let me talk; he told my mom I was stealing some stars from the box. At that moment I was in tears, without my voice, so I didn't defend myself. I remember my mom spanked me and asked the owner for forgiveness. I will never forget this experience. What really upset me was the fact that my mother spanked me without letting me explain myself and what really happened. (Claire)

Perhaps adults accept the word of other adults because those adults are professionals — doctors, teachers, etc. If, however, they do so merely because those others are fellow adults, they may be said to be following an adult taken-for-granted rule that Sacks (1972) might phrase as: When children and adults offer differing versions of the truth and an adult can believe another adult, do so.

In the following story, a child is both lied to (by her brother) and not believed (by her mother).

As a child I was prone to believe what my younger brother told me. This caused hard times on occasion. For example he was able to get me to trade him my walkie-talkie, with brand new batteries, for his. First he would tell me how much better his walkie-talkie was. Then he would say 'I'm going to be nice and trade with you though,' and of course I would gladly hand over my walkie-talkie for his. Soon my batteries would be dead. When I asked my mother to get me new batteries she would scold me for leaving my walkie-talkie on all night.

Whenever I protested that I had done no such thing, she would say, 'Then how come Adam's batteries never go dead?' It would take me a couple of weeks to get her to buy me new batteries. However, as soon as she did, Adam would get me to trade again. I did not realize that I had been tricked until long after my interest in walkie-talkies had gone. (Amanda)

Despite its rejection by adults, children's knowledge may endure. Children, however, may come to see that knowledge is not self-evident to others in the way it is to them. They may also discover that in certain situations they know more than adults do — and that there may be little they can do to establish the validity of their superior knowledge.

Being Denied Information

As children strive to gather knowledge in order to learn how the world works and to guide their activities, they may be hampered by being denied relevant information. Like lies, denials of information can distort or forestall knowledge. Such denials, nonetheless, may be urged on parents in literature directed towards them. Greenspan, for example, advises parents telling children about sexual intercourse,

> Let them have their illusions. . .there's no need to overwhelm them with information. (1993, p. 240)

To take illusions for knowledge, however, is to be at a disadvantage in thought as well as action.

Children may both recognize that adults impede their search for knowledge and fault them for doing so.

> Adults always thought they were right, I was wrong. The best example I can think of for this is the way adults spoke to me. For instance, if I was not allowed to do something and asked for the reason, frequent answers were 'Because I am your mother' or worse, 'Because I said so.' Also frustrating was when I would try to defend myself when adults were angry with me. If I even opened my mouth, I would hear, 'Don't talk back to me!' Adults often also said such things as 'You're just a kid' or 'You don't know how lucky you are to be a kid and have no real problems.' (Gini) [5]

---

[5] A fuller version of this story appears in Chapter 1.

In the following story, Cora describes the adult practice of 'sending the children away,' a method of denying them access to experiences, including the meaning and consequences of their own. Whether or not such a method is employed 'for the children's own good' and in the service of not 'overwhelming them with information,' its consequence is that children are denied information that might prove useful in understanding their experiences.

> I was 4 years old. . .and at my baby-sitter's house. She was a sweet lady, her name was Mrs Greenwood. Mrs Greenwood was getting lunch ready and she told me to run upstairs and to wake up her son. So off I go bounding up the stairs to wake him up. As I tried my hardest to wake him up all of my attempts failed. I got tired of shaking him so I went back downstairs to tell Mrs Greenwood that I couldn't wake him up. She said that it was all right, that she would go up to wake him while I ate my sandwich. She came downstairs with a stunned look on her face and sent me across the street to play with the two boys. We were in the cellar eating our sandwiches and watching what was happening next door. It turns out that her son was dead. Emotionally it didn't affect me because I was too young and I didn't understand death. *No one ever told me what really happened. What I was told by a friend next door was that he had hanged himself. This is one subject I had never dared to bring up to my parents and I still haven't even to this day.* (Cora, emphasis added)

Cora's experience may have left her, as she claims, emotionally unaffected, but it did not leave her untouched; rather, she had an experience whose meaning she partially pieced together from what she could glean from others and partially concealed, both from herself and others.

Adults may assume that children cannot 'handle' knowledge of death. Such an assumption is belied by empirical investigation (see, for example, Bluebond-Langer, *The Private Worlds of Dying Children*, 1978, and Matthews, 'Children and Death', 1994). Furthermore, adults who attempt to control children's access to knowledge may be unsuccessful — and not realize it. If adults *assume* they have been successful, children may be left on their own to deal with their knowledge, with the added burden of pretending to not have that knowledge.

> One example of my 'youngness' is a very painful memory. When I was 6 years old my grandfather passed away. Even though I was considered too young to understand what was going on — I did. I not only knew what was going on, but I understood what a funeral was. My parents, however, did not let me go to the funeral; they felt that I was too young. I always regretted not being able to go to my grandfather's funeral. I was not too young. (Cora)

When adults deny information to children, children may be left to grapple with difficult matters without assistance from adults as well as with limited or distorted knowledge. Alternatively, children may, though perhaps not quite so routinely, gain access to concealed information but conceal from adults that they have done so, thus denying to adults the information that adults' secrets are not secret. Adults' failure to attribute to children the competence to discover what adults are concealing facilitates children's concealment but, as well, forestalls adults' assistance in children's coming to terms with what they have learned. Although denial of information may present problems for children, children who gain access to previously concealed information may, as they do so, also gain the knowledge that adults do indeed conceal information, an important piece of knowledge in itself.

Discrepant Information

Adults who lie to children or deny them information, for whatever reason, know that they are doing so. Discrepant information need not result from deception — though it may. Children may be faced with discrepant information when the claims of one adult change over time, when the claims of adults differ from one another, or when, as with the above examples of being taken to lie, adults' claims differ from the child's own knowledge and experiences. James describes adults' claims — what he comes to redefine as 'excuses' — changing over time.

> I had wanted a dog for as long as I could remember. When I was 9 I asked my parents why I couldn't have one. They told me that I had to first show them that I was responsible enough for a dog. That summer I got a paper route to show them how responsible I could be. I kept the stupid thing for a year, then asked again for a dog. They still said no only this time they thought up another excuse. I was so mad at them that I quit the paper route and didn't talk to them unless I absolutely needed to for a long time. (James, Elizabeth's informant)

Lies presuppose the possibility of truth; denials presuppose the possibility of affirmation; discrepant information tosses one among alternatives, resolution to be sought beyond the immediate situation. Steve describes the struggle for knowledge when the claims of adults differ.

> Steve told me that his parents had a divorce when he was 3 years old and he lived with his mother and still does today. He thinks that having parents who are divorced made it difficult for him to choose who was right because they both would say different things. He would always wonder, 'Is Mom right or is Dad really telling the truth?' He would always go towards Mom's side just because, he said, you get

a different impression of the person you live with. The incident Steve remembers is when he was 4 years old. He had been on the steps all night with his sleep-over bag waiting for his dad to come pick him up for the weekend and his dad never showed. That was a hard time for him because he did not understand why Dad didn't want to see him and Dad always thought of suitable excuses. This is when he would get confused, because Mom was telling him that his Dad was a mean man for not picking him up and Dad was telling him his car broke down. (Lucy)

Steve sought to resolve, albeit with only partial success, the competing claims of his parents by drawing on knowledge of his mother that lay outside the immediate situation ('you get a different impression of the person you live with').

What counts as knowledge for some adults may not so count for other adults. Children's knowledge is somewhat circumscribed by what counts as knowledge for those who are transmitting it to them. Adults' formulations of the nature of gender roles and of age-related competence (described in Chapter 4 as grounds used by adults to exclude children from activities) are illustrative of discrepant information. Such formulations may be presented to children as knowledge but may be more accurately seen as beliefs designed to support a particular world view or set of activities.

What are boys and girls known to be 'really' like?

My brothers were allowed to do far more things than I was. I would always complain that that was not fair and my parents would justify themselves by telling me that it was because I was a girl. Well now I was beginning to think that being a girl was some sort of punishment. And of course they laid the one on me 'Girls are supposed to cook and clean and take care of their husband.' I was never the domestic type nor did I like waiting on people. I can remember my grand-mother saying (and she still does) that if a guy ever liked me she would talk to him and after she was finished he would no longer be interested in me. I began to get a complex that I was no good, especially at being a girl. (Ann)

One. . .difficulty that came with dinner was the aftermath. Before we had the dishwasher, my mother would wash all the dishes and I would dry them. I could never understand why my father and brother never helped with the cleanup. My mom would say, 'Well, he (my brother) has other chores that he does.' His one whole chore was to take out the rubbish, which my father usually did anyway. The hard-est part was understanding why boys didn't help with the cooking and cleanup. (Fern)

Children may either accept the validity of the knowledge transmitted to them, find themselves with an unresolved discrepancy, or challenge what they are told by invoking their own knowledge.

> My father told me when I was about 7 years old that girls are supposed to do all the household chores. I had to wash the dishes, do the laundry, clean the bathroom, make the beds, dust, iron and anything else that was considered women's work. I asked him why is that so? He told me that boys aren't supposed to do those kinds of things because they can make them become feminine. I don't think my father had the right to say that. I didn't believe him. If my brothers could go to a job and cook and clean dishes, they could do it at home too. (Andrea)

When children learn gender roles, they are dependent in part on the images that adults present to them. As they assess the knowledge that adults impart to them against the background of their own experiences, they may not be convinced by adults' formulations (just as adults may not be convinced by one another's).

Similarly with claims of age-related competence and rights, children may question what is presented to them as knowledge. The notion of 'too young' may be offered to children as derived from knowable criteria but children's attempts to understand those criteria may disclose the notion, as used by adults, as opportunistic rather than knowledge-based. As an explanation, 'too young' is vague, broad, all-purpose, difficult to refute, and, it appears, not particularly satisfying for at least some to whom it is offered. The ambiguity of the phrase and its selective use to facilitate adult projects do not necessarily go unnoticed by children.

> It seemed whenever I wanted to do something I was either too old to do what the youngest child was doing, or too young to do what the oldest child was doing. It never made sense to me. I could not understand how I had to wait a few years before I could do what my older sister was doing yet be too old to do what my younger sister was doing. There never seemed to be any benefits out of being the middle child. (Cindy)

> It was difficult to know when I was 'old enough' for my parents. I remember that at 7 years of age I was old enough to water the plants, to make my bed, to help my mom to clean the dishes, and to take care of my room but I wasn't old enough to go out and ride my bicycle and play at my friend's house. This always was difficult for me because my parents believed that my age was a matter of convenience. Then when I was 15 years old I was old enough to take care of my younger brother and to take care of the house but not to go out with my

friends, to wear the clothes I wanted to wear, or to have a boyfriend. (Claire)

Adults have a certain degree of power to define knowledge both for them-selves and for children but children, despite the limits of their power to define situations for adults, may reject adults' formulations.

Children may be quite sophisticated in recognizing discrepant information.

> One afternoon I walked down to the kitchen and told my mother I was bored. Out of the blue, she started to scream at me, telling me that if I was with my biological mother (I am adopted) I wouldn't be bored. I thought she was crazy. I couldn't understand why she wanted to hurt me so much. I didn't want to know any other mother. I never wanted to hurt her. She seemed so preoccupied with my being adopted. I always knew it would be something she'd have to work out by herself. (Nora)

In this story the child might be seen by adults' criteria as more knowledgeable than the adult.

When adults' claims are accepted as knowledge — both in everyday life and by those who study children — children's knowledge is distorted and obscured. When children's knowledge is brought forward for serious consid-eration, insights into the actions of adults *and* children become available. Knowledge can be viewed as an interactional resource in adult–child relation-ships, usable in varied and complex ways by all participants. For children, knowledge may be routinely limited by adults. How then can children con-struct knowledge out of lies, rejections of what they perceive to be truth, with information denied and discrepant information? Apparently they can, although the fact that they do so may go unattended by adults and their results may run counter to adult expectations and hopes.

Two Pleas for Telling the Truth to Children

In her philosophical analysis of lying, Bok, while rejecting the idea that people must (or can) always tell the truth, argues for strong limits on lying, especially to children.

> Rather than accepting the common view. . .that it is somehow more justifiable to lie to children. . ., special precautions are needed in order not to exploit them. (1989, p. 218)

She offers the following guidelines for lies told 'for the good of others.'

> The way to tell rightful paternalistic lies from all the others would then be to ask whether the deceived, if completely able to judge his own

best interests, would himself want to be duped. If he becomes rational enough to judge at a later time, one could then ask whether he gives his retroactive consent to the deceit — whether he is grateful he was lied to. (1989, p. 215)

Throughout this chapter informants imply or state explicitly that they do not give their retroactive consent and are not grateful for having been lied to.

In the following excerpts, Goldman too denies retroactive consent for experiences in his childhood. When Goldman was a child, his father read to him from Morgenstern's book *The Princess Bride*. As an adult Goldman abridged and edited the book and includes in his preface a description of his feelings when his father read a particular part of the story to him.

[I]n my, I suppose you have to call it 'soul,' there was that damn discontent, shaking its dark head.

He then describes his much later understanding of that discontent.

All this was never explained to me till I was in my teens and there was this great woman who lived in my home town, Edith Neisser. . .And I remember once we were having iced tea on the Neisser porch and talking and just outside the porch was their badminton court and I was watching some kids play badminton and Ed had just shellacked me, and as I left the court for the porch, he said, 'Don't worry, it'll all work out, you'll get me next time' and I nodded, and then Ed said, 'And if you don't, you'll beat me at something else.'

I went to the porch and sipped iced tea and Edith was reading this book and she didn't put it down when she said, 'That's not necessarily true, you know.'

I said, 'How do you mean?'

And that's when she put her book down. And looked at me. And said it: 'Life isn't fair, Bill. We tell our children that it is, but it's a terrible thing to do. It's not only a lie, it's a cruel lie. Life is not fair, and it never has been, and it's never going to be.'

Would you believe that for me right then it was like one of those comic books where the light bulb goes on over Mandrake the Magician's head? 'It isn't!' I said, so loud I really startled her. 'You're right. It's not fair.' I was so happy if I'd known how to dance, I'd have started dancing. 'Isn't that great, isn't it just terrific?' I think along about here Edith must have thought I was well on my way toward being bonkers.

But it meant so much to me to have it said and out and free and flying. . .That was the reconciliation I was trying to make and couldn't.

Informed by his insight, Goldman provides the following information for children reading or being read *The Princess Bride*.

Look. (Grownups skip this paragraph.) I'm not about to tell you this book has a tragic ending. I already said in the very first line how it was my favorite in all the world. But there's a lot of bad stuff coming up, torture you've already been prepared for, but there's worse. There's death coming up, and you better understand this: some of the wrong people die. Be ready for it. This isn't Curious George Uses the Potty. Nobody warned me and it was my own fault. . .and that was my mistake, so I'm not letting it happen to you. The wrong people die, some of them, and the reason is this; life is not fair. Forget all the garbage your parents put out. Remember Morgenstern. You'll be a lot happier. (1973, pp. 186–8)

7 Knowledge: The Case of Santa Claus

I saw Santa at the mall to have my picture done and tell him I was good to get gifts. I wrote him letters and one year got a letter from him. (When I was older, I realized the handwriting was my mother's.) One time I called him on the phone requesting gifts. I believed my toys came from Santa who bought them at Child World. I thought Santa's elves couldn't make the toys I saw on television but they wrapped and helped out with the store-bought toys. I was told that if I were awake he would not come. . .I was also afraid to get up too early because I thought I might see him leaving presents and then he would take them back. I would leave carrots for the reindeer and cookies and milk for Santa. My parents taught me that Santa came down the chimney but I questioned how he got into places without chimneys. They told me he could go into any house because he had 'powers.' A neighbor (younger than I) told me the truth. To confirm this idea of 'no Santa' I found my Christmas toys hidden in the basement and wondered where they came from. My parents still persisted there was a Santa. They told me that the elves were busy and so he dropped them off at the house to be wrapped. I did not believe them and I felt sad. Then I started being more helpful to my parents because I discovered they were buying my gifts. (Beatrice, Alicia's informant)

Beatrice's story describes a firm belief in Santa Claus, a wide range of evidence used to confirm this belief, the discovery that Santa Claus is not real, and the response to that discovery. Stories of Santa Claus that I have gathered[1] regularly display the structure and elements, if not necessarily the specific details, of Beatrice's account. These stories also describe adults' involvement, at times extensive and effortful, in what might be called, in a twist on Berger and Luckmann (1967), 'the social construction of non-reality.'

Santa Claus, an imaginary being created by adults taking great liberties with a historical figure, serves as a notable instance of adults deceiving children

---

[1] Data on the topic of Santa Claus came primarily from interviews directed to this specific aspect of the little trials of childhood.

and obscuring their access to knowledge.[2] (Similar or related issues arise with other adult-created imaginary beings, e.g., the Easter Bunny, the Tooth Fairy, the bogeyman, and monsters.) The deception entails detailed, complex, and long-term projects, supported by tradition, through which adults attempt to convince children of the truth of what adults know to be false.

Adults who are committed to maintaining for children the fiction of Santa Claus may find this chapter unsettling, questioning as it does a long-standing tradition typically viewed as beneficent. A quite different view of the tradition is provided by Miller,[3] who describes an event involving Saint Nicholas of which she says,

> There are many examples of how the repression of our suffering destroys our empathy for the suffering of others. Let me pick out *an ostensibly harmless illustration* and examine it in detail. (1990, p. 13, emphasis added)

She then offers a story of a celebration in Germany.

> A number of families had come with their children, lighted candles at the edge of the forest, and invited Saint Nicholas. Traditionally, this celebration is preceded by the young mothers informing Saint Nicholas of the attitudes and behavior of their children and the saint registering the sins in a big book so that he can speak to the children as if he were all-knowing. . .About ten children, one after the other, were first chided and then praised by Saint Nicholas. . .[Here Miller provides details of children's conversations with Saint Nicholas.] No one noticed the cruelty, no one saw the stricken faces (although the fathers were constantly taking flash pictures). No one noticed that each of the reprimanded children ended up not being able to remember the words of the little poem or song [they had prepared for Saint Nicholas]; that they couldn't even find their voices, could hardly say thank you; that none of the children smiled spontaneously, that they all looked petrified with fear. No one noticed that what was actually being enacted was a vicious power play at the expense of the children. . .The mothers didn't seem in any way unloving; they made an effort to help the children, to sing their songs or recite their poems. They were obviously concerned with providing their children with a lovely ceremony,

---

[2] For a very different view of Santa Claus, see Clark's *Flights of Fancy, Leaps of Faith: Children's Myths in Contemporary America* (1995). The author takes a very positive view of what she refers to as 'children's myths' but what I see as more accurately termed 'adults' myths *for* children.' Although she claims to be presenting children's perspectives, her data emphasizes adults' perspectives, assumptions, and claims about children.

[3] Alan Turin directed me to this story. He and Robert Kaven, knowing of my interest in the little trials of childhood, urged me to read Miller, for which I thank them.

an experience on which the children were supposed to look back with joy, emotion, and gratitude. (1990, pp. 13–18)

Miller's view may at first seem somewhat overstated, but consider the following stories of children in the US.

My informant said that he used to be dragged into New York City by his mother and two much older sisters for shopping. He was about 3 when his mother dressed him up in this nice outfit and took him Christmas shopping. He was forced to sit on Santa Claus' lap and hated every minute of it. The picture that we still have shows a little boy who has the saddest face on and looks so unhappy. He hated the dressy outfits, he hated the Christmas shopping, and he hated having to have his picture taken with Santa Claus. (Annette)

When I was 3, my parents thought it would be 'cute' to get my picture taken with Santa. I didn't agree. I cried through the whole thing and need to look at the picture to remind me of that fateful day every year. (Maryanne)

As in Miller's example, children in the US may be threatened with Santa Claus.

I remember my mother threatening me with telling Santa when I was bad; if I was being bad I immediately stopped. I believed that Santa would bring me coal for Christmas. (Althea)

My mother. . .managed to get me to behave by threatening to call Santa if I didn't behave. She told me the star button on the telephone was the direct line to Santa! (Daphne)

My parents told me that if I was good he would bring me presents on Christmas Eve and he would not bring anything if I was bad. Other adults told me he would only leave me slimy rocks that I could never wash off. He knew if I 'was bad or good.' This was an incentive to be 'good.' (Cynthia)

Threats may be offered seriously or as a 'joke.'

When I was 5 and my mom and I were living with my grandmother, I found out the truth about the fat, jolly old fellow who's supposed to deliver toys on Christmas Eve. I awoke on Christmas morning and walked downstairs to the kitchen where some of my relatives were. My uncle walked up to me and handed me a stocking full of coal and told me that's what Santa had left for me. I started to cry and was telling everyone that I hadn't been bad that year. I was very upset and decided to go watch TV. As I walked into the living room my face lit up to the surprise of a bunch of toys. From that day on I knew Santa wasn't real because he wouldn't have left me both coal and toys. I found out later that my uncle got the coal from a friend of the family. He sure got me good! (Lana, Helen's informant)

Threats may not be effective and may not be carried out.

Louise:	Victor, what do you think about Santa Claus?
Victor [age 11]:	He's nice. I like him. He comes even when I am a bad boy. (Louise)

One possible consequence of the threat that Santa Claus will not bring gifts is that those children who believe in Santa Claus and find that he does not leave them presents — perhaps because of parental poverty or neglect but for whatever reason — may reasonably conclude that they have been 'bad.'

Any presentation of Santa Claus as real of necessity requires deception. Bok, in her book *Lying*, writes, 'before we even begin to weigh the good and bad aspects of a lie, the falsehood itself is negatively weighted; while such a negative weight may be overridden, it is there at the outset' (1989, p. 50). Although adults may not recognize or may deny the negative weight of the deception associated with Santa Claus, they nonetheless take steps to override it. Focusing on what they deem 'positive' consequences, they justify tales of Santa Claus by citing the pleasure the fiction gives children, even insisting on such pleasure in the face of contradictory evidence. Children may, of course, gain pleasure from a belief in Santa Claus but its cost, for both adults and children, may be great. The cost may become evident when children learn that Santa Claus is not real.

The whole time that we as children believed our parents were telling the truth about Santa being real we were really being lied to. (Millie)

For a society that feels that lying is wrong, society lies about certain beliefs to children and calls it tradition. (Daphne)

The more the Santa Claus issue is studied, the worse it makes parents out to be. After the presents, the stories, the cookies, the photographs in stores, and the songs about him are stripped, only the lie the parents told their children remains. (Lois)

In the words of Bok, 'reasonable persons should maintain to the best of their ability. . .the dual perspective of liars and deceived' (1989, p. 105). The stories in this chapter offer the perspective of the deceived. I advise readers to suspend until the conclusion of this chapter their everyday views of Santa Claus as a positive force in children's lives and to entertain the possibility that children's belief in Santa Claus is based on what children see as wrong — lies and deception — and is a potential source of the little trials of childhood.

The Strength of Beliefs

Some children, for cultural, religious, or other reasons, are never introduced to Santa Claus as a real being. For such children, belief in Santa Claus may appear odd. In the words of a Jewish informant.

> I was told that Santa Claus wasn't real by my parents but they told me not to tell my friends who aren't Jewish. I knew about Santa from the cartoons, stories, and songs that everybody hears even though my family doesn't celebrate Christmas. I liked the idea, but I couldn't see how it could be real. I thought my friends were crazy. (Anita, Cynthia's informant)

Personal circumstances may also make such belief unlikely.

> I never really had the opportunity to believe in Santa Claus. Being the youngest of five children probably had something to do with it. All of my brothers and sisters already knew that there was no such person as Santa and keeping the secret was not easy. I cannot really remember a time that I did believe in Santa. (Glenda, Millie's informant)

Yet other children may not believe even when the opportunity is available.

> Geraldine doesn't remember believing in him so therefore she does not remember discovering that he was fake. She did, however comment, 'I wondered why my parents were trying to force me to believe that Santa was real when I knew he was fake. I wasn't dumb.' (Lois' informant)

> As far as I can remember I knew that Santa was an imaginary person that adults had made up in an attempt to get children to behave. (Edith's informant)

But other children may believe wholeheartedly and without question.

> I remember getting all excited that he was coming. My heart would beat a mile a minute and my eyes were like they were glued open. (Millie)

> As a child, when I was first told about Santa Claus, I believed that he was as real as you or I. My parents told me that he was a man who brought me presents and that was good enough for me. (Millie)

Althea commented about those she interviewed,

> These people believed in Santa Claus because nothing or no one ever gave them another perspective. Santa was fortified by everything they trusted.

Even children who otherwise question the world around them may accept the reality of Santa Claus.

> Looking back on my childhood, I realized that Santa Claus was one of the few things that I truly believed in. I was inquisitive and needed to know how and why things happened. How exactly was the earth created? What is the air made of? Why should I believe in God? These are some of the things that I remember wondering about as a young-ster. I thought that the answers to these questions were the key to understanding all of life. And magic was something that really dis-tressed me due to the fact that the magicians would never tell me how their tricks worked. But the magic of Christmas and Santa and his reindeer I did not question. For some strange reason, I just knew. I was so positive that it was real that I never really questioned it. (Louise)

Children who believe without question may seek explanations for occurrences that, for children who are coming to doubt, might further undermine their belief.

> Warren's father dressed up as Santa. He thought it was strange that his father and Santa wore the same after-shave. 'They both have good taste,' he remembers thinking as he sat on Santa's lap. (Althea's informant)

In offering the explanations they have formulated, children may display them-selves to others as naive (and thus 'cute') when, alternatively, they can be seen as being duped.

Children may resist challenges to their belief.

> I think I was probably 12 or 13 when I realized Santa was not real but I think that there is a difference between when I heard he wasn't real and when I actually realized it. I believed in him for so long that it took a while for it to get into my head. (Walter, Louise's informant)

> Tom. . .said that in his childhood he always wanted to believe in Santa Claus but he was made fun of when he did. His older brother and sister were at fault for this, he says. They would ridicule him when he wanted to go sit on Santa's lap or leave cookies out for him. Tom says he pretended to not believe in Santa Claus so that his older brother

and sister would leave him alone. Tom always felt like he was missing out on a big part of Christmas if he didn't believe in Santa Claus. He says that the media always encouraged his beliefs about Santa Claus when his brother and sister told him that Santa was not real. (Florence's informant)

Strategies for resisting challenges include pretending non-belief and seeking additional support for belief.

The strength of children's belief in Santa Claus is indicated by the wide range of activities to which the belief may give rise.

> The thing I remember most is writing my Christmas list and mailing it to the North Pole. I would get every catalog that was mailed to my house and sit in my room for days looking for the perfect gift for myself. I would compare prices, look at every page three times or more, and then finally make a decision. I would then write my list and give it to my mother so she could mail it to old Saint Nick himself. (Althea)

Were Althea to engage in similar deliberations in selecting a gift to be received from an ordinary mortal, she might be judged serious, competent, mature, a 'good shopper' — attributes that seem oddly out of line with a belief in Santa Claus. The stage is set for others to view her actions with amusement and for her feeling foolish once she learns that Santa Claus is not real. Alternatively, children who know that adults provide gifts can make more rational choices.

> I was not sad about [discovering Santa was not real] but I stopped writing letters and stopped asking for so many gifts. My parents had to buy my brothers gifts too. (Caroline, Alicia's informant)

Children's belief in Santa Claus is based on the evidence that they have available. Their apparent naiveté in believing stands in stark contrast to the competence they display in grounding their belief. They draw on a variety of kinds of evidence — some that is publicly disseminated, some provided privately by adults, some from their own experiences, and some from their independent inquiries. The kinds of evidence children have access to is in its nature (if not its validity) the very kind that adults might depend upon in their ontological deliberations and that adults might well be distressed to learn had been faked.

Adult-created (False) Evidence for the Existence of Santa Claus

The presents they receive may serve children as clear evidence for the existence of Santa Claus.

> Someone had to give the presents that were from Santa Claus, that was the only proof I needed. (Warren, Althea's informant)

Children may also rely on a wide range of other evidence that, unbeknownst to them, is designed by adults to create and support children's belief in Santa Claus. Such evidence, available both publicly and privately, provided by sources that children view as trustworthy, is, of necessity, contrived and based on lies and deception. It is fake and known to be fake by those who provide it.

Santa Claus appears as an unquestionably and obviously real being in public sources readily available to both children and adults: literature, songs, films, and television. He can be found in stores and on street corners.

> The image of Santa Claus is everywhere. He appears on Christmas cards, in cartoons, and magazine illustrations. Santa Claus is sometimes shown making toys in his North Pole workshop and also going over lists of good and bad children. Other photos show Santa Claus coming down the chimney with a bag full of toys over his shoulder. Santa is seen in department stores, holding young children on his knee and asking them what they want for Christmas. (Florence)

> We had many statues of Santa and pictures too. (Rhonda, Maryanne's informant)

> I saw him in books and was taught what was in books was honest and real. (Delia, Alicia's informant)

Teachers present activities in class that take for granted the reality of Santa Claus.

> In school I made paper stockings and hung them up for Santa. He left candy canes in them and a note on the chalk board. (Caroline, Alicia's informant)

On Christmas Eve, otherwise reliable weather forecasters report sightings of him.

> Warren told me about how the weatherman used to keep updates on where Santa's sled was on Christmas Eve. (Althea's informant)

Much can be known of Santa Claus: He works (making toys), assisted by others (elves). He possesses a moral sense, judging children's behavior as good or bad, and is knowledgeable.

> At the age of 4 or 5 I was taken to see Santa at a department store. He greeted me, 'Hello, Frances.' I asked my mother how he knew my

name. I don't remember her response but I do remember being impressed that he knew. I also remember bystanders smiling at my question. Years later my mother told me that I was wearing a tee-shirt with my name spelled out in candy canes on the front. (Waksler)

Letters can be sent to him through the public channels of the Post Office, are not returned 'Addressee Unknown,' and may even be answered.

I can remember my mother sitting us down and having us write to Santa and tell him what we wanted for Christmas. Then we would wake up Christmas morning with personal letters from Santa. (Samuel, Maryanne's informant)

Before I even went to the tree to open my presents I would go and read the note Santa left for me, just me! Just to think that Santa spent a couple more minutes from his busy schedule to write me a little note to say thanks [for the cookies and milk]. (Andrew, age 7, Althea's informant)

Gift tags written by Santa provide further tangible evidence of his reality.

Opening my gifts and reading the tags I would find they said, To: Alicia, From: Santa. (Alicia)

The requests made of Santa Claus can be honored.

When Barbara received the gifts that supposedly only Santa Claus knew that she wanted she never questioned her belief in him. (Tess' informant)

The evidence of one's senses can support Santa Claus' reality. One might see him or hear him.

Eleanor remembers hearing pitter-patter sounds coming from the roof and she thought they were the reindeer. (She later found out it was her parents in the attic pretending they were reindeer.) (Marie's informant)

There may be clear evidence that Santa Claus and his reindeer eat the food that is left for them.

I remember making cookies on Christmas Eve for Santa Claus. Before I went to bed, I would leave one on a plate for Santa with a big glass of milk. With the cookie I would leave a carrot for Rudolph the Red-nosed Reindeer. . .There would be a note that said thanks for the cookies and all the presents would be signed from Santa. (Fred, Millie's informant)

Especially strong evidence is provided by the 'traces' of Santa Claus intentionally created by adults. Such 'traces' are particularly convincing since they are commonly viewed as left unintentionally.[4] Consider, for example, crumbs left behind.

> Barbara and her sisters would leave out cookies and milk for Santa Claus and carrots and celery for his reindeer, and in the morning, Christmas Day, she would find a note from Santa Claus thanking her and her two sisters for the delicious cookies and also thanking them for the celery and carrots that they left for the reindeer. The two plates that they left the food on were full of crumbs. (Tess' informant)

Adults may use trace evidence to overcome children's puzzlement over certain actions attributed to Santa Claus. How, for example, can he come down the chimney or what happens if one doesn't have a chimney? Such puzzlement suggests that children's knowledge of what is physically possible — how the natural world works — is challenged by his putative method of gaining access to houses. The challenge is intensified by adults who fake 'traces' as evidence that Santa Claus can indeed come down a chimney.

> David remembers one Christmas when his parents had put dirt all around the fireplace to make them [the children] believe that Santa Claus had actually come down the chimney. (Florence's informant)

> My mother would. . .leave dirty footprints leading to and from the Christmas tree. (Samuel, Maryanne's informant)

> When Barbara walked into the living room she saw that there was a trail of footprints leading from the fireplace to the Christmas tree and

---

[4] Goffman writes, 'The expressiveness of the individual (and therefore his capacity to give impressions) appears to involve two radically different kinds of sign activity: the expression that he *gives,* and the expression that he *gives off.* The first involves verbal symbols or their substitutes which he uses admittedly and solely to convey the information that he and the others are known to attach to these symbols. This is communication in the traditional and narrow sense. The second involves a wide range of action that others can treat as symptomatic of the actor, the expectation being that the action was performed for reasons other than the information conveyed in this way. . .The individual does of course intentionally convey misinformation by means of both of these types of communication, the first involving deceit, the second feigning' (Goffman, 1959, p. 2). In Goffman's terms, 'traces of Santa Claus' are similar to 'expressions given off,' routinely taken to be unintentional, although rather than being embodied they are disembodied, read as evidence in the absence of the evidence-leaver. For a discussion of disembodied evidence, see Waksler (1991c).

then back to the fireplace and along the mantel where their stockings were hung. When she examined the footprints closer, she saw that they were made of a white powder that looked just like snow. (Tess' informant)

Adults' answers to children's questions involve both lies and distortions of information about how the physical world works.

I can remember when I was younger asking my grandfather if I could keep the cellar door open because we didn't have a chimney for him [Santa] to come down. He brought me downstairs and showed me the old start of a chimney and said that Santa comes through that. (Valerie, Maryanne's informant)

I can remember you asking how Santa got into the house because we didn't have a chimney. I had to think quick, and I told you that Santa has a magic key in order to get into the houses without a chimney. (Rhonda, Maryanne's mother and informant)

I would ask what if there were a fire? My parents said Santa went out the night before and poured water down the chimney to put out the fire. (Caroline, Alicia's informant)

Adults may alter their own behavior in ways designed to further confirm the existence of Santa Claus or to forestall doubts.

My dad would always clean the fireplace so that Santa could go down. (Adam, Cynthia's informant)

Donna's parents would pretend that they never saw or recognized any of the gifts that were from Santa Claus. (Tess' informant)

When I was real little, my brother and I did not get gifts from our parents on Christmas Eve when everyone else did so we asked Mom and Dad, 'Why does everyone else get gifts from you and we do not?' That next year we had gifts from Mom and Dad on Christmas Eve and gifts from Santa on Christmas Day. (Marie)

In the face of such evidence, it is not surprising that children may believe wholehearted. As Millie writes,

There appeared to be no reason to disbelieve. After all, how could all those people be wrong?

Children's Use of Evidence and Reason

Some children who believe in Santa Claus never question his existence until a decisive event gives them incontrovertible proof of his non-existence. Some such events occur by chance or accident, others by intention.

> I opened a gift with a tag that was marked from Santa Claus and later on that day I walked into the kitchen where my mother and grandmother were talking. I overheard what they were talking about. As it turned out they were discussing the outfit that I was opening and how long it took my mother and grandmother to pick it out. Right there I knew the truth. I was devastated. (Gilda, Marie's informant)

> It is a big thing to some children to be able to crush others' beliefs. (Harold, Maryanne's informant)

A child's distress attendant on belief may lead adults to disclosure.

> I found out about Santa Claus because one Christmas Eve I was very ill and I was scared that Santa wouldn't come. I thought that because I couldn't sleep Santa wouldn't be able to come. My mother had to sleep with me to keep cooling me down. I was very afraid he would be scared that I might see him and not come for that reason. I asked my mother if he would come and that is when she told me that he wasn't real. She said she didn't want me to be upset anymore so she told me. I soon fell asleep, and then the next morning the reality of what I learned hit me. (Althea)

Other children may believe but still puzzle over the existence of Santa Claus and seek proof or refutation, using as evidence both false evidence provided by adults (of the sort described in the previous section) and evidence and reasoning of their own. The following story displays the reasoning, based on a preponderance of evidence, that a child might employ to support the reality of Santa Claus.

> We always put out cookies and milk and it was always gone in the morning when we woke up. He always knew what we wanted for gifts and that was usually what we received. (We never asked him for outrageous things.) I always believed that if I saw Santa then he would disappear or something along those lines so sometimes when I woke up when 'he' came in the room I didn't look to see if it was him. I just knew. After 'he' left I would look out and there was a stocking full of presents. These things were my evidence that Santa was real. (Cynthia)

The words of trusted others also serve as evidence — the words of those children who also believe and, especially, the words of adults.

> All my friends believed in him and my parents told me so. (Andrew, Althea's informant)

> The kids at school also influenced me along with my parents. (Warren, Althea's informant)

Knowledge that parents and other adults could not afford such presents may serve as an especially telling argument for Santa Claus' existence.

> Andrew noted that he knew that his mother did not have that much money but he still managed to get all his presents. He told of one Christmas when he got a really expensive remote control car and he knew that his mom did not have the money to buy it. 'I knew Santa gave it to me.' (Althea's informant)

> One year I asked for a toboggan and a doll — they were very expensive for the times — and my family was not that well off. I got them both though. Who else but Santa could have gotten me the two things I wanted most? (Rachel, Althea's informant)

Children may be convinced of Santa Claus' reality by the evidence of their senses.

> Audrey said she and her brother used to sleep in the same bed on Christmas Eve when they were young so that they could get up early and open the presents. They used to tell each other that they heard the hooves on the roof at night. (Marie's informant)

> Charlotte thought he was real because she could hear his sleigh bells going by her grandparents' house and she could see Rudolph's glowing red nose. (Tess' informant)

> When Donna was little, she thought she saw him in her living room. (Tess' informant)

> I remember one Christmas getting up in the middle of the night and hiding under the dining room table to try to see if Santa would come. I snuck into the living room over by the Christmas tree and I thought I saw Santa moving around in the shadows. (Evelyn, Cynthia's informant)

129

Sense experiences may also serve to cast doubt on the reality of Santa Claus.

> I was 12 years old and my belief in Santa was faltering. . .This particu-
> lar year Santa woke us as usual and sleepily we went downstairs. After
> opening our gifts, I went into the kitchen to get a drink of water and
> there in the kitchen was Santa sneaking out the back door. I looked
> at the back of his boots and noticed they didn't cover his shoes. I
> could not believe what I saw. I exclaimed 'You are not Santa Claus,
> you are Uncle Frank. I can tell by your shoes.' (Ida, Helen's informant)

> I never really saw him, although I used to think that I heard bells
> outside my window when his sleigh went by. My never being able to
> see him caused me to wonder if there really was a Santa after all.
> (Millie)

Occurrences that link adults' actions with those attributed to Santa Claus may
lead to questions.

> My informant said that she remembers walking in on her parents
> wrapping gifts one night. She thought nothing of it at the time but on
> Christmas morning she wondered why the gifts that she watched her
> parents wrap were under the tree all signed from Santa Claus. (Edith's
> informant)

> I found out that Santa wasn't real when I was about 7. I was down-
> stairs in my bedroom and I heard shuffling around upstairs. I went
> upstairs and saw my mom running back and forth with packages. My
> dad was putting together plastic cars. The next morning my brother got
> those cars from Santa. I was a little bit depressed, but not as much as
> when I found out about the Easter Bunny. (Adam, Cynthia's informant)

In their search for evidence, children may use care in selecting informants.

> Audrey said that all of the children at school with her in the fifth grade
> thought that it was uncool to think that Santa was real. Knowing this
> she knew that she could not ask any of her friends for the fear of
> being laughed at. That is why she asked her mom. (Marie's informant)

Evidence may cumulate, producing the knowledge that Santa Claus is not real.

> As Warren got older, he put together the grandma incident, the coin-
> cidence that the handwriting on the tags was the same as his mother's,
> and the after-shave of Santa and his father and came to his own
> conclusion. (Althea's informant)

Charlotte said she found out that Santa Claus was not real when she was either 9 or 10 years old. She found out because that Christmas Eve when Santa Claus called she recognized that it was her father's voice (instead of her uncle's, who normally did the voice of Santa calling). And she also got a note from Santa Claus that said, 'Thank you for the cookies, I was very hungary [sic].' And she noticed that it said 'hungary' and not 'hungry.' When she showed the mistake to her mother, her mother said, 'Oops, I spelled it wrong'!' She also heard her parents downstairs very late on Christmas Eve and so she went downstairs to see what they were doing. She saw them bringing up presents from the basement and when they saw her they told her to go back to bed. And the next morning the presents that she saw them with were under the tree addressed from Santa Claus. And also the carrots that she left out for Rudolph were put back into the refrigerator the next morning although Santa Claus left her a note saying that Rudolph loved them. (Tess' informant)

Some children discover that Santa Claus is not real through their own explicit efforts. They may, for example, set off in search of evidence.

The way that I found out was that I was snooping for presents in the house and I went into the hall closet to find a Winnie-the-Pooh record player. I knew the record player was for me because my brother was older and he did not like that kind of stuff. When Christmas morning came around and I opened the present marked 'To: Marie, From: Santa Claus,' what was it? It was the record player I found in the closet. From that point on I knew that my parents were acting as Santa. (Marie)

Children may ponder the matter and pursue their quest for truth by designing experiments.

Zoë, age 7, asked whether or not she believed in Santa Claus, said that she would be able to decide if she were poor. If Santa still delivered gifts, then he is real; if he didn't then he is not. However, since she isn't poor, she doesn't know. She told of a friend who conducted an experiment, leaving a piece of rope in the chimney. She described the experiment as inconclusive. (Personal communication, 12/19/93, Waksler)

I wrote a letter to Santa and only told him the gift I wanted (I did not tell my parents); if that gift did not come he wasn't real. The gift never came, so I figured it out! I also saw a list that my parents had with a note on it to buy a Barbie doll before the sale was over. (Caroline, Alicia's informant)

I decided to tie a piece of string around my big toe and leave string all through the house to see if I could 'catch' Santa. I thought it was a great plan and, right before I went to bed, I left string all over the house. In the night I felt a tug at my toe and I ran down the stairs to find my mother caught up in all the string that I left out for Santa. Needless to say, I was very disappointed to find out that Santa Claus was really my mom. (Flora, Millie's informant)

How do children come to seek empirical evidence and use scientific reasoning to confirm or refute the existence of Santa Claus? They appear to figure out the process themselves, perhaps in consultation with other children, perhaps through inferences drawn from other experiences they have had. Clearly with respect to Santa Claus, adults do not encourage the process but rather actively discourage and impede it. The following conversation shows how children's investigations and experiments are clearly hampered by adults' false trails and false information.

An Example of a Child's Reasoning: Interview with Victor, Age 11
by Louise

Louise: Victor, what do you think about Santa Claus?
Victor: I think he is fake.
Louise: Why is that?
Victor: I don't know. I guess because when I go upstairs, I see presents that say 'From Santa' and it's not even Christmas yet.
Louise: Why else?
Victor: Because reindeer can't fly, and there is no such thing as magic.
Louise: How do you know?
Victor: Because my great-grandfather was a magician, and there was always a reason behind his tricks.
Louise: When did you first realize that Santa was not real?
Victor: When I was about 9.
Louise: What do you think of Santa Claus now?
Victor: I think he is just some made up old fat guy.
Louise: Do you think there was ever really a Santa Claus?
Victor: No, because it is impossible for anybody to deliver all those presents, unless he was really rich.

Louise continues, 'During the interview, by the tone in his voice, and the way he reasoned the whole situation out, I got the impression that Victor was trying to convince himself more than me or anybody else. And after the initial interview with him, he admitted that he wasn't positive that Santa did not exist, he only thought so.'

Distress at Learning that Santa Claus is Not Real

Some children never believe in Santa Claus; others express little or no concern in learning that he is not real.

> I remember not caring whom I got my presents from. I found out by accidentally seeing my parents wrapping presents. I saw a present for me, a Fisher-Price stereo. I didn't care who bought it; I wanted it anyway. (Lois)

Other children are angry when they learn that Santa Claus is not real. In the following story, Kate describes her anger, interestingly enough directed towards the truth-teller, not the liar.

> In the third or fourth grade, Anna from my class, a girl who had been bullying me since kindergarten, confronted me with her 'facts' and 'truths' about there not being a Santa Claus or Easter Bunny. I was so frustrated that she told this that I went home and told my parents. After my parents told me that there wasn't a Santa Claus or Easter Bunny, I became furious at Anna and even more furious and resentful at her parents. If their daughter knew that there was no Santa Claus and Easter Bunny then it was their responsibility to instruct her not to ruin other children's fun by telling them that there isn't a Santa Claus or an Easter Bunny. They had obviously shirked this duty and I as an innocent child felt that I suffered a loss because of their neglect. (Kate)

Yet others experience varying degrees of unhappiness and distress.

> I cried when I found out that he wasn't real. I loved to believe in him. (Francine, Cynthia's informant)

> I was reading a book for class. The book said that there was no Santa. I was devastated! I thought that Christmas would be no more. I talked to my mother and begged her to please keep Christmas going. She assured me that it would always go on, even if I knew there was no Santa. (Alice, Maryanne's informant)

> I remember asking my mother because I heard someone talking about it in school. She asked me if I really wanted to know. When I said yes, I was extremely disappointed with the answer. (Maryanne)

> Millicent says that she was 7 years old when her big brother told her the truth about Santa. She said that after her brother told her Santa wasn't real, she started kicking him and beating him up because she wanted to believe in Santa. She refused to believe what her brother

said about her parents really being Santa Claus; she decided instead to keep thinking he was real. But about a year later when Christmas came around, Millicent found a present under her parents' bed that had her name on it and was signed 'From Santa'! She was so upset she started crying and brought the present to her mother and asked her why she had lied to her all this time about Santa. She did not talk to her parents at all for weeks. They explained to her that Santa was only a fantasy figure used to make Christmas more exciting. Millicent felt stupid for believing that Santa came down chimneys and reindeer flew in the sky. She was mad at her parents for lying to her. (Florence's informant)

The older kids at school went around and told all the younger kids that he wasn't real. I didn't believe them so I went home and asked my mother and she sat me down and told me. I guess she wanted me to hear it from her and not some jerks at school. I guess I asked my mom because in some strange way I wanted to prove them wrong. . .It will be different [now that I know] but there isn't anything I can do. (Andrew, age 7, Althea's informant)

Learning the truth may leave a child feeling foolish in relation to other children.

I found out through one of my friends at school. I felt like such a fool for believing for so long and not figuring out for myself. I never felt anger toward my parents, though. (Millie)

Eleanor says she was 7 years old when she found out that Santa Claus was really her parents. She found out on the bus one afternoon coming home from school. She overheard older kids talking about Santa, saying people were stupid if they believed in him and only babies believed in Santa. (Florence's informant)

Robert has just recently discovered that Santa is not real. He is 8 years old and found out from one of his friends. He told me that his friend made fun of him for still believing in Santa and that he is too old to still think Santa is real. Even though Robert is the youngest in a large family of seven children, his family kept the secret. Robert says he is a little sad to find out about Santa Claus but is glad he found out now before more kids made fun of him for still believing. He says, 'Christmas will never be the same now that Santa is gone.' (Florence's informant)

Upon learning that Santa Claus is not real, children may have practical concerns, e.g., that presents or valued activities will also cease to exist.

The main thing I was concerned with was whether or not I would still get the presents from Santa if there was no Santa that really came. (Millie)

Melissa recalls being sad because she knew the kids on the bus were telling the truth. She says that Christmas she did not even put out her stocking or cookies because she thought Santa wasn't coming anymore. But when she woke up on Christmas morning she found her stocking hanging in its usual place, filled with candy, gifts and presents under the tree. She remembers jumping up and down because she realized that Christmas could still be the same as it always had been even if she didn't believe in Santa fully. (Florence's informant)

I used to make cookies with my mother to leave for Santa and I was afraid that now that I knew Santa wasn't real that I wouldn't be able to do that with her anymore. She told me that now we could make those cookies for ourselves. (Valerie, Maryanne's informant)

Children may be especially distressed that they have been lied to and deceived. They may perceive the adults who perpetrated the deception as the source of disillusionment and disappointment and be angry with them.

Learning that Santa was not real was upsetting to me. Realizing that my parents had been fooling me for ten years caused a brief rush of disappointment, but I was over it quick enough. It was not as easy for my informant Fred, who stated, 'I remember being told by one of my friends that Santa Claus was not real. I fought back and said that he was too, because my parents told me so. I was taunted by all the kids in my class for being a baby because I still thought Santa was real. I was so upset that I ran out of the classroom crying, wondering how my parents could do this to me.' (Millie)

I found out from one of my friends and felt like hitting him. I never thought that my parents would lie to me. I felt like my whole Christmas was going to be ruined. It took me a while to get over it and trust my parents again and they say that we as kids should never lie. (Paul, Millie's informant)

When I first learned that Santa wasn't real I was kind of angry at my parents for lying to me all these years. I had always thought everything my parents told me was the truth and now suddenly it wasn't. . .I believe it was my first time that I had ever known my parents to lie. (Althea)

When I realized Santa Claus was just a spirit and not a person I was very upset and confused. I couldn't believe my parents would lie to me about something that would eventually hit home really bad. I believed there was a Santa Claus for a very long time. When I realized there wasn't one I felt betrayed and hurt. I hated my parents. (Helen)

In the following story Kay describes herself as the victim of a 'hoax' and calls attention to a double standard for lying. In both wanting and not wanting to know the truth, she faced a dilemma.

Kay said she learned that Santa was not real because she 'saw her parents wrapping the presents one Christmas Eve.' She proceeded to say that her older sister confirmed this sudden realization. 'When I saw them wrapping presents I went upstairs and asked my older sister if there was a Santa Claus. She looked straight into my eyes and said "No." I did not really believe it at first but then I started to put the whole hoax together. I realized that there were about fifty different Santas around town and they were all different colors.' Kay said, 'I wondered why my parents went through all of that trouble to make me believe something that was not true if I was just going to be told the truth anyway.' She also wondered, 'Why was I put on time-out for lying?'. . .Kay said she was disappointed and sad. She said, 'I thought my parents were mean for lying to me, but I thought my sister was mean for not lying to me.' (Lois' informant)

Nonetheless, children may discover advantages in not believing.

When I was 8 one of my friends told me Santa wasn't real. I denied this until the end! Everyone said he wasn't real and brainwashed me into finally thinking he wasn't. I felt disappointed and lost some of my Christmas spirit. Since I'm an only child, I now figured I could get more gifts since my mother was buying them and Santa didn't have to deliver toys to any other house. (Alicia)

Children who never believed may come to see not believing as an advantage.

Glenda thought that she was spared the humiliation that she saw lots of kids suffer when they found out the truth. . .She seems to think that she missed some of the mystery but none of the fun. (Millie)

Adults may be aware of children's distress, as is evidenced in the following statements by adults.

I can remember the Christmas that three of your cousins found out about Santa because of my big mouth. I went and said that I knew Judy would love the tea set and how we had gone to a lot of trouble to get it. She turned to me and said that she thought Santa had a

workshop where they made all the toys. I have never felt so bad. She
started crying and your other cousins heard and were upset. (Paula,
Maryanne's mother and informant)

I am dreading the day that my two sons find out about Santa. I enjoy
keeping up the fun with the children. I am not looking forward to the
day that they find out the truth about Santa. This is a fun charade to
play with them. (Alice, Maryanne's informant)

Alternatively, adults may make light of their deception.

I asked where the cookies went and my mother said, 'Now you know
why Dad is so fat!' (Caroline, Alicia's informant)

Whether or not they know of or take seriously the distress that children can
experience, adults continue to justify and perpetuate the deception. In the
following comment, Millie calls for honesty, citing what she describes as the
'heartache' attendant on learning that Santa Claus is not real, but then retreats,
struggling to preserve the fiction.

In a child's life Santa is a big part, but at an older age it seems as
though maybe honesty in the beginning would have been the best
policy — honesty not about Santa but about how there is more to
Christmas than the presents and the man in red. Christmases would
not have been any less special and it may have saved someone a lot
of heartache in the long run. The shock of finding out from someone
other than our parents caused some adults who were interviewed a lot
of pain and heartache. Maybe this could have been avoided if other
holiday things had been emphasized. (Millie)

Children's belief in Santa Claus appears in my data as a firmly entrenched
tradition maintained by adults in the face of children's potential distress and of
the lies and deceptions of adults required to support it.

Reformulations of 'Reality'

When children learn that Santa Claus is not real, both children and adults may
adopt a variety of strategies to minimize or conceal the lying and deception
that occurred. The following story describes reformulations of reality offered
in response to a child's distress.

I was 9 years old when I found out the truth about Santa Claus. I had
always believed in Santa. I never had a reason to wonder about him.
I always received what I asked for from him, he always took bites out

of the cookies I left for him, and I always found a carrot half eaten outside. So I was heartbroken when I found out that Santa Claus was really my mother and father. It was one week before Christmas when my older brother came running into my room saying I had to see something quick. He led me into my parents' room and showed me a big box in their closet filled with presents. They were all to me and my brothers and sisters but they were signed from Santa. I couldn't believe it! I wanted to go ask my parents why Santa had brought the presents early this Christmas, ask them why they were in their closet, but my brother made me swear that I would not tell them what I had just seen. That Christmas when I opened my presents from Santa there was not the usual excitement or screams. I simply said thank-you to my parents. I remember lying on my bed crying and my mom came in. I told her why I was crying and she explained to me that Santa was just a 'magical spirit' and was only real in my imagination. And pretending 'he' was real could be just as much fun. From then on my mom had me be her Santa's helper, helping her pick out gifts for the stockings and wrapping presents. Although Santa Claus is not real, he is in the spirit of Christmas, representing the meaning of giving, and I believe in him for the spirit. (Florence)

Florence's belief in the reality of Santa Claus is presented as still *true*, for he is 'real in her imagination.' He remains real 'as a spirit' and the 'spirit of Christmas' can be offered as a real, superior, and grown-up formulation. 'Pretending' to believe can be 'just as much fun' (though, if so, why was Santa Claus not presented as pretense from the beginning?)

Adults' reformulations may embody interesting ontological positions.

I remember being in the third grade when a boy in my class decided to tell everyone that his brother had said that Santa wasn't real. I was devastated and went home to question my parents as to what the truth was. My mom asked me what I believed and I said that I wasn't sure. *She said that if I believed that Santa was real, then he was. She then said that if I felt that Santa was just a person that people wish were true so much that they have him come alive that that was also a possibility.* I chose to believe that he was real at that point in time. (Edith, emphasis added)

Eleanor asked her mother if the kids on the bus were telling the truth. Her mother told her that she should not listen to them because *it was her own choice whether or not she wanted to believe in Santa Claus.* (Florence's informant, emphasis added)

Children can thus be taught that reality is a *choice*, that something is real if one believes it is, that reality is based on what one wants to be real. Reality itself may be reformulated.

Barbara confronted her parents with the question of whether Santa Claus was real or not and was told by her father that *Santa Claus is real in your heart.* (Tess' informant, emphasis added)

The notion of 'belief' may also come in for revision.

I think that I can fairly say that I have never fully stopped believing in him or what he stands for. (Edith)

The meaning of 'real in your heart' and of the claim to have not stopped 'believing' is vague, perhaps intentionally so, for vagueness can obviate the need for ontological clarification.

Children's reformulations may serve the purpose of demonstrating that adults did not *really* lie.

At this point in time I would have to say that I believe that Santa Claus was a real person that we wish were still alive today whom we try to bring back once a year in his spirit. (Edith)

When I was 9 years old, kids in my class started talking about Santa not being real. *They would say Santa died of cancer but he was real at one time so your parents really didn't lie.* (Caroline, Alicia's informant, emphasis added)

The reformulations of adults and children suggest that lies and deceptions may be viewed as needing to be explained — or explained away.

When children discover that Santa Claus is not real, adults may divert them from a negative view of the deception by directing their energies towards supporting the fiction for other children.[5] Children are thus offered partial admission into the world of adults, their disillusionment forestalled or minimized. In the story that starts this section, Florence speaks of being offered the opportunity to be 'Santa's helper.' Other stories describe similar complicity.

I was never mad at my mother for not telling me that Santa was not real. I just continued to make believe for my sister. (Maryanne)

It was my mother who first told me the truth about Santa. She could not believe that at the age of 9 I still believed in Santa. I was a little upset, but I thought that it would be fun to keep up this charade with my little sister. (Samuel, Maryanne's informant)

When I realized Santa was not real, I did everything I could to keep the secret alive so that my younger brother did not find out. (Millie)

---

[5] Elaine Kaven first brought this strategy to my attention.

> Audrey found out that her older brother knew that he was not real but he played along so not to ruin it for her. (Marie's informant)

> I didn't think of it as a lie, I mean too many people knew that he was fake. I just felt like I was being trusted with the secret. (Daphne's informant)

In the following story, disappointment and the perpetuation of the deception coexist, without apparent awareness of the inconsistency.

> When I found out the truth, I was disappointed. . .About the time I found out, I was taking my cousins to see Santa to confirm their belief. I wanted the younger children to still believe. I felt this was because Santa is a part of what Christmas is all about. (Delia, Alicia's informant)

Thus do children become accomplices in deception. Children's complicity may serve to diffuse the distress of both children and adults by uniting them in a common project. Instead of being addressed and rectified, the distress is forgotten and perpetuated.

> I do not exactly remember when or how I learned that Santa Claus is not real, but somehow I did realize the truth, though it really does not affect my Christmas or make it different in any way because I know that there is definitely a spirit of Christmas that seems to make even the grumpiest person happy if even for just one day. Christmas is still and will always be a very happy holiday for me and my family. (Tess)

> [My informant] says he treasures each and every Christmas that he can celebrate Santa Claus, and he is now passing on the tradition to his own family. (Florence)

'But I Want My Children to Believe'

Millie writes, 'The question that confuses the people that I interviewed is why did their parents make such a big deal out of Santa Claus? Why all the extras to make Santa seem so real?' Despite adults' claims that they create and sustain children's belief for the sake of those children, adults themselves may gain a great deal from the fiction of Santa Claus. They speak of their own pleasure at seeing children's excitement and delight and extol the 'magic' of Christmas. Children may perceive the importance to adults of Santa Claus and continue the fiction for adults' sake.

> Donna thought Santa Claus was real and then realized when she was 7 years old that he was fake. Though she knew that he wasn't real, she 'faked it' so that her father would not be upset. (Tess' informant)

When I was in the fifth grade I heard some kids saying that there was no such thing as Santa Claus. I was really upset by this and ran to my cousins to see if this was really true. They told me that yes the kids at school were right but that I couldn't tell my parents that I knew about it since they would get upset. For a long time I just kept pretending that I still believed in him but it was very hard. A few years later I did tell them and they didn't seem upset at all. (Elizabeth)

I was worried that my mother would be disappointed because I was an only child and my mother had no one to play this charade with. I went on for two years getting my picture taken with the K-Mart Santa, just so my mom would be happy. (Harold, Maryanne's informant)

Adults may indeed express disappointment when they learn that children no longer believe.

I learned something new while working on this paper. I just took it for granted that my 12-year-old sister still believed in Santa. Naive I know, but I just didn't realize that she didn't know. When I asked her, she told me that she stopped believing when she was about 8 years old. I couldn't believe it! I was kind of disappointed. (Maryanne)

One benefit that adults can derive from children's belief in Santa Claus is the vicarious recapturing of what as children they lost when their belief proved false. Furthermore, by emphasizing the *traditional* (and thus positive) character of Santa Claus, adults can minimize or obscure the deceptive and distressing aspects that they experienced and that they transmit. Adult informants thus describe their perpetuation of Santa Claus.

Christmas was so magical when I was a child. When I found out there was no such thing as Santa Claus, Christmas lost some of its magic. That magic was recaptured when I had kids and saw their delight in Santa. (Doris, Daphne's informant)

As a young child, Millicent says she remembers writing long letters to Santa Claus telling him what she wanted for Christmas. She recalls putting out cookies and a glass of milk for Santa Claus and a carrot for Rudolph on Christmas Eve. She says Christmas was the holiday she loved the most as a child and still loves the most to this day. But today, as a mother of three young children, her Christmases are spent writing back the letters her children have written to Santa and taking the bite out of the cookie and carrot the kids leave out for Santa Claus and Rudolph. She says she enjoys watching her children's eyes light up when they see all the presents. She says, 'Santa Claus is brought back to life through my children's eyes.' (Millicent, Marie's informant)

One way that I believe Santa lives is in the hopes to see the joy on my children's faces someday. (Maryanne)

Even adults not a party to the deception may nonetheless be reluctant to disclose the truth as they know it.

[My informant] said that she does try to portray Santa as a real person to those who she feels are undecided about it. (Edith)

The positive nature of belief in Santa Claus may be maintained even in the face of evidence to the contrary, as illustrated in the following comment by Edith. Her own data, cited earlier in this chapter, includes the statement that when she learned he was not real, 'I was devastated,' and her informant's statement that Santa Claus 'was an imaginary person that adults had made up in an attempt to get children to behave.' Nonetheless Edith writes,

I have and will continue to allow Santa to live through my memory by portraying him as I remember him to those who don't remember him or to those who don't know any different. . .I have led people to believe that he is real and will continue to do so *if I feel that it won't harm them in any way.* At the same time though I would never impose my belief on others who did not share it with me. (Edith, emphasis added)

She does not explicate what counts as harm.

The sorry state of the world can be invoked as justification for supporting the fiction of Santa Claus.

I didn't see the harm in having people, especially children, believe in something so wonderful in a world that is filled with hatred and violence. (Edith)

I think Santa's a good role model for children. He is something good for kids to believe in, and God knows they need something to believe in. (Walter, Louise's informant)

Both children and adults use the spirit of Santa Claus to show that there is good in the world, that not everything is bad or evil. (Anonymous)

The alternative thus offered to evil in the world is pretense; evil is natural, goodness imaginary.

Adults may want their children to believe in Santa Claus but fulfillment of their desires may be costly. As one informant noted,

From my data I can see that adults have been lying to children for many years. I also see that children as they get older start to do the same thing by going along with the myth of Santa Claus so that the smaller children can still believe. To me this seems to be like the adults are corrupting the children to turn into smaller versions of themselves. (Marie)

To lie and deceive is thus to become an adult.

* * *

Adults may define their statements and deceptions about Santa Claus as 'not really lying.' For Bok, however, to settle 'the moral question of whether you are lying or not. . .we must know whether you *intend your statement to mislead*' (Bok, 1989, p. 6, emphasis in original). Regardless of other intentions, the presentation of Santa Claus as real is *intended* to mislead and thus is a lie. As such, it compromises knowledge and the appropriate and reliable methods for achieving it. It may also have widespread consequences when children generalize from their experiences of Santa Claus. The following story was told to me; I recount it here from memory.

In response to her question, a child was told on the way to church that Santa Claus was not real. Throughout the church service, the child whispered her disbelief, 'Is it really true that Santa Claus isn't real?' She was assured that he wasn't. As she left church, she asked, 'What about God? Is he real?'

8 Teachers and School

My second grade teacher was the one that the other kids did not want. She was very strict and considered mean by my peers. Until that time I had been used to being favored by all my teachers and had enjoyed school. My teacher in second grade did not allow us to write on the board while we were waiting for the bus. She also did not like my friends and me to help her to pass out papers. I couldn't understand why she didn't want our help, but mostly I remember being scared. Second grade was the only time I would try to fake being sick in order to stay home from school. (Amelia)

In second grade I had this really mean art teacher. Her name was Mrs Crockett. No one liked her. Well, one day Timothy Grady spilled green paint all over my new shirt. I was devastated. I told the teacher on him and she yelled at me! She told me that it was my fault. She then told me that I did not care about my artwork. The reason I didn't care was because we had such a mean teacher like her! (Anne-Marie, Ursula's informant)

Viewed from children's perspectives, teachers and school may appear in ways that stand in stark contrast to adults' perspectives, as well as to their intentions. Children may experience the little trials of childhood when they meet with discrepancies between what is presented at home and at school and between teachers' perspectives and their own. They may be troubled by school rules and procedures and by relations with teachers. They may see themselves as victims of teachers' shortcomings and they may experience embarrassment and humiliation. When adults are unaware of the grounds of children's distress, and when adults apply and act in terms of their own inaccurate formulations, adults' efforts to help and to console children are likely to be ineffective.

The purpose of this book as a whole and thus this chapter is *not* to urge adults as a matter of principle to defer to children in all matters. Clearly some teachers' actions have strong justification and some children's trials seem inevitable. Not all differences in perspective can be avoided and neither teacher nor child is always or necessarily 'right.' Nonetheless, for those who want to *understand* children's experiences of teachers and school, the data in this chapter contributes to that goal.

Children's troubles may begin with the first days of school.

I cried each and every day of kindergarten. . .I couldn't bear the thought of leaving my mom alone, for she would surely miss me and maybe even cry. My great difficulty adjusting to kindergarten was not understood by adults. People advised my mother to leave me there in the morning, kiss me good-bye, and let me adjust. They didn't realize that I was worried about my mother. (Iris)

One hardship about school was being away from our mother. My sister Lila was always worried that something would happen to her while she was at school. Sometimes it got so bad that she wouldn't be able to eat her lunch or join her friends in recess. She said she rarely ever went to the nurse to fake sick like I did to get to go home. She didn't want to upset our mother by doing this. She said this was very hard for her, as it was for me as well. (Dorothy, describing her sister's and her own experiences)

Children who are sent off to their first day of school by sobbing adults may well have grounds for concern. Adults who misinterpret children's distress, attributing it to 'missing' their mothers or to immaturity, can provide no help in assuaging that concern.

Kindergarten may present its own special difficulties.

Janice remembered back to her days of kindergarten. She recalls: 'I hated it! They made us play ring-around-the-rosy all the time. It was the stupidest game and we had no choice, we HAD to play it.' (Janice, Ramona's informant)

At about age 6, when I first went to school, I discovered that the teacher stored all the good stuff on the top shelves of the closets, like paints and paste and the really fat permanent markers. Out of sight, out of reach. She also spoke with that familiar high pitched voice. . .She loved teaching us and watching us work quietly — I could tell by the frozen smile and twinkling, staring eyes. . .I'm not sure I liked being a 'victim' of 'the look'[1] because it made me feel little and like I was free entertainment. (Gwen)

When Vivian was in kindergarten, she lived too far away from the school to get home after the morning session. She had to stay in kindergarten all day long and do everything twice. She had two naps, two snacks, made two decorations on every holiday, and had to take two tests. (Vivian, Maida's informant)

---

[1] For a discussion of 'the look,' see Joyce's 'Watching people watching babies' (1991).

Against the background of their experiences prior to attending school, children may find school an odd place indeed.

Differing Perspectives: Home and School

When adults are unaware of the quite different experiences that children can have at home and at school, children may be left on their own to make sense of, come to terms with, or at least endure, these discrepancies. Words and deeds may be evaluated differently and have different implications in different contexts. Language acceptable at home may not be so at school.

> There was an incident that I will never forget. The class was making stand-up Christmas trees out of construction paper. Mine wasn't looking the way I wanted it to so I got frustrated and threw it away. Mrs Taylor came up to my desk and asked me where my Christmas tree was. 'I screwed up,' I told her. 'You what?' she said. 'I screwed up,' I told her. She then gave me this horrible look as if she were disgusted with me and told me to go to the back room and write 'screwed up' five hundred times. When I got up to number four hundred, I finally got the guts to stand up for myself. I told her that I didn't understand why she was making me write and that I have never gotten in trouble at home for saying 'screwed up.' I also told her that I honestly didn't think I said anything wrong. She just said 'OK, but I don't want to hear it again. You can stop writing now.' (Ariel)

Behavior that is allowed in one setting may be forbidden in another.

> There I was a big 6-year-old all the way up to the position of first grader. To me, first grade meant I became a big boy. Oh how I wish that was true. Even though I was higher up than a kindergartner, I found I was still treated as a little kid. The one particular incident that represented this was not being able to go to the store. When I was not in school, my mom let me go to the store to get her stuff that she needed. I could go alone and didn't need accompanying. The store was equally distant from both my house and my school. . .I point this out only to show what the situation was. Even though the store was so close, my teacher would not allow me and my classmates to go there. I was upset because at home I was treated like a big boy by being able to do this but at school I was treated like a baby. By not allowing me to go to the store, my teacher reduced my level of maturity that I had achieved at home. This difference in treatment made me mad and really killed my notion that first grade was the big time. What made me laugh was it took until the third grade for me to attain a privilege that I had already possessed at home for three years. (Ned)

Home and school rules governing the eating of food may differ.

> My own hard time occurred when I was in the second grade. I went
> to Catholic school and had a nun for a teacher. Each day after lunch,
> Sr Mary Frances would check our lunch-boxes to make sure that we
> had eaten everything that our parents had packed for us. If we did not
> eat all the contents of our lunch-box, we were not allowed to go out
> for recess on that day. There were times when I could not eat all the
> food that my mother packed me. Therefore I spent many recesses
> inside. Many children made fun of me. I never understood why my
> teacher would force us to do something that we did not want to or
> could not do. There were times when I thought that I was going to
> vomit because I was trying to force down all of my food. This type of
> rule could cause physical harm. At home my parents always stressed
> that it was important for me to eat enough food and the right kinds
> of food, but when I told them I was full they would not force me to
> eat more. My second grade teacher forced us to eat all of our lunch,
> and offered punishment if we could not obey her rule. How could she
> punish us for something so natural as being full? (Charlene)

What appears a reasonable lunch at home may be a source of difficulties when
brought to school.

> It was always expected of me to eat what was packed in my lunch at
> school. There was a difference between my lunch and the lunch the
> other kids had. One difference was that my father made my lunch. He
> used to make me a bagel with cream cheese and tomato wrapped in
> tinfoil. I used to be so embarrassed because everyone else had peanut
> butter and jelly in a brown bag except for me. I never told my father
> this because I was afraid he would get mad so every day I would ask
> the other kids for food or eat when I got home but before my dad
> came in from work. (Brunella)

Brunella's method of resolving these differences was to go hungry, suggesting
the seriousness with which she viewed her problem. Anticipation of her father's anger served to limit her options.

When children try at home what they have learned at school, they may
bring down troubles upon themselves.

> When I was 10 years old I had a teacher who told the class one day
> that we should all stand up for our rights. I took this too literally.
> When I got home I hung out a load of wash to dry and waited for
> Mom to come home from work. I could not wait to ask if I could sleep
> over a friend's house and go to school on the bus in the morning. She
> was already in a bad mood when she walked into the house. She told

me I was going to come home on the bus right after school the next day and stay with my sister for a while. So I stood up for my rights. I said, 'NO!' My mother's face showed sheer shock. She asked me what right I had to say no to her. I said my teacher told us to stand up for our rights in class. That was the end of that 'stick-up-for-your-rights' business when Mom and Dad were present. I ended up staying home anyway. (Gwen)

Perhaps certain school lessons should come with the caveat: Do not try this at home.

Differing Perspectives: Teacher and Child

Children and teachers may have very different views of the same situation. When teachers fail to *understand* children's perspectives — whether or not teachers accept those perspectives — not only may they be unable to help children effectively but they may also compound children's troubles. In the following story Hannah describes her teacher's attempts to make her talk loudly.

My third grade teacher used to make me stand up in front of the class every time I spoke to help project my voice. This didn't work. She wouldn't listen to me when I told her that I just didn't have a loud voice. She used to tell my mother that I had a self-esteem problem. The teacher said the reason I talked quietly when I answered was because I was not sure of my answers. This made me very mad because I knew my answers were correct. I just didn't like speaking loudly. It was as if the teacher was looking for an excuse to explain my behavior. I never did learn that year how to speak loudly and it is a problem people say I have now. Why can't I be just a soft-spoken person? (Hannah)

Children may thus find their very selves subject to unwanted revision by teachers.

In the following story the child and the teacher were, both literally and figuratively, perceiving the world in dramatically different ways.

Seeing Things Differently
by Amanda

I can remember the times when my visual limitations caused me hard times as if they occurred ten minutes ago. One incident that was particularly difficult for me to accept occurred in the first grade. One day I was going through my desk and found an old paper that I hadn't colored. The lines on the paper were hardly visible to me. In a panic I began to color the paper right away, for I thought that it was so old that the picture was fading. I reasoned that if I did not hurry the lines would completely disappear before I could finish. I passed the paper in when I had finished. I was very proud of it. The next day I got it back. There was a big red sad face at the top. I began to cry. After a while I noticed that there was only one green tree-top colored on the entire page. Suddenly it all made sense. My colors had disappeared before the teacher had gotten a chance to see them! So, I marched up to her desk and told her what had happened. She took my paper away from me and turned it over. There right in front of us was the result of all my hard work. 'You colored the wrong side,' she said. I was demoted to kindergarten the next day.

Another such incident that I remember clearly occurred in the second grade. This time I was given a paper with fill-in-the-blank sentences. The sentences themselves were not written big enough for me to read. I sat for a long time trying to figure out exactly what I was supposed to do with this paper. Finally I decided I should put words on the lines. Knowing that spelling was important to my teacher, I filled the lines with words I could spell. When I brought it up to my teacher to correct, she got angry. 'You are supposed to use the words at the top of the paper, not any word that pops into your head,' she scolded. Up until that very second I hadn't even realized that there were words at the top of the paper. My bewilderment turned to anger when she finished, 'Since you rushed through the paper the first time, you will have to stay in for recess to redo it.' I sat at my desk just being mad until she warned, 'If you don't get it done now, you will have to stay in every recess until it is done.' Well, I began right that minute, and two recesses later I had managed to put each of the words on a line (in the exact order in which they appeared at the top of the paper). When I handed the paper in, my teacher was still not pleased. However, she did not make me do the paper over again.

*   *   *

Her teachers' implicit explanations for Amanda's behavior (immaturity, stupidity, carelessness, undue haste) seem, in light of Amanda's explanations, misguided. Her teachers' formulations also forestall efforts to provide Amanda with useful information, e.g., that lines and crayon colors on paper do not fade as rapidly as she feared or that resources for improving her vision might be warranted. Indeed Amanda's attempts to make sense of her experiences *as she saw them* were taken as evidence not of her competence but of her incompetence.

Rather than providing Amanda with information, her second-grade teacher *assumes* that Amanda possesses knowledge, specifically, that 'using the words at the top of the paper' does not mean 'in the order in which they appear' but 'in terms of what makes sense in a sentence.' When teachers assume that students possess knowledge that they do not possess, the discrepancy can lead to children's distress.

> I was in the fourth grade and we were getting ready to send our art projects to an art show. My teacher gave me a picture that I had made and asked me to put my 'John Hancock' on it. I had no clue what she was talking about and I was scared to ask what it was for fear of seeming stupid. After a few minutes of wondering what to do I neatly printed my name on it and gave it back to her. She then explained to me that this meant to sign your name in cursive. I was so ashamed and wished that I had asked what it was in the first place. (Elizabeth)

When teachers understand children's perspectives, they have greater resources not only for easing children's distress but for teaching them. Without teachers' understanding and help, children may craft their own solutions.

> In fourth grade, when the teacher would leave the room she would pick a good student she trusted to go to the board. I hated when she would pick me. I would have to stand at the board and write down anyone's name who talked. If I wrote down a name, the kids would get mad and yell at me. If I did not write down anyone's name, everyone would talk. So, if I ever had to go up there, I would write down the names of the people who were talking and when I heard the teacher's high heels clapping down the hallway I would erase the names and tell her no one was talking. That made everyone happy. (Maida)

Rules and Procedures

Like any social setting, schools require rules — legal, formal, informal, and taken-for-granted — that may apply to all schools, some schools, a school in particular, and a specific classroom. Children's understanding of these rules requires 'extensive, sophisticated knowledge and the grasp of a wide array of subtleties and nuances of words and action' (Waksler, 1987, p. 150; see also Mackay, 1973 and 1974). Teachers transmit rules created by others. Teachers also create rules, some of which reflect their own personal preferences. What Mackay says of instruction also applies to rules: they can be 'the occasion for adults to exercise their preference for a certain meaning of the world for the child' (1973, in Waksler, 1991b, p. 31). Children — and other adults as well — may find some of these rules odd.

> We were not allowed to use erasers in kindergarten. We had big thick pencils without erasers. While on a class trip, I bought a big pencil that had an eraser. I used it one day in class and the teacher told me I could not use it. I asked her why and she told me it was not fair to the rest of the class that I had an eraser and they did not. I told her I would share but she asked me to put it away. (Maida)

Maida does not seem to have been able to discover an explanation for the rule forbidding children's use of erasers or why her sharing was unacceptable.

Not only what one uses but how one uses it may be the subject of rules.

> Throughout elementary school, my teachers constantly attempted to force me to change the way I hold my pencil. They insisted that I was not holding it correctly. I suffered much embarrassment when I was forced to use a rubber attachment on my pencil. It was shaped like a long pyramid so that my fingers were forced to hold the pencil correctly. The teacher may have been blind to the embarrassment I suffered because she was so set on correcting me. This situation brings up the question of who is right. Is there really a correct way to hold a pencil? Despite teachers' attempts, I continue holding my pencil 'the wrong way.' Now that I am no longer a child, I am not corrected by my teachers nor do I suffer their embarrassing methods of correcting the problem. (Ruby)

Coloring pictures may be subject to rules.

> In kindergarten, I colored a picture of a pear yellow. The teacher yelled at me and said pears aren't yellow. She then told me she didn't like that color and that it wasn't to be used in the wrong way. I know this sounds really stupid, but I was afraid of the yellow crayon until I was in third grade! I would color the rainbow red, orange, green, blue, and purple. (Anne-Marie, Ursula's informant)

The apparently simple rule of 'lining up' may be experienced as a hardship.

> By the age of 8 a number of my teachers had tried to 'socialize' me to stand in single file along with the others in line. They tried and tried but for some odd reason the 'socialization' never 'took.' I was a second grade 'social deviant.' I would stand to one side of the person in front of me. I stood quietly frozen, hoping to be overlooked. Once, I remember, my teacher looked straight at me with piercing eyes that scared the pants off me. I shuddered as she walked toward me. I could not force myself to stand behind the person in front of me. Maybe it was because I couldn't see around the person in front of me. Maybe it was because I felt confined and cramped being sandwiched between two people in line. Maybe I just wanted to be different. Suddenly Mrs Porter approached me, snatched my arm, and thrust me into the proper position in line, scolding me all the while. This was humiliating. Through my teary eyes I could see the children turning around to look back at my reddened face. I held my breath for a few moments and bowed my head, pretending that I was home playing with my favorite toys or watching television. Perhaps Mrs Porter simply

did not realize that I was not trying to be bad; I was not trying to make her mad at me. I was merely objecting to my 'socialization.' Of course I did not know this when I was 8 years old, though. I was unable to do something and somebody did not understand my point of view for I was 'only a child.' (Gwen)

Following one's peers may be a useful strategy for following rules but it can also lead to unsuspected rule-breaking.

When I was in first grade, my teacher asked a question. Every student she called on shrugged their shoulders and said they didn't know. When it got to me, I just followed everyone else; I shrugged my shoulders and said I didn't know. She was so mad because she knew that I knew the answer. She yelled at me and told me, 'We do not shrug our shoulders in this classroom and say we don't know the answer. Now answer the question.' That was the last time I ever did that. (Bettina, Ramona's informant)

The taken-for-granted rule of which Bettina appears to have been unaware and which she violated might be phrased as: You may shrug your shoulders and say you do not know if you indeed do not know or if you know that the teacher does not know that you know; otherwise you are expected to answer. As a first grader Bettina was expected to know this rule despite its subtlety and the fact that it is unlikely that it was ever explicitly formulated by the teacher.

Were rule-breaking not a possibility, a rule would not emerge. Rules and rule-breaking are thus inextricably linked. Rules are created because it is in the interest of some person(s) or group to have such rules (see Becker, 1963); it is likely to be in the interests of some other people or groups to not have those rules or to break them. Whatever the source of teachers' and school rules — even if children take part in their creation — rules may serve as the source of difficulties for children who do not support those rules or who find it in their interest to break them.

Child–Teacher Relations

As children seek to understand and craft relations with teachers, they may encounter difficulties. When, for example, teachers have taught a child's sibling, they may make assumptions about the second child based on their remembrance of the first. Some children may find the teacher's assumptions advantageous; others may not.

When I was in the sixth grade, I had a horrible teacher. She was mean and she would scream at us every single day. From the first day of school she took a dislike to me. I recall her saying, 'Clarke? Any relation to a former student of mine, Brian?' I remember cringing and telling her that he was my brother. That was the biggest mistake of the year. After that day, all she did was pick on me. My homework was never good enough and she said I was not trying. My brother was a terrible student and if he was wrongly yelled at, he made sure he spoke up about it. . .Then one day my friend was talking and the teacher blamed me and started screaming at me. I answered her back and told her it was not me. She slammed her book on her desk and said to me, 'You're a little imp, just like your brother!' I was so shocked. When I went home I told my dad about what happened and he had a meeting with her and the principal. The teacher sat there and lied to my father's face about ever making that comment to me. (Maida Clarke)

Children may find it difficult to be taken to be who they are when teachers assume them to be like someone else.

Some children love their teachers. Others do not, and the sources of their negative views may be surprising to adults. In the following story, what might be viewed as an ordinary instruction by a teacher is described as grounds for a child's ongoing fear.

I remember the first day of kindergarten. I got there a little bit later than everyone else. For some reason I did not have crayons at my desk and the kid next to me would not share. The teacher came up to him and said in a firm tone, 'Please share your crayons. You are not in nursery school.' After this, I was so afraid of her no matter how nice she was to me. (Erika, Ursula's informant)

Size, as well as other more diffuse feelings, may be a source of fear.

When I was in third or fourth grade, the teacher used to call us up to her desk and discuss our grades and our progress in the class. I always dreaded those days because I was only 10 and my teacher looked so big to me. She used to stare at me and make me feel uncomfortable. The way she said my name used to make me cringe. She tried to act so sweet but I knew deep down inside that she wasn't as sweet as everyone thought. To this day I still can't figure out what my problem with her was. The thought of her face still makes me nervous. (Anne-Marie, Ursula's informant)

Were they to become aware of children's perceptions of them, some teachers might want to change their presentations of self; others might see no need to do so. Erika's teacher might value firmness and see Erika's response as unwarranted, as Erika's problem. Teachers who do want to change the way children perceive them may upon occasion find their resources limited — Ann-Marie's teacher had little control over her size (although she might have been able to control the *appearance* of size). What is clear is that children do have perceptions of teachers, that those perceptions may be quite different from the way teachers think they are being perceived, and that children's perceptions may not necessarily be unwarranted. Anne-Marie's teacher might indeed not have been 'as sweet as everyone thought.' In understanding child–teacher relations it is useful to know how *each* views the other.

What some children view as positive others may view as negative. Lacking knowledge of children's differing perspectives, teachers are likely to find that the same practice may produce quite different responses from different children. Some children, for example, may be troubled by being ignored by a teacher — and further troubled by the failure of their efforts to remedy the situation.

> I remember always being overlooked by the teacher; all I wanted was some attention. One day I decided the only way to get the attention I needed was to make myself noticeable, so I stood up in the middle of a lesson and started to tell a story that I thought related to what the teacher was saying. She got very angry and moved my seat up close to her desk. I was so embarrassed. After that day I never volunteered my ideas to teachers, unless I was forced, and even then I would get very nervous. (Amelia's informant)

Other children may complain of being favored by a teacher.

> I guess it wasn't a bad thing to be liked by my teacher. It was just that sometimes I felt that I needed to be better than everyone else because of that. If I did not get an 'A' on an assignment I would feel like a failure. I thought that if I was so favored by the teacher it was because I could do so well. If I didn't do well I really thought that the teacher no longer liked me and I would never do good again. The pressure I felt was tremendous. (Clara, Amelia's informant)

> I thought that the teacher was acting like she liked me just to be mean. She saw how it made the other kids act but she still did not change. When she would use my papers as examples to the rest of the class all the children would laugh at me. I began to feel like the teacher was my only friend in the world. I would stay in during recess to do 'extra credit' in order to avoid the teasing of the others. That would only make her like me more. I wondered why my teacher wanted the other kids to hate me. (Ethel, Amelia's informant)

Children may find it politically useful for peer relations to act differently from the way they feel.

All the other kids really didn't like the teacher. I loved her. I thought that they were wrong when they said that she was 'mean' or 'not fair.' But I didn't want them to call me a 'teacher's pet' so sometimes I went overboard in acting as though I disliked her. I would often give her a hard time until she began to see me as a troublemaker. The problem was that I think she could tell that I really did like her. I felt bad when I was mean to her and didn't want to hurt her feelings but I wanted the others to like me. (Miriam, Amelia's informant)

That children have relations with teachers is certainly not a surprise; that they may work carefully to manage those relations may go unnoticed by adults.

I had this really neat pen that my grandma had given me and it was missing. Somehow it turned up in Pammy Hurst's pencil box. Even though Pammy was the complete opposite of me, we were friends. Good old Mrs Foster didn't like Pammy and thought she was definitely a thief. She held up the pencil box for all to see and allowed the entire class to rummage through it for any writing utensils they may have been missing. Being a 'good' student I was torn between taking my pen and losing Pammy's friendship or taking Pammy's side and helping her fight for her pencil box. . .and losing Mrs Foster's 'approval.' No matter what I chose to do, Mrs Foster would have done what she set out to do — punish Pammy. I ended up keeping my mouth shut and apologizing to Pammy afterwards at recess. She was mad but also understood my position. 'She has to like one of us,' Pammy said. Through her understanding, I was able to keep my 'identity' which Mrs Foster accepted. And although Pammy knew I disagreed with the situation, she helped to confirm the identity I had created to get what I wanted (acceptance). (Eleanor)

Teachers' 'Failings'

Children may fault teachers for acts of omission and acts of commission: for not interceding on behalf of children, for making (avoidable) mistakes, for embarrassing and humiliating children, and for being unfair. What some children deem a failing may not be so judged by other children or by adults; what are labeled 'failings' may indeed be viewed as 'strengths' by others, including those to whom they are attributed. Once again the differences between children's and teachers' perspectives are displayed.

Teachers' Failures to Intercede

When teachers fail to intercede on behalf of children, children may notice teachers' failures, fault them for their omissions, and be left on their own to suffer the consequences of their difficulties.

> When I was in kindergarten, we had to draw a picture of our families. At that time I did not have a mother. My mother had passed away when I was only 11 months old so I lived with my dad and my brother. At that time my father had been dating a woman for 4 years. They were going to get married the following year. I loved her like a real mother. Anyway, I drew a picture of my father, my brother, and my father's girlfriend. The teacher asked us about our drawings. I said my family was Dad, Jim, and Sarah. The teacher had known my mother passed away because she had my brother in her class at that time. The kids all asked me why I called my mother Sarah. I told them and one of my classmates shouted out, 'She can't be in your drawing, She's not your real family.' I looked at the teacher and she looked sympathetic but she just told him that it wasn't a very nice thing to say. She did not even send him out of the room. I was furious. I started to cry and she told me to sit down and that everything would be okay. I just remember looking at her for help and she excused the issue like it was just not a big deal! (Erika, Ursula's informant)

Adults too might fault Erika's teacher for her failure to intercede. In the following story, however, adults might find it more reasonable to fault the child's absolutist views of coloring than the teacher's failure to intercede.

> One thing that I couldn't stand was that the other kids always colored everything wrong. They would color their pictures with green skies and purple grass and stuff. It just wasn't right and the teachers never said anything. It made me so mad! (Janice, Ramona's informant)

Whether or not adults accept the grounds of children's complaints, what emerges from these two stories is that children can fault teachers for what children view as their failures to act and can experience distress from those perceived failures.

Teachers' Mistakes

Teachers may make mistakes in interpreting what is going on in situations or in grasping the underlying reasons for children's behavior. In the following story the principal's mistake suggests ignorance of the role of other children in what is labeled misbehavior.

> In the second grade I got into trouble. I was at a program in the auditorium and we were sitting boy/girl/boy/girl. The boy next to me wanted to sit where I was sitting. He told me if I didn't trade seats with him he would tell everyone that he saw my underwear. Considering what was going to happen to me if I did not do what he wanted, I

decided to trade seats with him. I got caught and was yelled at by the principal of our school. (Carol)

When children's explanations are not sought, are ignored, are viewed as irrelevant, or are not believed, teachers may be deprived of important information to explain children's behavior. Consequences for children may be painful.

When I was young, I had a problem with my legs. I walked on my toes until I was 8. In first grade, we had a song called the elephant song. We all walked around in a circle pretending to be elephants. The teachers pulled me aside and told me I had to walk on my heels. My parents and I had been working on physical therapy every night. Therapy was painful for me and I used to cry. My mom would have to stretch my muscles every night and they hurt. They did not know why I walked on my toes and they tried to correct the problem. I remember trying to tell them why I walked on my toes but it wasn't of any use. (Erika, Ursula's informant)

Children may fault teachers for mistakes consequent upon teachers' not listening or, when they do listen, of not believing what children tell them.

This happened when I was in second grade. I had to retake a quiz because the teacher thought that I was copying. The teacher saw me talking to my classmate but my classmate was the one who started asking me questions about the quiz. The teacher told me to walk up to her desk. The teacher was really mad at me and I felt really scared and hopeless. I was caught at the wrong moment. The teacher threw away my old quiz and made me take the quiz over. I was almost in tears. I had to do my quiz on her desk and without sitting. She didn't believe me that I wasn't cheating. She wanted to see me do the quiz in front of her. I was very nervous because I felt that she was pressuring me. When I finished the quiz I gave it to her. I was really mad because she was so unfair and mean to me. She didn't even give me a chance to explain what really happened. I think that even if she had given me the chance she wouldn't possibly believe me anyway. (Lorna)

The following story involves a teacher's spelling error in which she 'corrects' a child who has greater knowledge than she. It also displays adults' trust of one another, for the teacher did not correct the child's mother.

When I was in the first grade my teacher spelled my name R-o-s-a-l-i-e when it is really spelled R-o-s-a-l-y. I knew the right way to spell it and did so on all of my papers. Every time I would get a paper back, my teacher had corrected the spelling of my name. I really didn't understand why but hated seeing red marks on my papers so I began spelling my name her way. My mom discovered it and got really angry. I explained my actions to her by saying, 'My teacher told me I don't know how to spell my own name.' Needless to say, I never spelled it her way again. (Rosaly)

In his novel *Hard Times* (1854), Charles Dickens describes a similar interaction, that between a visiting teacher, Mr Gradgrind, and a student.

'Girl number twenty,' said Mr Gradgrind, squarely pointing with his square forefinger, 'I don't know that girl. Who is that girl?'

'Sissy Jupe, sir,' explained number twenty, blushing, standing up, and curtseying.

'Sissy is not a name,' said Mr Gradgrind. 'Don't call yourself Sissy. Call yourself Cecilia.'

'It's father as calls me Sissy, sir,' returned the young girl in a trembling voice, and with another curtsy.

'Then he has no business to do it,' said Mr Gradgrind. 'Tell him he mustn't.' (p. 8)

Unlike Rosaly's teacher, Mr Gradgrind is unmoved by parental preferences.

The Principal's Mistake
by Lily

When I was 5, I took dance lessons after kindergarten class. The dance class was a combination of tap and ballet. At the end of the dance program there was a recital. Our class routine was to dance to the song 'Good Ship Lollipop.' The costume was red and has all these shiny circles on it that were to represent gum drops. We had a red sparkle headband and black tap shoes. On Wednesdays at school we had 'Show and Tell,' where we could bring things in to show the class. Well, I couldn't wait for the day when I was going to be able to bring my costume in and dance in front of my kindergarten class. My mother wouldn't let me take the costume to school until after the recital. So after the weekend of the recital I brought the costume to class. I got all dressed up and did my dance in front of the class. The principal had been asked to come and watch me while I did my dance. Afterwards the principal sat me on his lap and started to joke around with me in front of the class. He asked if he could try on my headband but I replied that he was too big and it wouldn't fit him. He said that the headband would fit anyone's head. I still said no, he couldn't put it on, because I was the only one who could and would wear the headband. After saying that, my teacher was very mad at me. She scolded me, saying that I knew better than to say things like that and that I was to let him wear the headband. He promised me that nothing would happen to it. Feeling all this pressure I was left with no choice but to give in so I took it off my head and entrusted it to him. He then proceeded to put it on his head and dance around. The other kids in the class laughed at him but I was very sad by this and told him that he was dancing all wrong. Next thing I knew he had broken the headband when he took it off his head. I was so angry I began to cry. Why hadn't he listened to me? I had told him that it wouldn't fit his head. How could he have broken the one thing that meant so much to me? I just sat there and cried with the two pieces of headband in my hands. The teacher and principal told me to stop acting like a baby, that it was an accident. According to them there was nothing to do to fix it so it was useless to cry. I then heard them laughing in the corner. How could people be so cruel? I never wanted to go back to kindergarten again.

* * *

Teachers as Source
of Embarrassment and Humiliation

School can provide children with many occasions for embarrassment and humiliation. Apparently well-meaning acts by teachers are one such source.

> I can remember the horror and embarrassment my classmates and I felt when we witnessed and experienced 'The Birthday Paddle.' We were in the fourth grade yet we felt like first-graders when our teacher brought out 'The Birthday Paddle' whenever it was someone's birthday. The birthday child was forced to stand up in front of the class while the class sang 'Happy Birthday.' Then the teacher proceeded to spank the child's bottom with the paddle. I remember laughing along with the rest of the class at other students but I dreaded the day of my birthday. (Ruby)

Embarrassment may be a product of a teacher's lack of awareness.

> When the teacher would line us up by height, I would always be the last. I always felt embarrassed. I felt like I stood out because I was different. (Margie's informant)

Embarrassment may also be intended. As Allison describes her experience in the following story, her teacher not only intends to embarrass her but draws pleasure from so doing. Her concealment of embarrassment is described not as self-protection but as retaliation.

> One day in gym class in second grade I remember getting into trouble. I was a friendly type of person and I guess that I should not have been, at least not in that class. My gym teacher, Mr Renato, was a real

macho kind of guy. He used to wear tight jeans and tight T-shirts and he used to think that he was real cool. I did not like him that much but after this fateful day I disliked him even more. We were sitting all in a line on the floor. We were being told the rules of a game that we would be playing that day. It was called 'Steal the Bacon' and all of us knew how to play it so we were bored. I was looking around the gym and I noticed that my friend from sixth grade was walking by. My cousin Jane used to baby-sit for her and so I knew her from outside of school. I felt privileged that I knew her. She waved to me and so I waved back. I was not about to ignore her. Even though I was only in second grade, I knew the implications of not waving back to some-one I knew and also someone who was older than me. Mr Renato saw me wave to her and he became very angry. I was scared when I turned around and saw that look in his eyes. He said, 'Allison, since you think you are so smart and you do not have to play this game because you are too above us in mentality, you can go and stand outside next to the door. You do not deserve to play with us.' I was so humiliated because he had yelled at me in front of the entire class. I went and stood outside the door and I watched all of the kids playing the game and they seemed to have so much fun, but I did not let them see how upset I was. I especially did not want Mr Renato to see how upset I was because I thought that he would enjoy it too much and so I wanted to make him suffer. I know that the words he used were too much for me to handle and I did not understand what he was saying to me, except that I knew he was mad at me. Even though I did not understand what he had said, I still remember the words because I had been so upset with him. (Allison)

Allison describes herself as with little choice but to upset someone. Children may be feel both troubled and wronged when they are faulted and punished for making what they view as a 'reasonable' choice.

Children's 'failings' may serve as a source of embarrassment when teachers make those failings public.

I remember an incident in the third grade when I had lots of trouble learning to tell time. My teacher would always make a big deal out of it in front of the class and I was so embarrassed because I felt so stupid. He would always make sure that I was wearing a watch. In the beginning of my fourth grade year, when I had just come back from summer vacation, he tracked me down at recess to check my wrist to make sure I had a watch line. I still had trouble telling time a long time after and his 'humiliation method' didn't work! (Rosaly)

In gym class, the teacher used to make us do jumping jacks. I was one of those uncoordinated children who had two left feet. The teacher noticed I did not know how to do jumping jacks and called me to the front. He then proceeded to ask me if I would do ten jumping jacks in front of the class and show every one how not to do them. I still remember how embarrassing this was. (Aaron, Ursula's informant)

Teachers may intentionally use public humiliation both as a 'teaching method' and as punishment.

I remember a teacher I was very scared of because one time she caught me biting my nails. She forced me to bite my nails in front of the whole class. I was humiliated. (Henrietta, Natalie's informant)

Children's failings are not the only source of embarrassment and humiliation; public compliments may also prove troublesome.

In first grade the teacher would take me in front of the class and tell everyone how pretty my dresses were. I was really shy and this humiliated me. (Margie's informant)

In the face of protective or remedial measures that teachers take towards them and on their behalf, children may feel not protected but inadequate, incompetent, 'dumb,' and babied and publicly displayed to be so.

I was tested by a school psychologist because I was having a lot of trouble in math, more trouble than most kids were having. After completing the tests, which I had to be pulled out of class for, I was told that I had a learning disability that caused me to have problems with spatial and visual perception. This may not sound like something that could interfere with a child's well-being but it did with mine. You see, I started to get tutored before school every morning and the worst part of it was that I had to walk into class an hour after everyone else. This made me feel different, like I was some kind of underachiever. Well, as much as my teachers tried to help, they really didn't do a good job because this was before there were all of those programs in schools for kids with learning disabilities. I felt as if I was all alone and that there was a barrier separating me from all the other kids. My parents tried to help me feel like I was just as good as everyone else even though I tended to regard myself as dumb. (Pam)

Children may be aware not only of their own embarrassment but that of other children.

George said one of the worst memories from his childhood was when the teacher would call on a student who obviously did not know the answer. He said he felt so embarrassed for the kid. 'It was worst when the teacher would call the student up to the board and they did not know the answer. Whenever that happened to me I know I was embarrassed, so I can imagine how the other kids felt.' He said he hated watching them struggle at the board. He knew how they felt and wanted to help them. He said he never understood why teachers did that to their students. He can understand if the teacher thinks that the student was not paying attention and wants to prove a point. But to do it to a student who does not understand the problem, it seems mean to make them do it on the board. When he realized that I wanted to become an elementary school teacher he begged me never to do it to one of my students when I get a classroom. (Esther's informant)

Whether children are embarrassed and humiliated intentionally or unintentionally, for didactic or punitive reasons or by accident, they may indeed find their experiences trying.

Teachers' Unfairness

When teachers and children have different perspectives, children may judge teachers' perspectives as not only wrong but unfair.

The teacher always wrote home to my parents that I would be a good student if I was 'better behaved' and my parents would get very angry, thinking that I created problems in school. But it seemed to me that everything I did got me in trouble. I would answer a question that a friend next to me asked and be kept after school for talking and the person who asked the question would not even be spoken to. I felt like I was always picked on. (Amelia's informant)

Even when apparently inevitable, unfairness may still be a source of distress.

In kindergarten I remember when it was somebody's birthday we had a big celebration and all day long that child could be first at everything. That bothered me a lot because my birthday is in August. (Marcia, Natalie's informant)[2]

Children may recognize favoritism as a particular type of unfairness.

The teacher's niece was in Vivian's class. One day while out in the playground, Vivian had an ice pop. The teacher's niece went up to her

---

[2] A teacher with whom I discussed this story questioned the inevitability of this unfairness, suggesting that teachers can provide 'unbirthdays' for such children.

and told her she wanted the ice pop. Vivian said no. The girl stood there a minute, then she pushed Vivian into a huge puddle. . .Vivian said she was drenched from head to toe and covered in mud. There was no way she could stay in school and a policeman had to drive her home from school since she lived so far. Vivian told me, 'I still remember that Evangeline, her name was Evangeline, and she didn't even get in trouble. . .She got away with everything because her aunt was the teacher.' (Maida's informant)

In the following story, Larry complains of a reverse sort of 'favoritism,' that directed towards troublemakers.

Larry, a fifth-grader, told me, 'Mom says I have a good teacher, but I don't think so.' When I asked him why, his answer was, 'She doesn't spend enough time with the class. She spends too much time with the troublemakers. She just doesn't do what she should.' (Larry, Ramona's informant)

One strategy that teachers may use when some students 'misbehave' is to punish or deprive all students. From a teacher's perspective such a strategy may seem reasonable; from a child's perspective it may be deemed unfair.

Another hardship that I remember is from the year I was in fourth grade. We were having a Christmas party and the boys started to take the Nerds candy and shoot it through their straws across the room. The teacher finally saw it and got very angry. She yelled at the entire class and we weren't allowed to have Nerds in the classroom for the rest of the year. . .I didn't think this was fair because only certain people were doing it. Why should I be punished if I wasn't doing anything? (Ramona)

It may be very difficult for teachers to know whom to blame when blame is being distributed. For children, especially when as participants they have greater knowledge of what occurred, teachers' mistakes in assigning blame may be viewed as wrong and unfair as well as troubling and consequential.

Belinda recalls her experience with an unfair punishment that occurred when she was in the second grade. The students wrote out their spelling words each week. One of her words happened to be the word 'it.' While she was out of her seat, a boy changed her word into an inappropriate one. When she returned to her seat, she began to laugh at the sight of the word on her paper. This got the teacher's attention. When the teacher saw her paper, she immediately thought the girl was to blame. Without asking any questions, she hit the girl with a ruler. (Belinda, Ruby's informant)

Some unfairness would thus appear to be inevitable in classrooms. What teachers view as fair, children may view as unfair, and vice versa. Teachers and children can differ among themselves. When teachers of necessity turn their attention to some children, others — or even those attended to — may find it unfair. Unavoidable though it may be, teachers' recognition of unfairness allows them to minimize it or, failing that, to offer children some explanation or some remedy.

Dealing with School Trials:
Failed Strategies
by Lily

As a child growing up I had my share of bad times. I think one of the things that I had the most trouble with as a child was sharing. An incident I can remember was when I was about 6 years old and in the first grade. One afternoon every week we had an art class. This art class included cutting, pasting, coloring, or painting. The one thing you could count on was the use of scissors sometime during the art class. For some reason, they never provided enough scissors for everyone even though everyone was going to need to use them. At the time I really felt that if they had provided enough scissors, it would have prevented bad incidents from happening. Each art class a basket of scissors was placed on the front table. It was a first come first served basis, from which the scissors were to be shared at the different tables. I never was able to get to the basket fast enough to get a pair of scissors. When I did finally get to the scissors there were only left-handed scissors left. This was totally useless to me because I was right-handed. I never understood why they made so many left-handed scissors when the majority of students were right-handed. I found it too frustrating to figure out how to use the left-handed scissors on my right hand although I have to admit several attempts were made. The reason getting scissors was so important to me was because they were needed to achieve the ultimate goal. This goal was to be the first one done with the project so it could be used as a model for the other students, for the teacher always praised the first student done with their project. The problem came when I had to wait for a pair of scissors so I could finish my project. I mean to wait for someone at your table to finish using the scissors so that then you could have your chance was asking the impossible. To watch everyone else finish their project and then be the last one took all the fun out of doing the project. So, as a 6-year-old, I thought I would outsmart the situation. On Monday I brought my mother's pair of scissors that I knew if I let them out of my sight I would get in trouble at home. So when we started to get the supplies together that we were going to need for the project, I made a quick dash for the basket so no one would suspect what I had done. I then secretly took the scissors from my desk and started cutting away. When I finished cutting I put the scissors on the table. I picked up a marker and started coloring the project. The girl next to me then grabbed the scissors away from me. This started the whole argument as we pulled and yelled at each other over the scissors. Well, with the determination I had I was able to get the scissors back in hand. This girl then started to cry; this of course brought the teacher running. I was so mad at her. Why couldn't she just use someone else's scissors? I had no trouble sharing the school's things but when it came to my own, forget it. The teacher came over saying that in this classroom we share things. I tried to say that I wasn't finished using the scissors when she had grabbed them out of my hand but I looked a little suspicious with the scissors in my left hand and a marker in my right hand with the cap off and a good part of the project half colored. I had no choice but to give them up although I tried with everything I had to keep hold of them. I even tried the crying act with the yelling and then screaming by saying she grabbed them first and it was not fair. I was soon to find myself out in the hallway. The teacher moved a desk out in the hall and made me think about what I had done. She said maybe after a little time out I would be more reasonable and be able to join the class again. I was so angry at her. If only she had understood who was the one being unreasonable!

*   *   *

Lily's story weaves together many of the strands of troubles presented in this chapter: differing perspectives provided by home and school (regarding access to scissors); differing perspectives of teacher and child (on the goal of art projects); rules and procedures (sharing); child–teacher relations (the teacher's unwanted intervention); unfairness (used by Lily as a strategy for extricating herself from her predicament); and the teacher's failing (misunderstanding the situation). Lily's story also describes some of the strategies — albeit for her unsuccessful — that children may use to alleviate the little trials of childhood, strategies that are the topic of the next chapter, in which they meet with greater success.

9 Crying and Temper Tantrums, Lying and Subterfuge, and Other Strategies for Dealing with the Little Trials of Childhood

> It seems to me that because of my position I had to find ways to read my mother and other adults so I could manipulate them. (Tammy)

> As a small child, I knew how to get adults to 'approve' of me. It was quite simple: be cute, do what you're told, and don't question authority. My third grade teacher was a firm believer in my theory — and she loved me! If that old woman only knew how I felt about her, it would break her mean heart. (Eleanor)

Initially I did not plan to study strategies for dealing with the little trials of childhood — indeed did not know they were there to be studied — but their abundant and varied appearance in the data I gathered warrants specific attention. In previous chapters, strategies appear within the context of trials; in this chapter I consider them in their own right. Whether strategies meet with success or failure, their very existence suggests that children can take action to ease their trails, craft strategies with knowledge, skill, care, and attention, and employ them with pride and an appreciation of their own cleverness. Learning and making use of adults' weaknesses, children may also come to a somewhat lowered estimation of adults' knowledge and competence.

Crying and Temper Tantrums

Although children's crying and temper tantrums may certainly reflect distress, they may, alternatively or simultaneously, be used intentionally to lessen or avoid trials or to guarantee rewards for enduring them. Adults who assume children to be incapable of such use facilitate their success. In the following story the success of the strategy motivates its continued use even when the trial itself has abated.

> I was about 3 or 4 years old and had to go to the dentist for the first time. The expedition was a disaster. I was terrified of the doctor and

screamed whenever he tried to get me to 'open up.' When he finally succeeded in making me open my mouth, I bit his hand. After that visit, the mere mention of the word dentist would send me into fits of crying. Finally my mother came up with the brilliant idea of rewarding me for being brave and letting the doctor look inside my mouth. She promised me a trip to the toy store to pick out a special gift. I agreed and was thrilled with the results. As I got used to the dentist, my fears diminished. I recall thinking that if this were known to my mother, she would no longer buy me any more toys. It was then that I realized I could control the situation. By keeping up the pretense and continuing the dramatic performances of which I was capable, I could hold the advantage over my mother and keep things the way I wanted them. (Josie)

Crying may also prove useful in preventing or assuaging punishment.

Being sent to bed early was my major punishment. I never learned my lesson from an early bedtime. It just taught me to keep some toys under my pillow so I could play until I was tired. It also taught me how to fake cry and pretend to be sorry even though I wasn't sorry at all. (Holly)

Note also Holly's strategy of making advanced preparations to lessen punishment (hiding toys).

For children faced with serious punishment, crying may be viewed as providing some degree of protection (and adults may forbid crying for just that reason). In the following story Yvonne describes her use of what she insightfully refers to as 'half-pretend tears.'

Intentional Crying as a Strategy
by Yvonne

Punishment was always a major issue for me. I hated to be punished, hit, spanked, restricted, or yelled at, especially by my father, so I would try to avoid it by crying. I remember when I was in my elementary years and my brother and I got in trouble, my father would come flying out of the kitchen with a wooden spoon in his raised hand. He would swing it around as he ran after us and yell obscenities. My brother would run around and laugh at him, which made him even more angry. I would run to the nearest corner, usually in the living room, and sit crying. When my father approached me I would cry harder while pleading with him not to hit me. I figured if I put on my 'puppy dog eyes' and cried hard enough that he would feel bad for me and not swing that spoon in my direction. This did not always turn out in my favor but I was convinced that if I did not conjure up these half-pretend tears and fears, I would have gotten hurt worse. The worst part of this type of punishment was that later my dad would claim it hurt him worse but from my point of view I could not understand this until he tried to confine me to the house for a week.

Whenever I did something that I knew I would be in lots of trouble for when my father found out, I would make sure I had a sad, wet face when he got home from work. When I was 12 years old, my parents found out from some nosy neighbors that I had a boy in the house while they were not there. This was a big 'no-no' and considered very punishable if it ever happened. When the door shut at 5:00 p.m., I heard my father's voice from my bedroom. I began to shudder because I knew that he was being informed of my after-noon incident. I knew that I had to do something so he would not yell at me. I had to show up tearful but no matter what I did I could not cry. I snuck out of my room and went to my parents' medicine cabinet. I knew my father always kept eye drops in there for the mornings that he was hung-over. I squirted two drops in each eye, then splashed some water on my face. As soon as I heard my mother call for me to come downstairs, I made my face look red, sad, and regretful. I slowly walked downstairs with my head hung low and tried to conjure up my own tears, which came easily now because I was quite nervous. I tried to think of what I was going to say, but I stood there with my mind blank. Suddenly all kinds of words came out of my mouth. 'I'm sorry,' I said. 'I promise it'll never happen again.' I continued with, 'Please, don't hit me!' At this point, I think my act began to work. All he could say was, 'You're grounded until Monday!' All I could think was, 'A whole week?' I would rather have the spanking.

*　*　*

Noteworthy in Yvonne's second example is both the apparent success of her strategy and her perception of it as ultimately a failure ('I would rather have the spanking'). Children's ranking of hardships may differ from adults'.

Although initially I was inclined to view temper tantrums as little trials of childhood, troublesome for children and an expression of their distress and lack of control — and indeed for some children they may be — my data indicates that children may also use them intentionally, manipulating their portrayal of emotions as a strategy, albeit not always successful, for assuaging their trials (or for achieving their ends).

Talking about temper tantrums is a very easy topic for me. As a child they happened all the time. I remember one tantrum in particular. My mother, my sister, and I were on our way to watch the fireworks show in my town on the 4th of July. I was around 3 years old at the time. I was getting tired of walking so I wanted my mother to carry me. I kept bothering her to pick me up but she refused to do so. I began to cry and jump up and down but she still kept walking. I stopped where I was and held my breath until I turned blue and passed out. Of course after falling face first into the dirt I became conscious again but my mother would still not pick me up. I was furious!

Although I never had another tantrum as bad as the 4th of July incident, I did have a few more problems controlling my temper. Whenever my mother would tell me my cousins were coming over I used to kick and scream because I didn't want them to play with my toys. About an hour before they would arrive I would run into my room and hide all of my toys. I would refuse to tell anybody where they were until my cousins had gone. (Dawn)

Children may find, as did Dawn, that temper tantrums are less effective than other strategies (in Dawn's example, hiding toys). Tantrums, however, may indeed accomplish their goals. Interestingly, in the following story, the reason Doreen gives for being locked in her room (a temper tantrum) also serves as the means of her release. (Doreen does not describe the purpose and success or failure of the initial tantrums.)

One thing I clearly remember was the lock on the outside of my bedroom door. I used to throw terrible temper tantrums. When I started doing this my mother would lock me in my room. After about fifteen minutes, I would throw the card table that was kept behind my door onto the floor. I would make a loud crash, then I would crawl halfway underneath it and wait for my mother to come. When she opened the door I would run out. I can't remember what she would do to me after that, but I never could figure out why they never took the card table out from behind my door. (Doreen)

Tears and temper tantrums may, however, prove unsuccessful.

I found tears and tantrums to be a very ineffective method of coping with my restrictions because the tears and tantrums only served as a reinforcement of my parents' belief that I was a 'baby' because I acted like one in times of distress. (Jill, Greg's informant)

And thus children may seek other strategies. The following account displays the complexity involved in children's developing alternatives to crying and temper tantrums in the face of adults' ambiguous and contradictory suggestions.

In Search of Strategies
by Eileen

As a young child I often had much difficulty in expressing my inner emotions and feelings. I wasn't sure how to let people know how I felt. I didn't know how to put those feelings inside me into words. Instead, I would cry for long periods of time or throw temper tantrums to release the pressure and tension that would build up inside me. My parents thought it was a childhood phase and let it go on for many years without thinking a thing of it. As years went on, my parents began to become worried about my problem. They would often sit me down and explain to me how important it was that I tell them how I felt. They told me that I should learn to 'speak my mind' instead of holding it in. They told me it would make me feel much better. By the time I had begun school, my parents were still frequently having discussions with me about expressing my feelings and now my teachers had begun to do the same thing. By the time I had reached the first grade, I began to realize that my crying wasn't getting me anywhere anymore and I realized that it was all part of the plan between my teachers and parents to get me to 'speak my mind.' What they did was just ignore me when I cried or threw a temper tantrum. Maybe this would make me open up. Well, I guess it worked. I was so sick of being ignored. Things just weren't working out the way they used to. I decided to try things their way. This was when all the problems began.

I began to express my feelings. I began to 'speak my mind.' I told my parents and my teachers exactly how I felt about everything they did and everything they said. I let them know everything I was feeling and never left a single thought out. There was only one problem. I didn't know that there was a certain way I was supposed to express my feelings. I didn't know that I was supposed to speak softly instead of yelling. I didn't know I was supposed to censor myself as my feelings came pouring from my mouth. I didn't know I was supposed to say only things that my parents and teachers wanted to hear. I was just told to 'speak my mind' and that was exactly what I was doing. Nobody had ever told me about the details. It had been such an accomplishment for me. I thought everyone would be so proud of me because I had finally learned how to tell them how I felt. Evidently they weren't as happy and proud of me as I thought they would be. Every time I expressed my feelings, I would get myself into trouble. My parents would punish me by grounding me and making me stay in the house after school for weeks at a time. They used to tell me that it hurt them more than it hurt me. I could never understand that. There were a lot of things I just couldn't understand. I often would wonder, 'Why am I being punished after saying what I said when all along I've been told how important it is for me to say openly how I feel?' That just never made sense to me. It still doesn't make much sense to me.

This went on until about the fifth grade. I would 'speak my mind' and I would be punished for it. By this time I was tired of being punished. I wanted to go out and play with my friends. I didn't want to be grounded all the time. I knew that there had to be a way I could keep myself from getting into so much trouble. That is when the idea finally hit me. I thought if I didn't say anything, if I didn't express my feelings at all, if I just sat quietly when my parents and teachers said something or did something I didn't agree with, then I couldn't get into any trouble. It was as easy as that.

I tried out my new plan and it worked out wonderfully. When my parents or teachers made me angry, I would just sit there. I wouldn't speak, I wouldn't cry, I wouldn't show any signs of hidden feelings. I never said anything. This way my parents never had a reason to punish me. It was terrific. I was having a grand old time going with my friends and having fun and never having to worry about being grounded. There was just one problem. I didn't think this problem was that bad at the time. My feelings and emotions were growing inside me. Every day they built up more and more. By the end of the week, I was so frustrated that I just laid in bed and cried. I wished that there were someone who really wanted to know how I felt. I wished that there were someone who didn't care if what I was saying was a good thing to say. I wished that there were someone who didn't care how I told them how I felt or how loud I was when I told them. I wished that there were someone who really cared about me, as a person, a real person with real live feelings. But there was no such person. Mom and Dad wanted to know how I felt — as long as I told them the way they wanted to be told. But I just couldn't do it that way and so the only way to keep myself from getting into trouble, I decided, was to keep my mouth shut. After all, a little bit of crying by myself was better than being grounded in the house by myself.

Well, it worked then and I guess you could say it still works.

* * *

Although Eileen describes considerable effort devoted to crafting her strategies, she might have benefited from adults' understanding and assistance in developing ones less costly for her.

Lying and Subterfuge

In Chapter 6 I discussed how children may come to learn both that adults lie and that adults view as lies that which children take to be the truth. Learning that adults can lie in the service of adults' ends, children may divert this strategy to their own ends, including those of which adults disapprove. Children may, alternatively, discover the efficacy of lies through their own efforts or through consultation with others. Here I illustrate some of the sources whereby children can learn to lie and the uses they may make of their knowledge. Whatever the source of their knowledge, children may find lying a useful way to ease the little trials of childhood.

Children may learn both to lie and how to do so at the direct urging of adults.

The favorite line in my house was, 'Don't tell Dad,' even for my mother. I was always taught to tell the truth and found it very easy to do to everyone except my father, who was the one who stressed it the most. Whenever something went wrong, my family would gather, with the exception of my father, and try to figure out a good story, or 'lie' if you will, to tell my father about the situation at hand. . .I use 'lie' because we never told an absolute lie, like 'a burglar came into the house and broke the railing while taking my television down the stairs.' There was always some truth in the story. (Jane)

The teaching of politeness can serve as an occasion for 'lying lessons.' If children are instructed to tell the truth *and* to be polite, and if these two rules conflict, they may find themselves with both a dilemma and an opportunity for learning to lie. Sacks writes,

> If children are asked some question, one of whose alternative answers may occasion a rebuke and another not, then apparently they learn, and apparently it is learned that they have learned, to produce answers that are directed to avoiding the rebuke, which answer production can involve them in lying. (1975, p. 75)

In matters of politeness, children may well find a lie to be the answer that avoids rebuke.

Choosing politeness over truth, however, presents its own problems, both because one is required to lie and because one is expected to conceal what may be very serious disappointment. The following stories demonstrate the difficulties that can be submerged under lies.

> I can remember how many things were difficult as a child. . .One difficult thing was when my parents gave me all kinds of presents and I didn't like them. . .I remember once I was very sick at the hospital with an acute infection and my father brought me a coloring book with crayons. This coloring book wasn't the one I wanted with Snoopy and Charlie Brown. I remember taking it and thanking my daddy for the present. I started to color it in front of my daddy. He thought I was very pleased and delighted with the present but when he left I started crying and I threw the book and crayons on the floor. (Claire)

> When I was 6, I had an operation on my eye. The hospital I went into was huge. Everything smelled like medicine and all the furniture seemed drab. I had to stay in a room with five old men, which made me nervous because they were so sick and I thought they were going to die in front of me. I was so scared. When the operation was over, my father told me he would buy me any toy I wanted. I told him I wanted a Barbie doll with a motorbike. A little while later, he came back with a fake Barbie doll. I was so upset because it wasn't what I wanted but I couldn't upset my father so I pretended that I liked it

and didn't complain. I was so afraid of hurting his feelings, I played with it, but only when he was around. I didn't want him to think he had failed me. (Sara)

To understand the seriousness of lies urged upon children in the service of politeness, it is important to recognize that gifts are one of children's very few ways of obtaining desired goods. Great disappointment requires a great lie if the disappointment is to be concealed. Receiving presents thus is an occasion for children to experience serious distress, for the feeling of disappointment with certain presents received is conjoined with concealment of that disappointment, telling a lie, and intentionally constructing what one knows to be a falsely pleasurable definition of the situation. Children may, nonetheless, endure their own disappointment silently in order to keep adults from distress.

When adults demand that children 'be' a certain way and when such 'being' conflicts with children's projects, children may find lying a useful strategy for conflict resolution. (For another strategy, 'being crazy,' see Meynell, 1971.) In the following story, lying is used as a strategy for appearing to others as different from what parental restrictions allow, accompanied by a fear of parental discovery.

> One problem I had. . .is that I always had a very early bedtime. Most of my friends were allowed to stay up until 9:30 or 10:00, while I was always in bed by 7:30 or 8:00. When I was in first grade, the PTA in our town did a survey on how much television the children watched. Seeing as not all of us could write yet, our class had to do the survey orally. One of the questions in the survey was what time we went to bed at night. I decided to lie about my bedtime so my friends wouldn't make fun of me for having to go to bed so early. After the survey was completed throughout the school, the PTA held a meeting to discuss the results. My mother, who never missed a PTA meeting, was of course going the night the results were going to be discussed. I was terrified that she would find out that I had lied about my bedtime. (Sally)

Lies may also be useful simply to obtain what one wants.

> My brother would argue with me over what we were going to watch on TV. Just before our yelling would escalate to a real fight I'd scream 'Mommy, Tim hit me!' Of course my mother would scream and yell and say things like 'Tim, you're older. You should know better,' or 'Go and pick on someone your own size.' And I always got to watch what I wanted.' (Lisa)

Instead of or in addition to direct lies, children may employ subterfuge. Informants offer abundant and detailed stories of faking illness as an effective way of avoiding undesired activities in general and school in particular. Using their bodies as resources, children may craft false definitions of situations to gain their own ends and to manipulate adults. Adults desirous of a 'mental health day' may simply plead illness; without this resource, children may turn to an enactment of illness. This enactment, to children's distress, may fail.

> Every kid loves to stay home from school and watch television all day instead of being in school. A few of my friends would be absent at least once a month because they had a headache or just played sick. My mother would never let me stay home unless I had a temperature and it just was not fair. I tried to play sick many times but it just never worked. I did end up with the perfect attendance award each year but I would have much rather have had a day at home being a couch potato! (Theresa)

Faking illness may, however, prove remarkably successful. Considerable thought and effort may facilitate success, as is evidenced in the following story.

The Craft of Faking Illness
by Wilma

My most memorable experience as a child began when I was in the first grade. As a child I would do just about anything to get out of going to gym class. Sometimes this would mean getting out of school for the entire day. . .As a child I was pretty good at pretending to be sick. I had two major plans of attack.

The first scheme was 'The Fake Fever.' Whenever I told my mother that I wasn't feeling well the first thing she would do was to take my temperature. I had two different ways of dealing with this. If I knew she was going to take it, I would first drink a cup of hot water. The water would raise the temperature slightly but the amount it moved it was enough to convince her that I was not feeling well. Her next question would be if I thought I could make it through school. I would answer her in my sweet, innocent voice, 'I could try if you don't want to stay home with me.' The guilt would always get her, so she would usually tell me to stay home because I was probably coming down with something.

The second scheme took a bit more work on my part. As soon as my mother put the thermometer in my mouth, I would tell her that I needed to go to the bathroom. Once in the bathroom, I would start the hot water dripping. That way, when I was ready to wash my hands the water would be very hot. After washing my hands, I would stick the thermometer under the hot water. By this time the water was hot enough to raise the mercury enough to give me the temperature that I wanted for that day. By using the water I was able to control how 'sick' I was going to be.

In my home town, the school nurse had a rule that, 'If a child has a temperature of 100 degrees or more the night before a school day, he/she should not attend school the next day.' Keeping this rule in mind, I would put on the same stunt as in the morning. This way I wouldn't have to go to school the next day. Knowing that I wasn't going to school the next day gave me, not my brother or sister, the benefits of a weekend night. This meant I was able to watch television until 9:00, I didn't have to put out my clothes for the next day, and I was allowed to have a bedtime snack. Then, around 10:00 the next morning, the fever would miraculously disappear and I was free to play for the remainder of the day.

My most vicious scheme for staying out of school was the 'Fake Stomach Ache.' I would usually decide the night before if I wanted to be sick the following day. Once my mind was made up, I would complain a little the night before that I had a stomach ache and nausea. Before I went to sleep I would set my Mickey Mouse alarm clock for fifteen minutes earlier than usual. That way, I would be up around the same time as my mother. My mother usually woke up ten minutes before she actually got out of bed. At this point I would be up when she was still lying in bed. I would then walk to the bathroom and turn on the light, something I never did in the morning when I had to go to the bathroom. Next I would take a Dixie cup from the dispenser and fill it with water. This was not ordinary water. The water I used was from the toilet. If I had taken it from the faucet my mother would have heard the water running. After I scooped up the water and checked to make sure Mom was still in bed, I would hold the Dixie cup as high as I could, fake a couple of burps, and slowly pour the water back into the toilet. The water falling in would give the sound of vomit. I would then quickly flush the toilet, and start whining for my mother to come quick. Mom would come running and sit with me in the bathroom to make sure I was 'finished.' Then she would say, 'Guess who's not going to school today?' Once she had said that I would pretend that I wanted to go to school because of a special activity we had that day. But Mom would always insist that I had to stay home, and once Mom made up her mind, I never fought her decision.

Another memory I have about faking sick was that I never pretended on my father's day off. Since my dad was a veterinarian I was always afraid that he would figure out my tricks whereas I knew my mother would never doubt me because, like my mother always said, 'You are the only one who knows how you feel.'

* * *

Wilma's story displays extensive knowledge and effort in setting the scene of her 'illness' and careful assessment of who can and who cannot be duped. The skills she displays are by no means atypical of the many 'faking illness' stories

I have gathered. These stories describe a range of skills employed to construct complex scenes, some of which are detailed by Wilma in the foregoing story and in the following excerpts from a story by Ruth. These skills include:

- *Sophisticated acting abilities*
  'When I wanted to stay home sick I would put on a big act.'
- *Advanced planning*
  'Usually the night before I'd start to complain of not feeling good.'
- *Use of props*
  'To try to avoid the thermometer I would always put a hot wet face cloth on my forehead. This way when mom felt my forehead it was hot and sweaty feeling.'
- *Knowledge of the 'look' of illness*
  'I'd try to look still half asleep by messing up my hair and pale by putting powder on my face' and 'I would complain of a sore throat or a stomach ache because how can you prove either of those?'

Given the thought and effort Ruth describes devoting to her subterfuge, one might suspect that she viewed school attendance as a serious problem but she concludes her story, 'I was a student who generally liked school, so there weren't many days when I pulled this stunt, but when I did it was successful.'

Abigail describes with apparent pleasure the challenge of faking illness, suggesting that while staying home may be the primary goal, fooling adults can sweeten victory.

> Playing sick was my favorite activity. It was a challenge. My parents were very strict about missing school and usually if I did not play it up as much as I could I would have to go to school. Even when I was sick for real with a high temperature, I would have to do extra sneezing, extra coughing, and extra complaining in order to stay away from school. I would usually mentally set myself to get up at about 3:00 or 4:00 in the morning, and when I did I would start coughing so loud and hard that when my parents looked at my throat it was indeed red. I would also put cotton swabs up my nose to make myself sneeze. Sometimes I would put a penny under my tongue to raise my temperature when I was given a thermometer. Somehow the metal of the penny made the temperature go up. One day I put a thermometer under the hot tap water and it exploded! I was terrified, and my mother was not happy with me! Eventually I got to be pretty good at playing sick. (Abigail)

Given the problematic nature of faking a high temperature, Marian developed the following strategy.

> One of my most favorite things to do was to tell my mother I had a bad earache. That way she couldn't do anything but feel sorry for me.

You don't usually have a temperature when you have an earache! (Marian)

Faking illness can serve functions other than release from school. In the following story, Tammy describes it as a strategy to defer bedtime, using knowledge of her baby-sitter to manipulate her.

My baby-sitter had always been a stickler for exact bedtimes and I had never been able to devise a way to get around them — until a brainstorm hit. I remembered how upset she was when I had been sick. When she announced my bedtime, I started to cry and held on to my stomach. I moaned and told her that I felt like I was going to be sick. She immediately brought me a blanket, a glass of juice, and a hot water bottle. She dashed upstairs and returned with my pillows, which she put behind me. She then handed me a pan and told me in a calm voice that if I felt as though I were going to throw up, I should put the pan up to my face. I had discovered my baby-sitter's soft spot and I played on it. Once again I had read into an adult and found a way in which I could get what I wanted. Because of my baby-sitter's fear, every time she sat for me I pretended to be sick and thus extended my bedtime until 10:00 or 11:00 at night. (Tammy)

Those who regularly fake illness may over time run an increasing risk of discovery and find it advisable to change their strategies. Lisa opts for faking injury.

As I got older I realized this tactic [of faking illness] might not work much longer so I realized I needed to try something new. So I planned a nasty fall down a flight of wood stairs. I'd stand at the top of the stairs and drop all of my books and notebooks down them and then I'd stamp my way down them making as much noise as possible and then lie at the bottom, sprawled out among my things, looking helpless by the time anyone in my family could reach the top floor. I did this usually the day before gymnastics in gym. I hated gymnastics. With a twisted ankle or a hurt arm I was hardly expected to do tumble sets or bounce on a trampoline or walk on a balance beam. I avoided a lot of gym classes that way. (Lisa)

Although lies and subterfuge can be successful, they are not necessarily so, and repeated use can compromise success. Children may find it to their advantage to have a broad repertoire of strategies upon which to draw.

Concealment

When adults are unaware of what children are doing or not doing, they are hardly in a position to impede children in their projects or punish them for their actions or inactions. Children may find it a useful strategy to facilitate adults' unawareness by concealing participation in desired but prohibited activities and concealing avoidance of undesired ones, thereby easing their trials.

   Not wanting to go to bed or not wanting to stop their activities, children may be motivated to develop a range of strategies for concealing their wakefulness and carrying on clandestine projects. In the following story concealment follows failed efforts to 'negotiate' (through fighting).

> One area that I remember from my childhood starts at age 6 and continues to about the time I turned 9 or 10. This issue was going to bed at 8:00 p.m. during the school year. I remember that I was allowed to play with my neighborhood friends after school and then again after dinner and homework but the minute the street lights came on I had to go in. I remember coming home and fighting with my Mom and Dad to let me and my brother stay out and play. All the other kids could stay out and they went to bed after 8:00 p.m. Somehow that didn't faze my parents. So my brother and I eventually gave up the fight. After my Mom and Dad put us to bed, my brother and I would get in our doorways and talk or listen to Mom and Dad downstairs. Sometimes he and I would play a card game such as 'War.' I would creep up, deal the cards, and then get back to my doorway. We would hold up each card and whoever lost would throw their card to the other person. We would continue until we were tired. I don't remember if my parents ever knew we did this; if they did they never let us know. (Judy)

Watching television when one is presumed to be sleeping may be accomplished, though it may require careful planning.

> When my brother entered middle school he could stay up and watch television when I had to go to bed. I saw this as unfair because he still had to get up for school just as I did. Why could he stay up and I could not? This made no sense to me. To solve this problem I would go to bed as I was expected to, Mom would tuck me in as usual, but when she went back into the living room with my brother and father I began to activate my plan. I would stay in bed for a few minutes, then make my way into the bathroom. There was this one position that I could sit in and from that angle I could see the television in perfect view. I would sit there many nights and watch a few shows. There were times when I really got scared or felt that I was taking a risk and was about to be caught. When my father would get up to go

to bed I would run into my room so he wouldn't find me. After he was gone into bed I'd scram back into the bathroom. Right before my mother would get ready to put my brother to bed I would go to bed. I only wanted to stay up until he did. I really could've been caught. Every time anyone would leave the living room to get food, for a phone call, or do the littlest thing I would scramble into my room; that way if anyone looked at me I would look asleep. My parents may have known this all along but they never let me know. (Ruth)

Perhaps adults know what children are doing and ignore it because their goal is to have children in bed and quiet, actual sleep being less important. Or perhaps adults are simply oblivious. The notion that children are 'too young' or 'too innocent' to engage in such deceptive practices provides children with a shield behind which to carry out this and other strategies.

One particular form of concealment, 'hiding the evidence,' may prove an effective strategy for coping with undesired food. Although in the following story this strategy was detected and thus was unsuccessful, other informants describe success.

One particular night that I remember quite clearly is the night that we had liver and spinach for dinner. How I despised the smell and taste of liver and the slimy, sour flavor of the spinach. But the clincher was the fact that I had to drink a whole entire glass of warm goat's milk. Once again I was the last to leave the dinner table and I was having a really miserable time. I played with my food until everyone else finally left the room and went in to the family room to watch television. As I felt very frustrated and angry because I could not watch 'The Brady Bunch' with my family, I desperately tried to think of excuses that would save me from this cruel dilemma. Suddenly I thought of the incredible solution to my problem. I waited patiently until I was sure that I could hear my parents and brother talking in the family room. As soon as I was certain that they all were in there, I bolted for the bathroom with my glass of goat's milk. Ingeniously, I poured the goat's milk into the toilet and then quickly pulled the handle. What a wonderful sound that toilet made! As I sneakily made my way back to the kitchen I decided to continue my mission. This time I wrapped the smelly liver and green, mushy spinach in a napkin. I then made another successful trip back to the bathroom and repeated the same procedure as before. I was feeling quite pleased with myself as I carefully walked back to the kitchen a second time. However, this time I was not as lucky and was met by a pair of angry blue eyes that happened to belong to my mother. I was quickly reprimanded by her because somehow she had realized exactly what I had been up to. I was soon sent to bed without any dessert and wasn't allowed to watch television for the rest of the week. I remember how angry and upset

I was with my mother for not being able to understand that I really hated to eat food that did not appeal to me. I felt that it was my right to be able to eat whatever I chose to and it was definitely not her right to punish me for my preferred actions! I honestly thought that I was not doing anyone else any harm by choosing to 'do away with' my dinner. (Regina)

With limited resources for concealment, children may improvise.

I was in the first grade when I received my first pint carton of milk. I was never a big milk drinker and that milk tasted horrendous. My parents insisted that I have milk at lunch. Every day I would save my milk carton so the teacher wouldn't find a full carton in the garbage. I would hide them in my room. Eventually my room began to smell very bad. I wouldn't tell my parents what it was but of course they found my many full cartons of sour milk. My parents sat me down at the kitchen table. I thought I was on death row but instead they talked to me about it. They really shocked me by understanding and telling me that I didn't have to get a milk carton at lunch anymore. Instead I'd have a glass of milk when I came home. (Holly)

Holly's 'shock' at being understood suggests that children may, accurately or not, come to *expect* that adults will not understand their concerns, thereby justifying their use of strategies.

In the following story of concealment — of both an accident and the prohibited activity within which context it occurred — options are carefully assessed.

One difficulty that I thought of took place when I was about 8 years old and I was with my friend Ernie and my sister Kim. We were visiting Ernie and were playing our favorite game. We got out the Monopoly money and pretended we all had a job. One of us chose to be the bartender while the other two went to the bar after work. Ernie's parents had a great bar set up in their recreation room. We said we were playing pool when actually we were making fake drinks. The bar was supposed to be off limits because of all the wine glasses but we were always very careful and knew well enough not to leave fingerprints on the glasses. Our game was going along fine on this particular day until a glass fell off the bar onto the floor. The three of us quickly began putting our heads together to think of an explanation so Ernie wouldn't get in trouble. We were going to say we were dancing and we bumped into the bar and knocked over a glass. That wouldn't work because more than one glass would have fallen. I was going to take the blame because I figured Ernie's parents wouldn't yell at me. But Ernie and Kim figured we'd only be kept from playing there and it was the only place we could really get away from the grown-ups. My sister was the one to come up with the idea we all agreed upon. She said we should just get rid of the evidence — bury the broken glass. We all knew the bar wasn't used very often so no one would really miss the glass for a while. We gathered the glass in a paper bag and set out to bury it. We decided the best place would be the most obvious. The dog often dug up the ground under the deck so there were always plenty of holes and dirt piles. We crept under the deck and dug a fairly deep hole. When the hole was big enough so the dog wouldn't find it, we dumped the glass out of the bag and in the hole. We were also smart enough to think of how to cover the hole. We made it look as if the dog had done it — no hand prints in the soil. After our mission was accomplished, we snuck back to the recreation room and started playing pool. (Eleanor)

The plan settled upon by Eleanor and her friends entails knowledge of and attention to detail worthy of an adult criminal. (An interesting comparison might be made with Letkemann's *Crime as Work*, 1973.)

As a strategy, concealment allows children to carry out their own projects while appearing to adults to be following adults' rules. For children who find negotiations with adults fruitless, concealment holds clear appeal.

A Selection of Other Strategies

The foregoing descriptions of crying and temper tantrums, lying and subterfuge indicate the complexity of strategies that children may craft. The range of strategies is suggested by the following stories of the assistance of others, tattling, manipulation of adults, neutralization of punishment, ignoring adults, and revenge. The success of strategies may require of children detailed knowledge of those towards whom they employ their strategies and those upon whom they can depend for help in carrying them out.

Assistance of others may be offered or sought.

Even when I had food I liked, I never used to like to eat much and we (my sisters and I) would have to sit at the table until we were done with everything that was on our plate. Well, I must have been the slowest eater in the world. Everyone would get up and start to clear the table and I would still be sitting there eating. Actually I would be playing with it, and trying to make it look like there was less on the dish, but it never seemed to work. I remember I use to shove the food in my mouth and fill my cheeks like a chipmunk, and it would take me forever to swallow it all. When my younger sister used to come in the room to get more dishes I used to give her my salad off my dish because she loved it. I would be so thankful that she would eat if for me. I do not know if my parents ever knew then but till this day my older sister still tells the story of how I use to stuff my cheeks and give my younger sister my salad. (Cindy)

Dogs may serve as especially willing others.

Every night at dinner I was poured a full glass of milk. I made it very apparent to my family that I did not like milk at all. And it was the truth, I truly did not like the taste of milk. Yet every night I was told to drink it. . .But one night at dinner I absolutely refused to drink it anymore because I was so sick of drinking something I hated so much. So after everyone left the table I discovered that my dog did not mind finishing the glass of milk for me. My dad thought, from that night on, that I drank the whole glass of milk myself. (Lydia)

Tattling holds both promise and risk as a strategy for diverting attention (and perhaps punishment) to others. It may draw other rewards as well.

One thing that I did as a child was tattletale. I would listen and watch as my brothers would plan schemes and carry them out. Then I would tell my parents and watch them get punished. . .If I ever did plan anything I would tell my brothers and they would test it out. If it didn't work, I would still tell on them. I knew that if I told on my brothers I would get some kind of praise or recognition in return. I would get to stay up later, watch my favorite television show, or go somewhere with my grandparents or parents, and my brothers couldn't because they were being punished. I knew the advantages of being a tattletale and saw the disadvantages of being punished for doing something wrong. (Nan)

Tattling may, however, entail risks. In my observations of a kindergarten class, I found that in response to tattling a teacher might:

1. deal with the rule-breaker and ignore the teller;
2. deal with the rule-breaker and discipline the teller;
3. ignore the rule-breaker and discipline the teller;
4. ignore the rule-breaker and ignore the teller.

Children who choose tattling may not with any accuracy predict the results of their telling and may, instead of bringing punishment on the head of another, call it down upon their own (Waksler, 1987, p. 147).

Manipulation of adults may be an implicit part of a range of strategies or may be used as a strategy in itself.

I learned how to live up to the image my parents created for me. I'd act right up to it even if it's not the way I'd act at all. My parents have this wild image of my being the child of the family with a 'good head on her shoulders, with common sense.' I do fit into this category to some degree but my parents think I fit it constantly. I used to and still use their image to my advantage. If I do something wrong I act so upset that I didn't use my common sense that they feel sorry for me and think I won't let it happen again. If my sister or brother got into trouble I could make a deal about it to make myself look better and them worse. The reputation parents create can be a very useful tool for manipulation. (Holly)

Parents may be played off against one another. Divorce may provide a setting wherein manipulation of adults is especially effective.

When my parents first made their separation official, I had difficulty accepting that I could not have everyone together. It was always my brother, my mother, and me or my brother, my father, and me. The times I spent alone with my dad seemed so lonesome. I think my dad sensed this and tried to do everything he could to make me happy. He only got to see me on Sundays and did not want that day to be unhappy so he always planned these wonderful days of picnics, zoo trips, movies, or special dinners. He always got me gifts on these days to make me happy so I began to look forward to these visits and figured that I could get a lot out of what seemed to be such a terrible situation. When my dad or my mom did not get me what I wanted I would threaten to go to the other one. This worked pretty well for a while. When my parents caught on, they collaborated and worked against me. I did not get all that I wanted but I began to realize that it was not as important to me. (Yvonne)

My Mom and I had regular arguments about everything under the sun. I recall thinking about how unfair it was that I couldn't tell her my side. There was a lot of resentment locked up inside me because of my stifled feelings. Then, one day during a fight, I lost my temper.

'If you won't let me speak my side, I'll. . .I'll go live with Dad!' I yelled. As soon as the words were out of my mouth, two tears rolled down my mom's face.

I don't remember ever planning out what I was going to say. I don't even remember ever thinking of the words I uttered that day. However, somewhere inside me I knew that they would have a big effect on her. They did. From that day on I was allowed to speak my side. Unfortunately, I realized through the fight that I could use my parents' divorce as a weapon against my mother. If she wouldn't buy me something or if she wouldn't let me go somewhere, I'd use the threat of going to my father. Deep inside I knew that I never would, but if I told that to my mother, my manipulation tactic would no longer work. (Tammy)

Neutralization of punishment may serve as a strategy to lessen trials. Holly (earlier in this chapter) described hiding toys in preparation for confinement to her room. In the following story, Ruth describes another way to neutralize punishment.

> I'd hit my brother real hard and he had a red mark across the face, which my mother saw was obviously from being hit. I was sent into my room for the afternoon. This was a horrible punishment because I love to be outdoors. I was in confinement to my room so I decided to make the best of it. I amused myself for a while then I decided to take a nap. When my mother came to allow me to go to dinner I was sound asleep. She may have been upset because sleeping did not seem like much of a punishment. My mother let me sleep and finally I woke up on my own. After I had slept all afternoon there was no way that I would be able to go to sleep that night. I require very little sleep. My parents were well aware of the fact that I did not require much sleep so they were probably afraid of how they were going to get me to bed that night. I recall being up half the night with my mother. I was complaining that I was not tired. She only decided to use the confinement method of punishment for a few times because it was probably more of a pain to her that night than it was a punishment for me. (Ruth)

If children deem it a trial to be yelled at, one neutralization strategy is to laugh at adults who are yelling (described earlier in this chapter as employed by Yvonne's brother). This strategy is risky, for it may lead to more severe punishment, but informants have described with pleasure the effects of their laughter: adults' confusion, adults' faces growing red with anger, adults trembling with rage. Avoiding negative consequences of this strategy may lead children to pursue other strategies, e.g., leaving the scene.

Ignoring adults requires that children attend to the consequences of prior actions and make intentional use of what they have learned.

> For as long as I can remember, I've always bitten my nails. I've always bitten them as low as I could until they started hurting me but the minute they began to grow back I would bite them down again. My mother has never really said anything about it but my father has always hated it. I constantly heard (and still do hear) demands from him to stop biting them. 'Take you fingers out of your mouth' and 'Stop biting your pretty nails' was all he ever said to me. For my whole life he has told me to stop biting my nails but I don't know why. I never paid attention to his demands but I guess he always thought that one day I would listen to him. I always thought it was funny that he told me to stop biting them so many times. They weren't his nails, I wasn't in any serious pain because of it, and biting my nails wasn't hazardous

to my health, so why should he care what I did with them? To this day, every time I see him he tells me to take my fingers out of my mouth but I continue to ignore his requests. (Naomi)

In Naomi's presentation, her father's apparent obliviousness to the ineffectiveness of his own actions serves her as a resource.

Revenge may alleviate hard times.

Rebecca could remember a teacher that she had in the fifth grade. One time she was talking out of turn. The teacher used to pace the aisles and his form of discipline was rapping you on the head with his class ring. Rebecca recalls that it really hurt. She never told her parents but she vowed that she would never like him again, and she remembers feeling like she got even when she got an A on a report that she had to do on a book that she never read. What made her feel like she got even was the fact that he wrote on her paper that she had really insightful comments. (Albert's informant)

In the first grade, I sat in the back of the room next to a window (my last name was Smith, so I got put in the back of the room). Since I was next to the window, I tended to pay more attention to what was going on outside than what was happening in the class. My first-grade teacher absolutely hated me. She would always try to catch me day-dreaming by calling on me and asking a question related to what she had just been talking about. I knew that she never liked me. She would call on me and I always knew the right answer. I was always smart enough to figure out the right answer without having to pay attention in class. She could never get mad at me because I always knew the right answer. (Libby, Debra's informant)

Children may thus employ a wide range of strategies to forestall, minimize, or help them endure the little trials of childhood. As they do so they draw upon their knowledge of the physical world, the social world, adults in general, and particular adults.

A Note on Sources of Children's Strategies

Do children learn strategies from adults or create them on their own? Do children exchange ideas about strategies? Are strategies a part of children's culture (Opie and Opie, 1959)? Since few informants directly address these questions I here can do no more than offer a few tentative answers gleaned from the stories I gathered. It appears that adults may explicitly teach some strategies, e.g., lying, that children may then divert to their own purposes. Adults may also serve as a direct source of strategies, as when one parent suggests how to 'handle' the other. Some informants describe strategies as their own creations, Regina speaking of her own insight ('Suddenly I thought of the incredible solution to my problem') and Tammy citing 'a brainstorm.' The successes and failures of friends and acquaintances may be instructive, Theresa stating, 'A few of my friends would be absent at least once a month because they. . .just played sick.' Elder siblings may serve as 'ground-breakers', younger siblings learning by observing what elder siblings can and cannot get away with. Children may be advised by other children; siblings may hold what one informant describes as 'sibling conferences.' Eleanor describes group deliberation ('The three of us quickly began putting our heads together to think of an explanation'). Unintentional behavior that is followed by positive consequences may come to be used intentionally. Trial and error may be employed. The etiology of children's strategies appears a fruitful topic for future research.

* * *

The emergence of strategies reflects the differences between children's and adults' perspectives, projects, and values. It may also reflect the impossibility of children's direct negotiations with adults.

> My mother always had complete control over me and my two younger brothers and sister. I was unable to talk back or disagree with her. She would not let me get in one word. Mom would say, 'End of discussion — period' without even listening to my side of things. This was unfair because my mother was always right no matter what. (Theresa)

Adults may negotiate in bad faith — and thus not really negotiate.

> A big thing with me was that if I had no one to play with at home, I wanted to go to my friends' houses all the time. It was these times when my parents and I would have talks to make a compromise but they would listen and stick to their original decision and I would not get my way, EVER. (Lillian)

'Negotiation' with children is a topic about which professionals may offer advice. In *The Emotional Problems of Normal Children*, Turecki acknowledges, with disapproval, that non-negotiable topics may be deceptively presented to children as if negotiation were possible. Advising a mother who says, 'I'm not sure I understand why it's wrong to reason with a child,' he responds, 'It's not wrong, but there's no point giving the same explanation over and over again, or getting into a lengthy negotiation *when you know perfectly well that you aren't going to change your mind*' (Turecki, 1994, p. 62, emphasis added).

In any negotiation so framed, a child's position is clearly less than weak. Greenspan in *Playground Politics* also recognizes adults' power in negotiation: '[A]t least some of the time, let your child argue. Even if you eventually have to pull rank and turn her down, at least she has gotten a fair shot at convincing you that she's right' (1993, p. 80). Children, however, may discover that the 'shot' — and thus adults — may not be 'fair' at all.

What might children conclude from what they perceive as the need for strategies for dealing with the little trials of childhood and what might they conclude from the success of their strategies? In discovering that adults assume that children possess neither the guile nor the competence nor indeed the need to engage in such endeavors, children may come to see not themselves but adults as unknowledgeable, unaware, deluded, 'innocent.' Describing her faking illness to stay home from school, Diane writes,

> Mom would soothe my needs, tuck me into bed and tell me I could stay home from school. What a sucker my mom was when I was young.

10   What Can Be Learned?

I never thought of my childhood as being hard or difficult until we discussed it in class. I have come to the conclusion that when children argue with their parents they are fighting a losing battle. Parents are older; therefore they are always correct (at least they think so). There is really no hope for children because the parents always pull their 'rank' on you and you must do as they say. So if children just agree with their parents and go along with what they say and do, their childhood will be filled with wonderful memories and they will not remember the hard ones so much. (Theresa)

When I look back upon childhood, I think of happy moments such as birthdays, getting your first bike, and receiving your first bed. Hardships seem virtually non-existent. When thinking back, however, if you dig far enough into your memory bank, being a child was not much fun at all. As a child you are totally dependent; you must do whatever your parents want, when they want it, no questions asked. There are no choices to be made when you are a child. You are treated like a mindless cute little thing that can be dressed up, rather than a human being or an adult-in-the-making. It seems to me that when people do in fact treat their children like adults, society feels that they are not caring and sensitive when in reality the child is better off treated with respect. (Celeste)

If children indeed experience the little trials of childhood and develop strategies for dealing with them, what are the theoretical and practical implications of their so doing? How might sociological and everyday conceptions of children — and of adults — be altered to incorporate a recognition of children's perspectives and children's trials? In this chapter I call attention to some issues of particular relevance in addressing these questions.

Telling people what they *should* do is not part of the mandate of sociology as I conceive of it. Recommendations presuppose values, goals, and practical contingencies, all of which are relative to the contexts in which they apply. Sociology does, however, offer the kind of understanding on the basis of which recommendations can be constructed. Thus readers may, within the framework of their own values and concerns, draw from the materials in this book what Bentz describes as 'a vision of a better way of life hidden in the documents' (1989, p. 236).

Telling *sociologists* what they should — and should not — do is quite another matter. Sociologists who uncritically adopt adults' formulations of children's perspectives, subscribe to the glorification of adults, and are a party to the obscuring of children's experiences, distort sociological understanding of children, adults, and the workings of the social world. In 'Studying Children: Phenomenological Insights' (1986) I argued for sociologists taking children seriously as topics of study — not as *objects* of socialization, not as proto-adults, but in their own right, as participants in the social world, with their own perspectives and projects. I identified two overarching biases that characterize adults' views of children: that children are 'unfinished, in process, not anywhere yet' and 'routinely wrong, in error, and don't understand' (1986, pp. 73–8). Testimony to the existence of these biases — and to their erroneousness — is offered throughout the stories in this book, wherein, despite adults' views to the contrary, children apparently *are* somewhere and *do* understand. Only by suspending adults' biases can sociologists hope to apprehend children's lived experiences and respect what Husserl (1962) calls 'the originary right of the data.'

Adults' Distortions of Children's Perspectives

Mackay (1973) and Atkinson (1980), among others, attribute adults' lack of knowledge of children — and thus distortions of children's perspectives — to their uncritical use of taken-for-granted beliefs about children. As a consequence, even when children 'act like adults' their actions may be trivialized. As Atkinson notes,

> [A]ctivities which are treated as tied to the category adult are seen as not having been 'done for real,' as having been done 'unknowingly,' when performed by someone not seeable as an adult. (1980, p. 44)

Certain features of children's lives — e.g., activities they 'do for real' and 'knowingly' — can only emerge when the suspension of adults' formulations of children's experiences makes way for them.

Adults' distortions of children's perspectives can obscure the fact that in adult–child relations intersubjectivity may be far more limited than adults suspect.[1] Adults may *assume* a unity of perspectives[2] between adults and children,

---

[1] For a general discussion of intersubjectivity as problematic, see Waksler, 1995.

[2] Speaking of the unity of perspectives, Husserl writes '. . .there constantly occurs an alteration of validity through reciprocal correction. In reciprocal understanding, my experiences and experiential acquisitions enter into contact with those of others, similar to the contact between individual series of experiences within my (one's own)

an assumption that is brought into serious question by examining children's perspectives. Children themselves may conceal discrepancies, leaving adults with an erroneous sense of shared understandings. Analysis of children's perspectives on and judgments about the social world indicates that although their perspectives are on some occasions in agreement with those of the adults with whom they associate, on other occasions they are in opposition.[3] When perspectives conflict, adults may use their power to ensure that their own perspective prevails. When children's views are extremely discrepant with adults', adults may not even imagine what children's perspectives might be. The following view of school years, for example, may well contrast with adults' views.

> My main goal in life was to tackle the jump rope strategies and become cootie-free[4] during recess. (Felicia)

Matters that adults — and perhaps children themselves — think 'ought not' to be of great significance to children may nonetheless be so and, without adults' intervention, endure.

> When I think of hard times in childhood, I immediately envision my brother taunting me. He used to call me 'Vooey Tooey' in a real high-pitched voice that struck a nerve in me so terribly that I would go into a screaming rage. Sometimes at night he would lean against the wall separating our bedrooms and whisper 'Vooey Tooey' in that squeally little voice. I would spend half the night crying. Nothing in my life has ever irked me as dreadfully as that torture. It lasted for at least ten years and he always got the same reaction out of me. Looking back, it seems ridiculously silly that such a minute activity could have mangled my nerves. However every now and again, for fun, my brother will say those two little words in that horrible voice and it makes me cringe and cover my ears. (Violet)

---

experiential life; and here again, for the most part, intersubjective harmony of validity occurs, [establishing what is] "normal" in respect to particular details, and thus an intersubjective unity also comes about in the multiplicity of validities of what is valid through them; here again, furthermore, intersubjective discrepancies show themselves often enough; but then, whether it is unspoken and even unnoticed, or is expressed through discussion and criticism, a unification is brought about or at least is certain in advance as possibly attainable by everyone' (1970, p. 163, brackets in original translation). 'Reciprocal correction' is hampered when children's perspectives are denied or rejected.

[3] For an example of adults' and children's differing perspectives on child abuse, see Wattam, 1989.

[4] 'Cooties' as used in this context refer to *imaginary* versions of body lice of that name. Children claim that 'cooties' can be transmitted by other children intentionally or unintentionally. Remaining 'cootie-free' is viewed as a desirable goal; transmitting 'cooties' to disliked others can also be valued.

When adults are unaware of children's perspectives, they may formulate explanations very different from those that children might offer. 'Sibling rivalry' offers an instructive example. The following story begins by describing what adults might see as an obvious instance of sibling rivalry.

> I feel that the most devastating time in my childhood was when my younger brother was born. I was $3\frac{1}{2}$ years old and my grandmother was taking care of me at the time. We got a phone call from my father saying that my mother had gone into labor so my grandmother and I hopped into a cab and went to the hospital. At the hospital it seemed like we waited an eternity. Then finally the doctor came out and said, 'It's a boy!' I was so upset at the fact that I was going to have a brother that I burst into tears. (Celeste)

As Celeste continues her story, a different picture emerges.

> I began screaming that I wanted a sister and to send my brother back. To me this moment was very traumatic because up to this point my parents had provided me with basically everything I wanted and this time they screwed up big-time. As soon as the tantrum began my father came over to talk to me. He told me that even though I had a brother I could still have fun with him. Not in my eyes. I couldn't dress him up, I couldn't play dolls, and most importantly I couldn't play house. That day my parents just didn't, or couldn't, understand what I was going through. Fortunately I eventually got over my hatred of my brother and we are now good friends. I guess my father was right. (Celeste)

Despite Celeste's description of her father as ultimately having been 'right,' at the time of the experience he appears to have been in error, consoling her with what she saw as false promises, distorting both the source and the depth of her distress.

Sibling rivalry may gloss a range of children's experiences in which 'rivalry' is a minor or non-existent element and other features are more salient. Where adults 'see' sibling rivalry, children may 'see' quite different things. The following story demonstrates especially clearly the different perspectives that adults and children may have on 'sibling rivalry.'

> My sister, who was 6 when I was born, just recently told me that she had resented me for being born until she got a brand new pink coat. That made up for having a new girl in the family. (Karen)

Without denying that Karen's sister might also have been experiencing sibling rivalry, I want to call attention to *her* trial as implied in the remedy she describes: receiving something *she* really wanted — perhaps wanted as much as her parents wanted the new baby. For Karen the matter appears to be one of *fairness*. Examination of children's perspectives on what passes among adults for 'sibling rivalry' may disclose more mundane and practical matters that children find troubling and that adults may quite readily remedy. (My own actions have been affected by this 'story of the pink coat,' for now I give gifts to the *siblings* of newborns, the siblings *not* being bar- or bat-mitzvahed, the siblings *not* in the hospital. Adults may look at me somewhat oddly but no child has complained. Perhaps I am interfering with children's learning to deal with not receiving gifts when others do, but I suspect they will have other opportunities to learn this ultimately unpleasant lesson.)

Adults' distortions of children's perspectives are not necessarily accidental; indeed they may be useful in enabling adults to carry out their own plans and projects by including children without children's consent and even to their distress. The idea that adults routinely 'know better' than children and the idea that children's projects are not 'really' important can be used to justify adults' fostering their own projects in the face of children's opposition or distress. Were adults regularly to take into account children's perspectives, they might feel it incumbent upon them to reassess and perhaps change their own behavior, compromising or deferring desires that they would prefer to have prevail. They might discover themselves in error and children right. Taking children's perspectives into account, adults might, alternatively, continue their practices, and indeed feel quite justified in so doing, but might thereby give lie to the presumed altruism of adults and willing participation of children.

Discrepancies in perspective between adults and children would seem to be as inevitable as they are between adults and adults. In a variety of situations children's and adults' desires may even be mutually exclusive, making compromise impossible. The following story illustrates the mutual exclusivity of a teacher's project (classroom management) and a child's (sharing a secret).

> My informant said that she was sitting at her desk in school doing seat work when suddenly she remembered she had something very important to tell her friend. She began to whisper quietly because there was no talking allowed during this time. However, she had been doing seat work for what seemed to her to be hours and was very anxious to tell her friend the secret. The teacher caught her and sent her to the corner for the rest of the day without any interaction with the rest of the class. At the time and even now she felt as though the punishment was harsh. She had not gotten in any trouble that day and was a good student. Although she can't remember what the actual secret was about, she still feels that at the time it was important. (Loretta's informant)

Children may experience quite understandable distress when their perspectives are ignored, their important projects not only aborted but punished, and disagreements resolved by adults' use of power.

The images of children that abound in everyday life emerge as *social constructions* of children by adults, in many ways distortions of children's own constructions of themselves and their experiences. The recognition of these images as social constructions may, in the words of Goode, serve 'to point out the possibility of reconstructing [children] and our relations with them. . .' (1994, p. 117), both in sociological theory and in practical action.

Glorification of Adults

Unexamined taken-for-granted ideas passing as knowledge may foster a glorified view of adults — and thereby burden adults as their practices are measured against largely unrealizable standards. Children too may be burdened, required to distort their own experiences if they are to sustain glorified images of adults. In her book of advice to children, *When Grownups Drive You Crazy*, Leshan displays just such glorification.

> As I begin to talk about your parents, let me say that the love between parents and children is just about the best thing there is in the whole world, and in most ways your parents (as well as the other grownups in your life) prove their love to you every day by all the things they do for and with you. (1988, p. 6)

Her formulation is obviously ideological, not empirical, and hardly true of all children's experiences. The *assumption* of parental love impedes children's understanding of experiences that do not warrant the assumption. Is it possible that some parents do not love their children? Is it also possible that some of the things that parents do 'for and with' children are 'for' parents and only reluctantly 'with' children? Leshan writes,

> There are even times when most children wonder if their parents really wanted to have children. When Ron hears his father talking to his grandmother on the phone and hears him say, 'It would have been a much better vacation if we'd sent Ron to camp,' he decides it's true, his parents wish he'd never been born. It probably doesn't mean that at all. It's just that parents — all parents — need time to themselves. (1988, pp. 70–1)

Of course adults have concerns, projects, and wishes that do not include children. A parent who read a draft chapter from this book wrote,

> My sympathy went out to parents, who have needs too, and may not always be capable of the right course of action, perhaps because they are tired, troubled, ill, pregnant, dealing with another child, or whatever. Yes, adults put children to bed because they need time without children! (Donna)

When, however, adults define everything they do as 'for the good of the child,' the experiences of both adults and children are distorted. If, instead, children are allowed to see adults as having their own needs and desires, children may expand their knowledge both about needs and desires and about adults.

But to deny that there indeed may be parents who wish their children had never been born is to limit the resources of children who find themselves in such a situation. Although Leshan's advice appears well-intentioned, any advice is flawed if it *assumes* what may, in some instances, be false. How can children understand their experiences when only a single formulation of those experiences is presented *and*, to them, appears inaccurate? The option offered them is to define their experiences against the background of a glorified view of adults regardless of what their experiences are.

Glorification of adults may include the assumption that adults routinely know more than children, a claim that seems especially open to challenge. Children may certainly be perplexed by adults.

> Throughout the interviews my informants would say, 'I wonder why my parents did that' or 'I wonder if they really knew how that made me feel.' (Lydia)

However, like oppressed groups who find it to their advantage to understand their oppressors, children may find it useful to understand adults and may devote effort to doing so. One understanding they may arrive at is that adults, despite their claims to omniscience, know less than children. Support for this 'reduced' view of adults can be garnered from adults' apparently *not* knowing of children's strategies for dealing with the little trials of childhood — *not* knowing that children are awake when presumed to be asleep, hide food instead of eating it, only pretend to take medicine. Elaine, describing the importance of changing strategies to avoid discovery, says,

> They [adults] catch on eventually. They're just a little bit slow.

Are adults indeed ignorant, are they simply inattentive, or do they choose for their own purposes to pretend ignorance? If the latter, children may perceive the ignorance but not the pretense. Some informants, however, describe their suspicion that adults knew of their strategies and did nothing about them. Children — and adults — may benefit from children's clandestine activities but what sense are children to make of adults' feigned unawareness?

Children's experiences may also lead them to reject the view of adults as kindly, finding them instead, as in the following story, spiteful. Analyzing two of her interviews, Rochelle writes,

> In both of these examples it becomes clear to me that one reason it is hard being a child in relation to teachers is because children are constantly expected to do things without knowing why they have to

do them. In both of the previous examples mentioned, the children were uncomfortable yet the teacher made no attempt to put the children at ease. Perhaps an explanation of why I had to sit next to a boy [seats were paired and there was an odd number of boys and girls] or why Jack needed to practice reading aloud [he was judged to need help but found it embarrassing to read aloud] would have been beneficial for both of us. We knew that there was a reason we were being forced to do these things and since one wasn't provided by the teacher we were left to assume that they were doing it merely out of spite.

There are both benefits and costs associated with the glorification of adults. One noteworthy cost is that adults' are faulted for what children, offered explanation, might judge differently. Another cost is that both adults and children may feel compelled to distort their experiences.

Double Standards

Adults may hold children to different — and higher — standards than they hold other adults or themselves. Children may not be allowed simple mistakes (e.g., spilling milk, breaking objects, missing the bus, or, in the story to follow, forgetting) but instead find their acts subject to judgment, viewed as intentional, and used as vehicles for instruction.

> In the first grade I had the meanest nun that ever walked on the face of this earth. She was very strict and was yelling at us constantly. Each week a different student had been assigned to take down the milk crate and get some milk for snack time. Well, it was my turn to do it and that Monday I was not in school. Tuesday came and along with it came snack time. I completely forgot that it was my turn to get the milk until I saw Brian come back with the milk crate full of milk. I immediately went to the teacher asking why I couldn't go get the milk. She started yelling at me, saying that it was my responsibility to remember to go down for the milk so now I couldn't do it for the rest of the week. I was so angry with her. It wasn't fair. I had completely forgotten and she could've at least reminded me, but I guess that was impossible. I mean she was the 'Wicked Witch of the West.' (Cora)

Children may not be forgiven unwise spur-of-the-moment choices, required instead to pay consequences that adults may avoid.

> Bethany remembered back to third grade. Her teacher's name was Miss Bruce. There was this kid in her class named Joe whom Bethany had a 'crush' on for two years. Joe went up to Bethany and asked her if she had a tootsie roll. Bethany said, 'No, it's a titsie roll.' Joe got mad

and said, 'Oooh, I'm tellllling.' Bethany begged him not to tell because she knew she would get in trouble. Needless to say, Joe told. Miss Bruce came up to Bethany and asked her to tell her what she said. Bethany told her in a mumble. Miss Bruce made Bethany write a letter to her parents explaining why she would say such a thing. Bethany did not want to. She was scared of how her parents would react. She didn't really know why she said 'titsie roll,' she just thought it was funny at the time. (Ariel's informant)

'Pure' accidents may be punished.

Christopher told me of the time that he had been at his house celebrating New Year's Eve with his older brothers and sisters. The family had just received a trampoline for Christmas and the children had been given these sparklers to play with in the backyard. Well, Christopher's sparkler was burning close to his hand so he decided to throw the sparkler in the woods before he burnt his hand, so Christopher threw the sparkler in the air. The sparkler landed on the new trampoline and burned a large hole right in the middle of this barely one-week-old gift from Christmas. Christopher's father heard all of the children making a great deal of noise in trying to get the sparkler off the trampoline and came out in the backyard to see what was going on. The siblings quickly told Christopher's father what had happened and who was to be blamed for this act of destruction. Christopher was immediately taken to his room and beaten by his father's belt for his actions. Christopher told me the reason that this act of punishment stayed in his mind so vividly is that he felt that this was a pure accident and he had never been beaten by his father before for an accident. Christopher was 5 years old at the time that this took place and he feels that this is why he is so careful to this day about 'accidents' happening to him. Christopher said that he is careful now almost to the point of being paranoid about accidents happening to him that are his fault. (Anthony)

Inadvertent acts may be treated as advertent.

I was a good student and have always been told that I was a peacemaker. I'll never forget the time I whistled in class. I was just learning how to whistle and one day in the class I wasn't thinking and tried to whistle. The teacher stopped the class and said, 'Who whistled in class?' I was horrified and couldn't admit that I was the one. The teacher then told the whole class that if the person who whistled didn't tell, everyone would have to stay in for recess the next day. I went home and immediately told my mom what had happened. She suggested I write a note of apology. I did this and my teacher was shocked it was me. She sent a letter back to me saying that she was sorry she upset me! I was stressed out by this whole thing in second grade. (Enid's informant)

Children may also have fewer resources than adults for making amends or rectifying mistakes (although the letter of apology, as just cited, may add to their repertoire). It is unlikely that a 3-year-old can send flowers, replace a broken object, or clean up serious messes. Indeed such tasks may fall upon adults, contributing to the seriousness with which they take children's mistakes.

Adults can be daredevils in situations where children are judged fools.

A 5-year-old dashed across a busy street. When asked why, he said, 'The chance was there and I just had to take it.' (Personal communication from a somewhat shaken baby-sitter)

Clearly children's actions can jeopardize their lives and adults may quite obviously see themselves justified in seeking to prevent such actions. Prevention, however, may be more effectively achieved when adults see themselves as responding not to stupidity or misbehavior but to a sense of adventure.

Children may become aware of adults' double standards when they find adults violating rules to which children are held. Consider the following examples of such rules and informants' examples of adults' violations.

- *Don't talk with your mouth full.*

  One thing that my Mom did that bothered me was when she was on the phone and we would just be finishing dinner and she would talk to the person while chewing her food or with a mouthful. (Kara)

- *Don't slurp your food.*

  One of the women I interviewed said that nothing used to annoy her more than the way her mother ate. She said her mother used to 'suck' her food down. When she would eat her cereal she would suck all of the milk out of the spoon, then eat the cereal. This made her so furious that she to this day will not eat breakfast with her mother. It's just one of those things that always bothered her. (Rita)

- *Eat neatly.*

  A girl I interviewed said her mother cannot eat without spilling something on herself. 'She ends up spilling food on her lap, shirt, or any other article of clothing she happens to be wearing.' (Alma)

- *Don't interrupt.*

> Several people that I spoke with said that it annoyed them when, as children, adults would interrupt them when they were speaking. A man that I interviewed said, 'It was as if I wasn't there or that what I had to say was not important. If they wanted to talk while I was speaking they just did and ignored me.' I can recall many instances of this from when I was a child. My parents would often ignore what I was saying to start a conversation of their own. I was always angry at this because if I had interrupted their conversation then they would have been angry and I would have had to stop talking. (Andrea)

Offended children may have no recourse to ways of correcting or reprimanding errant adults. Thus they may see adults' escaping the negative consequences that would follow similar actions by children. Of the circumstances in which his mother's neglect led to the death of his pet frog, Ned wrote,

> I received an apology and the promise of a new frog but I felt justice wasn't served. In my eyes her murdering my frog wasn't half as bad as the fact that she received no reprimand. I knew that if I had done something like that, I would have faced intense scolding and lengthy punishment. She didn't miss television, she didn't go to bed early, and she got off the hook with no strings attached. My figuring was that just because she was an adult didn't mean she should go free. Why should her age and position (as my parent) produce immunity in incidents such as this? This question (in a little more basic wording) really had bothered me. I viewed this whole frog episode as rather unfair. I can remember thinking that when I became an adult just like Mom, I could avoid punishment just like Mom. After about a month I got a new frog, but I also had a slightly different view of adults. (Ned)

Observing double standards, children may discover not only that adults are able to avoid the consequences of their failings but also that adults do indeed have failings. As expressed in the words of one informant, 'I always thought of my parents as gods, they could do nothing bad or wrong. But when I discovered that they were lying to me it destroyed my perception of what they were' (Nan).[5]

Obscuring the Little Trials of Childhood

The little trials of childhood can be obscured by a variety of adults' practices, including justifying children's hardships, belittling their trials, imposing on

---

[5] The full text of this story appears in Chapter 6.

children the very trials that adults suffered themselves, and revising accounts
of their own childhood experiences. Sociologists too may obscure children's
trials, to the detriment of knowledge. As Bentz writes,

> Childhood adversities and their effects must be an integral part of
> socialization theories. Otherwise, theory may contribute to a kind of
> social amnesia, which fortifies adverse childrearing practices. (1989,
> p. 10)

The materials presented throughout this book serve as grounds for assessing
the theoretical and practical consequences of this obfuscation.

Justifying Children's Trials:
'But It's For Their Own Good'

Adults can certainly offer many reasons for their actions towards children and
may justifiably claim that what they do is 'for children's own good.' I in no way
mean to deny the existence of such altruistic motivation but do want to raise
three points deserving of consideration: (1) Regardless of adults' reasons, children have the experiences that they have and may view some of these experiences as hardships; (2) Adults may indeed be motivated solely by children's
well-being, but stories presented throughout this book suggest that adults'
own concerns may be an additional, a primary, or even the only motivation
for certain practices; (3) Some of the practices that adults recommend as important for children seem to be subverted by children without adults' knowledge and without their notice of any consequences, calling into question the
'goodness' of those practices.

Children may question adults' presentation of practices as 'for children's
own good.'

> When the topic was raised of speaking of the difficulties of childhood,
> I began to recall, as an adult, all the numerous times adults made my
> decisions for me. My privileges revolved around their conveniences
> but I was never allowed to voice this accusation. They always 'knew
> what was best for me.' (Holly)

What is 'for children's own good' is a judgment, about which adults may differ.
When children and adults differ, it is not self-evident that adults are necessarily
right.

Belittling Children's Trials:
Children's Pain as a Source of Adults' Amusement

Why do adults smile when hearing stories of the little trials of childhood
or when recounting such stories of their own? (I still do so myself, although

with decreasing frequency.) That amusement can accompany such stories is illustrated by those of my informants who conclude their descriptions of trials by characterizing them as 'funny now.' Ambert, discussing students' auto-biographies, notes the same trivialization.

> A frequent remark went like this: 'Of course, when I think about this now, I laugh, but it was really a terrible problem for me at that age.' (1994, p. 3)

Why are experiences that are described as 'terrible' taken to be amusing rather than heartbreaking? Were such stories told of *adults'* 'terrible' experiences, would they also be met with smiles? Against the background of the matters raised in this book, it seems odd that adults are amused rather than saddened. Finding children's trials amusing can, however, forestall alternative formulations — that children have suffered or that adults have treated children badly.

The following story illustrates the juxtaposition of adults' amusement and a child's suffering.

> It was a warm morning in the spring, and I was in the first grade. That year, I had, I thought, the world's greatest bus driver. Candy corns at Hallowe'en, candy canes at Christmas time, we all adored her. I especially liked her because on those dreary, rainy mornings she would stop in front of my house and beep the horn for me as I hated walking in the rain. This morning was not rainy. Or dreary. This was a great morning for me since my Nana was visiting. I got ready for school and my mom and Nana both gave me a hug and a kiss good-bye and stood in the doorway to watch me walk to the bus stop, then wave as the bus drove by my house. But as I got about halfway to the bus stop, I saw the bus. It had already been to my stop. I was too far from the bus stop to run to the bus and too far away from my house to run back there and hope that, as she did on those dreary rainy days, she would pick me up there. I froze for what seemed like an eternity, feeling frightened, scared, confused — like a deer in the road in the dead of night with the bright yellow headlights shining in my eyes. My instincts told me to run, and I did. I ran straight behind me and hid behind the big green generator box. I crouched, praying that no one would see me. I waited forever, until the bus was far enough down the road so I could hardly see it or hear the beeping noise it made each time it came to a halt to let on more children. I stood up, already crying, and began to walk home. I crept up the front steps, opened the aluminum screen door, and closed it quietly behind me. I walked into the kitchen where my mom was finishing her cup of coffee. 'What happened, angel? Did you miss the bus?' With tears streaming down my face, and a very shaky voice, I told her what happened. 'I was halfway to the bus stop and the bus drove by me but I know she

saw me because I waved my arms and yelled but she just looked at me and kept driving.' My mom, feeling so sympathetic, gave me a big hug, told me not to worry, and drove me to school shortly thereafter. *It wasn't until a few years ago, after feeling full of guilt over the situation for so long, that she told me that she and my Nana had seen the whole episode from the window and laughed.* (Betty, emphasis added)

Although adults may laugh at childhood experiences — their own or those of others — amusement may fade quickly when the distress of those experiences is granted legitimacy. This pattern, recurring in my data, is illustrated in the following story.

A friend of mine laughingly described an incident in which she had brought home to her house a new friend whom she was trying to impress. When the two went up to her bedroom, she found all her clothes piled in the center of the floor. Her mother explained that she had done this to emphasize that she ought to clean her room. I asked my friend if this had bothered her at the time. Her laughter stopped and she spoke of the embarrassment and mortification she felt. (Maxine)

Children themselves may view their trials as serious, consequential, and not in the least amusing. As Dora notes of those she interviewed, 'My simple conversation with these people produced some very powerful statements.' Some of the following excerpts from my data may reflect conventional phrasings[6] rather than literal feelings and actual plans but do not therefore warrant dismissal. Even with allowance made for hyperbole, the comments suggest the serious nature of children's concerns.

I was devastated. (Nancy)

That was a very traumatic day for me. (Rita)

I wanted to crawl under a rock so that no one I knew would see me. (Opal)

All I ever wanted to do is run and hide. (Vanessa, age 10, Penny's informant)

I wished I could just disappear into the floor. (Nancy)

This was the most humiliating thing in the whole world. (Rita)

---

[6] Christina Papidimitriou helped in the clarification of this point.

This had to be the worst thing in the world. (Betsy)

My informant 'wished the kindergarten would burn down.' (Wanda)

My informant said that this totally embarrassed her because she thought that this made her look like an 'idiot.' (Betsy)

I thought I would die from embarrassment. (Dora)

I was so embarrassed and people were staring. (informant cited by Andrea)

That [incident described] is the worst; that can really tear a person apart. (Cathy)

Although the situations that give rise to these statements might strike adults as unworthy of such extreme claims, adults themselves may well be familiar with experiences that lead them to make similar statements — experiences that they judge to be far from trivial.

Reproducing Childhood Trials

Instead of forswearing practices from their childhood that they found distressing, adults may reproduce them in their dealings with children. The following line concludes an emotional story of a child's trying to conceal injuries and avoid the deceptively characterized ministrations of others.[7]

It is funny because I now find myself telling my 8-year-old sister or any child the same stories. (Nan)

Adults certainly may attempt to avoid subjecting children to those very practices that as children they themselves found distressing. When, however, such attempts do not embody an understanding of the more general phenomenon of the little trials of childhood, those attempts may fail, one trial simply substituted for another.

When I interviewed my mother about her hard times as a child, the first thing she said was, 'I used to have to eat liver once a week, no matter what, and I hated it! I had no say whatsoever and that is why I have never ever made you or your sister eat liver. I actually have never cooked it in my life and I never will!' My mother was also made

---

[7] The full text of this story appears in Chapter 3.

to finish everything on her plate before she got up from the dinner table. I find it very interesting how my mother made my sister and me finish our plates, even though she knew how awful it was. I also find it very interesting that even though my mother did the same thing to her children that her mother did to her, she still never made us eat liver. (Annette)

The reproduction of childhood trials may occur unintentionally or may, for a variety of reasons, be adopted intentionally. One such reason offered is that trials 'build character,' a claim implying that the vicissitudes of life will not be sufficient to provide enough character-building experiences. The reproduction of childhood trials may, however, be of more benefit to adults than to children, functioning to support claims that adults' childhood trials were 'not so bad after all,' that they were 'really' of value, and that no blame is due adults responsible for them. The materials throughout this book challenge such claims.

Revising Accounts of Childhood: 'I Wouldn't Change a Thing'

Justifying, belittling, and reproducing the little trials of childhood can be facilitated when adults revise accounts of their childhood to support common-sense 'adult' views of what childhood is like (and thus what theirs must have been like). Social rules appear to govern adults' accounts of their childhood,[8] with only certain kinds of stories — the very good and the very bad — counting. The little trials of childhood, if recognized at all, are likely to be presented lightly, perhaps (as discussed above) with amusement. Informants note just such revised accounts.

I feel as if this is what my mother is doing, looking back at her childhood as an adult and her memories of hard times are not as hard now as they were when she was a child. (Annette)

Accounts may be manipulated to deny the reality of one's childhood feelings and minimize the negativity of one's childhood experiences. Affect can be separated from experiences and replaced by 'adult' views of children's affect. Yolanda writes,

I think when I was a child things seemed a lot worse than what they really were. (Yolanda)

---

[8] How much of therapeutic talk about childhood is governed by such social rules and what is to be gained therapeutically by attending to the little trials of childhood is beyond the scope of this book.

Adults thus may deny that childhood experiences, including their own, are 'really' as painful as they 'seemed' at the time — *unless their doing so is granted legitimacy.* My research has been based on offering just such legitimacy. Although adults might not ordinarily offer stories of the little trials of childhood *as trials,* they seem able to do so, and to do so with enthusiasm. Carlotta describes this process.

> What is it like to be a child? I asked this question first and the responses were very positive in nature. All three informants expressed the freedom you have as a child. Freedom from working, freedom from monetary problems or stresses, freedom to play. One of them expressed how nice it was to be a child and have your mother cook and clean for you. After all these positive responses, I asked them to remember the hard times they encountered as children. All the positive responses were gone and it did not sound as good to be a child anymore. (Carlotta)

Adults may intentionally 'forget' certain kinds of childhood incidents or change the emotional charge and significance that those incidents possess. Nonetheless, such 'lost stories' seem not to have strayed far and are readily retrievable when they are given legitimacy by being acknowledged.

The view that adults' formulations are real and children's are not is challenged when accounts are freed from adults' revisions. Their freeing is described by Dawn.

> I remember discounting these hardships because I assumed that when my parents told me I 'was making a big deal out of nothing,' they were right and knew everything because they were my parents, and everyone knew that 'parents know best.' Now that I look back, these hardships were a big deal for me.

Dawn also suggests that adults may teach children to revise their accounts. Such instruction clearly may benefit adults. The benefit — and cost — to children are less clear.

The revision of accounts of childhood is both evident and perplexing when stories of trials are juxtaposed with claims that 'I wouldn't change a thing.' The following comment was offered by an informant whose personal accounts describe 'feeling frightened, scared, confused,' being 'devastated' and 'infuriated,' and a situation in which 'I ran upstairs, and hid under the covers, terrified.'

> There are many things in my childhood that didn't quite go as planned or things that didn't come out as I had planned. But if someone gave me the chance to do it all again, I wouldn't change a single thing! (Betty)

Ralph, telling a story of his parents' not understanding his fears, says,

> There were definitely times when it was hard to relate to my parents
> and it was tough to be a kid because no matter how scared I was, I
> had to do it [what they asked] and just live with the fear.

He then continues,

> There are definitely a few things that I can remember from childhood
> that make my stomach turn. But don't get me wrong, I loved being a
> kid and I wouldn't change a thing about it. I think from all the bad
> things I did, I at least learned from them.

Why wouldn't one want to change such experiences? Explanations such as the
following — unsatisfactory even, apparently, to the teller — are offered.

> On the whole, my childhood experiences weren't too drastic. There
> were things I hated doing but I realize that they have helped shape
> me into better person. Or something. (Alan)

Why?

Why do adults justify children's trials as 'for their own good'? Why do adults
belittle children's experiences? Why do they reproduce with children the very
practices that as children they found so objectionable? And why do they revise
accounts of their childhood? Since my data does not address these questions
directly, I simply offer for consideration a few possibilities. (1) If one learns to
be an adult by being a child, one can learn that adults act in these ways and
thus when one becomes an adult one can reasonably act in these ways. (2) If,
as I have suggested elsewhere (1986), adulthood is an *achievement* rather than
a *state*, in its very nature tentative, then beliefs and actions that facilitate one's
accomplishment of adulthood may prove useful. The reproduction of behavior
that was experienced in one's childhood and the treatment of children as
children can serve as ways of displaying that one is *now* an adult. (3) Such
practices for 'dealing with' children work, if by 'work' is meant accomplishing
adults' goals. These practices can be used to facilitate adults' actions towards
children since they are already 'in place.' Note, however, that other practices
may also work, and with less attendant distress for children. (4) One way for
adults to respond to the little trials of childhood they experienced is to pass
them on to children, for adults may find it more manageable to pass them on
than to endure them as features of their own past.[9] Perhaps, then, taking

---

[9] For one account of this process, see Miller, 1991. The reproducibility of child abuse
over generations might serve as another sphere for exploring the speculations offered
here.

childhood experiences seriously is problematic because it challenges adults' power, projects, self-definitions, recollections, and adulthood itself.

When adults interact with children, they may be guided by general principles or even explicit formulations of what they are to do and say. When they are not, or when they are caught by surprise, they may find themselves falling back on the ways that adults treated them as children.

> While I was growing up I remember a thousand instances when I would say to myself, 'I'll never act like them. I'll always understand my kids.' Now, when I'm baby-sitting or when I spend time with my niece and I hear myself say something like 'You should know better' or 'What I say goes — I'm the boss' or any of the hundreds of other 'grown-up' phrases I heard for the first sixteen years of my life I want to kick myself. I feel so stupid — so adult-like — so GROWN UP — so foolish! That really scares me. (Lisa)

To recognize such 'grown-up' phrases and actions allows one to judge them and, if desired, to change them.

Practical Implications: Alleviating the Little Trials of Childhood

Adults who choose to alleviate the little trials of childhood in ways that are beneficial to *both* children and adults are advised that the matter is a complex one, not amenable to simple solutions. The following suggestion, for example, appears both impracticable and, even were it desirable or possible, likely to substitute little trials of adulthood for those of childhood.

> Darlene told me that when she grows up, 'I am never, ever going to lie to my kids and I will always spend lots of time with them, no matter what! I am going to play and play with my kids and never put them in a time out!' (Darlene, age 10, Annette's informant)

Advice offered by professionals may be similarly simplistic. Thus Leshan, for example, suggests,

> Helping your parents *remember* is just about the best way to change the things that drive you crazy. And when they remember, a lot of things that drive you crazy may stop happening, or at least you will understand them better and will be able to deal with them in a more comfortable way. (1988, p. 11, emphasis in original)

> Most of what parents think and do with their own children started when they were children, and if you can begin to understand that,

you will find you are less confused and feel less guilty. After a bad time, like being spanked by your father, perhaps you could ask him, 'Did Grandpa spank you when you did something he didn't want you to do?' It might start your father remembering how it made him feel. (1988, p. 9)

Given the many functions that may be served by adults' revisions of their childhood accounts, some adults may take less than kindly to children's 'helping' them remember and children may find that they have made their own trials worse.

Mike's adoptive dad was a violent alcoholic who took his frustrations out on his son, both physically and mentally. One day Mike walked in the house and his dad began yelling and cursing at him with his fist balled up. Mike had been confused by this type of behavior for so long that this time he asked his dad, crying, how he could treat his son this way. His drunk father's response was 'You're not my son!' This reminder of the lack of a biological link between Mike and his father marked a true turning point in Mike's life. He never again looked at that man as a dad. (Violet's informant)

Urging upon children what adults might take to be confrontations leaves children open to consequences not anticipated by those who *assume* that 'in most ways your parents (as well as the other grown-ups in your life) prove their love to you every day by all the things they do for and with you' (Leshan, 1988, p. 6).

In a section entitled 'Is Love *Really* All You Need?' Berger and Berger, discussing social action and social change in a pluralistic society,[10] state, 'Good will is not enough' (1975, p. 366). The data throughout this book support their claim, for 'loving children' need not guarantee understanding them; indeed, it may obscure understanding and serve as the very grounds for children's trials.

When I was in the third grade my parents decided to get a divorce. My little sister was in kindergarten and didn't really understand what divorce meant. The day after my parents told us, my sister was at school telling everyone how neat she was because her parents were getting divorced. I on the other hand hadn't even told my best friend. Evidently, my little sister's teacher told the school psychologist what was happening. He came into my class and asked to talk to me. While I was out (according to my best friend) my teacher told the whole class that my parents were getting a divorce and that everyone should

---

[10] If adults and children are viewed as having distinct and different perspectives, sociological theories of pluralism and diversity may prove applicable to adult–child relations.

be nice to me and pray for me (it was a Catholic school). When I came back, everyone stared at me and whispered to each other. My best friend told me what happened and I ran out of the room crying. Not only were my parents getting divorced, now I was a social outcast! I didn't go back to class that day but for the rest of the school year (about one and a half months) during morning prayers my teacher added a special thought to me and my family during our troubled time. I loathed that moment and my teacher the rest of the year. (Audrey's informant)

Good will without knowledge may not only be ineffective but may be experienced by recipients as itself a trial.

From informants' stories I have gathered suggestions — some explicitly given, others implicit — for adults desirous of alleviating the little trials of childhood. I offer a sample of them to illustrate the directions that change might take.

- *Allow children alternatives, even ones that adults find unappealing.* It did not make any sense to me that I had to eat food that I did not like but I was allowed to put ketchup (a lot of it) onto the food that I did not like to kill the taste. (Theresa)

- *Allow children options that they will be granted when they are older.* To this day I still hate peas and baked beans but Mom does not make me eat them anymore. (Theresa)

- *Avoid ineffective methods.* I hated to be grounded. I did not think it did anything for me. It never helped me learn my lesson. My mother used to always ground me. The amount of times I have been grounded is countless, which just proves I never learned my lesson. (Inez)

- *Beware of the consequences of ineffective methods.* When my mother sent me to my room to 'think about' what I had done wrong, what I thought about was how much I hated my mother. (Anonymous, paraphrased from class discussion)

- *Recognize that children may have experiences that you have not had.* I like reading the story about the girl and swimming lessons. I think that I found it interesting because I never had to take swimming lessons. Ever since I can remember, I've known how to swim. I could never understand why some children were so afraid of the water. I think it was good for me to read this story so that I won't be like her mother. It sounded like the mom never had to deal with being afraid of the water. (Debra)

- *Put yourself in the place of children.*
  I can clearly remember having hard times as a child and using some of these same strategies to deal with them. This class has made me think a lot about my childhood. I had forgotten what it was like. I think adults should put themselves in the place of children when working with them. I think I am beginning to get a better understanding of how children think and act because I am remembering how I used to act. (Ariel)

- *Examine your own (unrevised) childhood.*
  I think that we as adults, when we are dealing with children, need to be more conscious of how the situations make the child feel. That might mean digging up the bad memories that have eaten at us since childhood and, for a moment, putting ourselves in children's shoes. (Ralph)

Other suggestions are implicit throughout this book. The appropriateness and effectiveness of any suggestion can only be assessed *in situ* but what is common to all the suggestions cited above is respect for children's experiences.

Not all of the little trials of childhood can be avoided but they can all be understood. Sympathy, apology, restitution, compromise, and change may become more prominent features of adult–child interactions when adults attend to the many ways that they can recognize and respond to the little trials of childhood.

A Concluding Note

When I began collecting stories of the little trials of childhood, I thought of them as relatively minor, smiled unabashedly as I read them, saw them as 'cute,' and found them interesting. The cumulative effect of the stories I gathered has led me to take more seriously the events described therein. I have continued to think of these experiences as 'little' trials but increasingly I am questioning their littleness. As one informant said of them,

> They are like having a bad dream; it seems horrible to the individual having it but it may not seem this way to someone being told about the dream. (Lou-Anne)

The particular power of the stories presented throughout this book is to allow those told of the little trials of childhood to understand 'that it seems this way' to those who experience them.

Bibliography

(For an extensive bibliography of sociological works about children, see Waksler, 1991b.)

ADLER, P.A. and P. (1978) 'Tinydopers: A case study of deviant socialization', *Symbolic Interaction,* **1**, 2, Spring, reprinted in WAKSLER, F.C. (ed.) (1991) *Studying the Social Worlds of Children,* London, Falmer Press, pp. 77–94.

AMBERT, A. (1994) 'A qualitative study of peer abuse and its effects: Theoretical and empirical implications', *Journal of Marriage and The Family,* **56**, February, pp. 1–12.

AMBERT, A. (1995) 'Toward a theory of peer abuse', in AMBERT, A. (ed.) *Sociological Studies of Children Volume 6,* Greenwich, CN, JAI, pp. 177–205.

AMES, V.M. (1955) 'Mead and Husserl on the self', *Philosophy and Phenomenological Research,* **XV**, 3, March, pp. 320–31.

ATKINSON, M.A. (1980) 'Some practical uses of "a natural lifetime"', *Human Studies,* **3**, pp. 33–46.

ATTANUCCI, J.S. (1991) 'Changing subjects: Growing up and growing older', *Journal of Moral Education,* **20**, 3, pp. 317–28.

ATTANUCCI, J.S. (1993) 'Timely characterization of mother–daughter and family–school relations: Narrative understandings of adolescence', *Journal of Narrative and Life History,* **3**, 1, pp. 99–116.

BECKER, H.S. (1963) *Outsiders: Studies in the Sociology of Deviance,* NY, Free Press.

BENTZ, V.M. (1989) *Becoming Mature: Childhood Ghosts and Spirits in Adult Life,* NY, Aldine de Gruyter.

BERGER, P.L. and BERGER, B. (1975) *Sociology: A Biographical Approach,* 2nd expanded edn, NY, Basic Books.

BERGER, P.L. and LUCKMANN, T. (1967) *The Social Construction of Reality: A Treatise in the Sociology of Knowledge,* Garden City, NY, Doubleday.

BLUEBOND-LANGNER, M. (1978) *The Private Worlds of Dying Children,* Princeton, NJ, Princeton University.

BOK, S. (1989) *Lying: Moral Choice in Public and Private Life,* NY, Vintage, A Division of Random House.

CARROLL, R. (1988) *Cultural Misunderstandings: The French–American Experience* (tr. C. Volk), Chicago, University of Chicago.

CAVIN, E. (1990) 'Using picture books', in MANDELL, N. (ed.) *Sociological Studies of Child Development Volume 3,* Greenwich CT, JAI, pp. 225–43.

CAVIN, E. (1994) 'In search of the viewfinder: A study of a child's perspective', *Visual Sociology*, **9**, 1, pp. 27–41.

CLARK, C.D. (1995) *Flights of Fancy, Leaps of Faith: Children's Myths in Contemporary America*, Chicago and London, University of Chicago.

COOLEY, C.H. (1962) *Social Organization*, first published 1909, NY, Schocken Books.

COSER, L.A., NOCK, S.L., STEFFAN, P.A. and SPAIN, D. (1991) *Introduction to Sociology*, 3rd edn, San Diego, Harcourt, Brace, Jovanovich.

CUFF, E.C. (1994) *Problems of Versions in Everyday Situations*, Washington, DC, International Institute for Ethnomethodology and Conversation Analysis & University Press of America.

DELFATTORE, J. (1992) *What Johnny Shouldn't Read: Textbook Censorship in America*, New Haven, Yale University.

DEVAULT, M.L. (1991) *Feeding the Family: The Social Organization of Caring as Gendered Work*, Chicago, University of Chicago.

DICKENS, C. (n.d.) *Hard Times for These Times*, first published 1854, NY, Walter J. Black.

FRANK, A.W. III (1981) ' "Pooh talk": Formulating children's conversational troubles', *Semiotica*, **37**, 1/2, pp. 109–20.

GARFINKEL, H. (1967) *Studies in Ethnomethodology*, Englewood Cliffs, NJ, Prentice-Hall.

GOFFMAN, E. (1959) *The Presentation of Self in Everyday Life*, Garden City, NY, Doubleday Anchor.

GOFFMAN, E. (1963a) *Behavior in Public Places: Notes on the Social Organization of Gatherings*, NY, Free Press.

GOFFMAN, E. (1963b) *Stigma: Notes on the Management of Spoiled Identity*, Englewood Cliffs, NJ, Prentice-Hall.

GOFFMAN, E. (1967) 'Embarrassment and social organization', in GOFFMAN, E. *Interaction Ritual: Essays on Face-to-Face Behavior*, Garden City, NJ, Doubleday, pp. 97–112.

GOLDMAN, W. (1973) *The Princess Bride*, NY, Ballentine Books (abridgement of Morgenstern, S. *The Princess Bride*).

GOODE, D. (1994) *A World Without Words: The Social Construction of Children Born Deaf and Blind*, forward by I.K. Zola, Philadelphia, PA, Temple University.

GOODE, D.A. with WAKSLER, F.C. (1990) 'The missing "who": Situational identity and fault finding with an alingual blind deaf child', in MANDELL, N. (ed.) *Sociological Studies of Child Development Volume 3*, Greenwich, CN, JAI, pp. 203–23.

GOTTLIEB, A. (1994) 'What's on your mind, kid?' *The New York Times Book Review*, 23 October, p. 13.

GREENSPAN, S.I. with SALMON, J. (1993) *Playground Politics: Understanding the Emotional Life of Your School-Age Child*, Reading, MA, Addison-Wesley.

HEAP, J.L. (1990) 'Applied ethnomethodology: Looking for the local rationality of reading activities', *Human Studies*, **13**, 1, pp. 39–72, January.

HUSSERL, E. (1962) *Ideas: General Introduction to Pure Phenomenology* (first published in German, 1913) NY, Collier Books.

HUSSERL, E. (1964) *The Phenomenology of Internal Time-Consciousness*, lectures given 1904–1910 (first published in German, 1928) Bloomington, Indiana University Press.

HUSSERL, E. (1970) *The Crisis of European Sciences and Transcendental Phenomenology* (first published in German, 1954) tr. with an intro. by D. Carr, Evanston, IL, Northwestern University.

JOYCE, M.C. (1991) 'Watching people watching babies', in WAKSLER, F.C. (ed.), *Studying the Social Worlds of Children*, London, Falmer Press, pp. 113–18.

KINNEY, J.R. with HONEYCUTT, A. (1938) *How to Raise a Dog in the City and in the Suburbs*, NY, Cornerstone Library.

KOLB, W.L. (1944) 'A critical evaluation of Mead's "I" and "Me" concepts', *Social Forces*, **22**, March, reprinted in MANIS, J.G. and MELTZER, B.N. (eds) (1967) *Symbolic Interaction*, Boston, Allyn & Bacon, pp. 291–6.

LANE, H. (1976) *The Wild Boy of Aveyron*, Cambridge, MA, Harvard University.

LANE, H.C. (1992) *Mask of Benevolence: Disabling the Deaf Community*, NY, Knopf.

LEBOYER, F. (1976) *Birth Without Violence*, NY, Alfred A. Knopf.

LESHAN, E. (1988) *When Grownups Drive You Crazy*, NY, Macmillan.

LETKEMANN, P. (1973) *Crime as Work*, Englewood Cliffs, NJ, Prentice-Hall.

LEWIS, J.D. (1979) 'A social behaviorist interpretation of the Meadian "I"', *American Journal of Sociology*, **85**, 2, September, pp. 261–87.

MACKAY, R.W. (1973) 'Conceptions of children and models of socialization', in DREITZEL, H.P. (ed.), *Recent Sociology No. 5*, NY, Macmillan, pp. 27–43, reprinted in WAKSLER, F.C. (ed.) (1991) *Studying the Social Worlds of Children*, London, Falmer Press, pp. 23–37.

MACKAY, R.W. (1974) 'Standardized tests: Objective/objectified measures of "competence"', in CICOUREL, A.V., JENNINGS, K.H., JENNINGS, S.H.M., LEITER, K.C.W., MACKAY, R., MEHAN, H. and ROTH, D.R. (eds), *Language Use and School Performance*, NY, Academic Press, pp. 218–47.

MANDELL, N. (1984) 'Children's negotiation of meaning', *Symbolic Interaction*, **7**, 3, pp. 191–211, reprinted in WAKSLER, F.C. (ed.) (1991) *Studying the Social Worlds of Children*, London, Falmer Press, pp. 161–78.

MARTIN, J. (1984) *Miss Manners' Guide to Rearing Perfect Children*, NY, Atheneum.

MARTIN, J. (1989) *Miss Manners' Guide for the Turn-of-the-Millennium*, NY, Pharos Books.

MATTHEWS, G.B. (1994) *The Philosophy of Childhood*, Cambridge, MA, Harvard University.

MATZA, D. (1969) *Becoming Deviant*, Englewood Cliffs, NJ, Prentice-Hall.

McHUGH, P. (1968) *Defining the Situation*, NY, Bobbs-Merrill.

MEAD, G.H. (1964) *George Herbert Mead on Social Psychology*, Chicago and London, University of Chicago.

MEYNELL, H. (1971) 'Philosophy and schizophrenia', *Journal of the British Society for Phenomenology*, **2**, 2, May, pp. 17–30.

MILLER, A. (1981) *The Drama of the Gifted Child*, originally published as *Prisoners of Childhood*, 1979, tr. R. Ward, NY, Basic Books.

MILLER, A. (1990) *Banished Knowledge: Facing Childhood Injuries* (first published in German, 1988) tr. L. Vennewitz, NY, London, Doubleday.

MILLER, A. (1991) *Breaking Down The Wall of Silence: The Liberating Experience of Facing Painful Truth* (first published in German, 1990) tr. S. Worrall, NY, Dutton.

MORGENSTERN, S. *See* GOLDMAN, W. (1973).

O'NEILL, J. (1994) *The Missing Child in Liberal Theory: Towards A Covenant Theory of Family, Community, Welfare and the Civic State*, Toronto, University of Toronto.

OAKLEY, A. (1980) *Women Confined: Towards a Sociology of Childbirth*, NY, Schocken.

OPIE, I. and OPIE, P. (1959) The Lore and Language of School Children, London, Oxford University.

POLLNER, M. (1975) '"The very coinage of your brain": Anatomy of reality disjunctures', *Philosophy of Social Science*, **5**, pp. 411–30.

RODMAN, H. (1965) 'Middle-class misconceptions about lower-class families', in RODMAN, H. (ed.) *Marriage, Family and Society*, NY, Random House, pp. 219–30.

ROLLIN, B. (1970) 'Motherhood: who needs it?' *Look*, **34**, 19, 22 September, pp. 15–17, reprinted in SKOLNICK, A.S. and SKOLNICK, J.H. (eds) (1971) *Family in Transition*, Boston: Little, Brown, pp. 346–56.

RYMER, R. (1993) *Genie: A Scientific Tragedy*, NY, HarperPerennial.

SACKS, H. (1972) 'On the analysability of stories by children', in GUMPERZ, J.J. and HYMES, D. (eds) *Directions in Sociolinguistics*, Holt, Rinehart and Winston, reprinted in WAKSLER, F.C. (ed.) (1991) *Studying the Social Worlds of Children*, London, Falmer Press, pp. 195–215.

SACKS, H. (1975) 'Everyone has to lie', in SANCHES, M. and BLOUNT, B.G. (eds) *Sociocultural Dimensions of Language Use*, NY, Academic Press, pp. 57–79.

SCHNEIDER, D.M. (1968) *American Kinship: A Cultural Account*, Englewood Cliffs, NJ, Prentice-Hall.

SCHUTZ, A. (1964) *Collected Papers II: Studies in Social Theory*, edited and introduced by A. Brodersen, The Hague, Netherlands, Martinus Nijhoff.

SCHUTZ, A. (1967a) *The Phenomenology of the Social World* (first published in German, 1932) tr. G. Walsh and F. Lehnert, n.p., Northwestern University.

SCHUTZ, A. (1967b) *Collected Papers I: The Problem of Social Reality*, edited and introduced by M. Natanson, The Hague, Netherlands, Martinus Nijhoff.

SCOTT, M.B. and LYMAN, S.M. (1968) 'Accounts', *American Sociological Review*, **33**, 1, pp. 46–62.

SPIEGELBERG, H. (1973) 'On the right to say "we": A linguistic and phenomenological analysis', in PSATHAS, G. (ed.) *Phenomenological Sociology: Issues and Applications*, NY, John Wiley & Sons, pp. 129–56.

STAINTON ROGERS, R. and W. (1992) *Stories of Childhood: Shifting Agendas of Child Concern*, Toronto, University of Toronto.

STONE, G.P. (1962) 'Appearance and the self', in ROSE, A.M. (ed.) *Human Behavior and Social Processes*, Boston, MA: Houghton Mifflin, pp. 86–118.

TURECKI, S. with WERNICK, S. (1994) *The Emotional Problems of Normal Children: How Parents Can Understand and Help*, NY, London, Bantam.

VANDERBILT, A. (1954) *Amy Vanderbilt's Complete Book of Etiquette*, Garden City, NY, Doubleday.

WAKSLER, F.C. (1986) 'Studying children: Phenomenological insights', *Human Studies*, **9**, pp. 71–82, reprinted in WAKSLER, F.C. (ed.) (1991) *Studying the Social Worlds of Children*, London, Falmer Press, pp. 60–9.

WAKSLER, F.C. (1987) 'Dancing when the music is over: A study of deviance in a kindergarten classroom', in ADLER, P. and P. (eds) *Sociological Studies of Child Development Volume 2*, Greenwich, CN, reprinted in WAKSLER, F.C. (ed.) (1991) *Studying the Social Worlds of Children*, London, Falmer Press, pp. 95–112.

WAKSLER, F.C. (1989) 'Erving Goffman's sociology: An introductory essay', *Human Studies*, **12**, 1–2, June, pp. 1–18.

WAKSLER, F.C. (1991a) 'The hard times of childhood and children's strategies for dealing with them', in WAKSLER, F.C. (ed.) *Studying the Social Worlds of Children*, London, Falmer Press, pp. 216–34.

WAKSLER, F.C. (ed.) (1991b) *Studying the Social Worlds of Children: Sociological Readings*, London, Falmer Press.

WAKSLER, F.C. (1991c) 'Disembodied evidence: The social significance of inanimate phenomena', paper presented at meetings of Eastern Sociological Society.

WAKSLER, F.C. (1995) 'Introductory essay: Intersubjectivity as a practical matter and a problematic achievement', *Human Studies*, **18**, 1, January, pp. 1–7.

WALPOLE, H. (1931) *The Castle of Otranto*, first published in 1764, in STEEVES, H.R., *Three Eighteenth Century Romances*, NY, Charles Scribner's Sons.

WATTAM, C. (1989) 'Investigating child sexual abuse — A question of relevance', in BLAGG, H., HUGHES, J.A. and WATTAM, C. (eds) *Child Sexual Abuse*, England, Longman, pp. 27–43.

WRONG, D.H. (1961) 'The oversocialized conception of man in modern society', *American Sociological Review*, **26**, April, pp. 183–93.

Appendix: What is Hard about being a child? Responses from a first-grade class

After Joan Duffy, a first grade teacher, and I discussed the little trials of child-hood, she raised the topic with her students during one of their regularly scheduled group discussions of their ideas, feelings, and concerns. She asked them what was hard for them as children, things that adults might not know or ask children about, offering a few examples from her own childhood and some general prompting with broad topics, e.g., illness, toys. What follows is the list generated by her first-grade class. I offer her method, based on natur-ally occurring classroom talk, as one that generates data from young children in a way that does not seem to put them at risk but that they (as well as researchers) might indeed find of value.

- being blamed for something you didn't do
- when people don't listen to you
- having to eat things you don't like
- sometimes telling the truth is hard
- not getting things you want
- before getting shots or stitches
- not laughing when someone is hurt
- really long car trips
- being teased
- being teased when you're crying
- when parents argue or fight
- having to stop what you're doing when you're not done
- when parents don't agree in what they tell you
- sometimes it's embarrassing when older people kiss you in front of other kids
- when parents are on a trip
- when people steal from you
- when your things get broken
- when you miss out on things you want to do
- when a person or an animal dies
- when a new baby gets a lot of attention
- getting chickenpox and you miss doing things

- missing school when you're sick
- waiting for your birthday
- waiting for special times to happen
- getting ready to perform
- bad dreams
- when you hear scary noises
- younger kids getting into your stuff
- when older kids are mean to you
- when people you play with don't help clean up
- when other kids won't share
- when other kids break promises
- when older kids get to do what you want to do

Index